Bible Translation Basics

Communicating Scripture in a Relevant Way

SIL International®

Series Editor
Mike Cahill

Volume Editor
Rhonda Hartell Jones

Production Staff
Bonnie Brown, Copy Editor
Judy Benjamin, Compositor
Barbara Alber, Cover design

Cover Photo
Rick Floyd

Bible Translation Basics

Communicating Scripture in a Relevant Way

Harriet Hill
Ernst-August Gutt
Margaret Hill
Christopher Unger
Rick Floyd

SIL International®
Dallas, Texas

Copies of this and other publications of SIL International® may be obtained from

SIL International Publications
7500 W. Camp Wisdom Road
Dallas, TX 75236-5699

Voice: 972-708-7404
Fax: 972-708-7363
Email: academic_books@sil.org
Internet: http://www.ethnologue.com

Contents

Table of Tables

Table of Figures

Acknowledgements

Over the past years, many have felt the need for a basic course that applied the growing wealth of insights from communication theory to Bible translation. In July 2005, a small group of Bible translation consultants met at the European Training Programme campus in England to draft the outline of such a course.

Over the following years, a smaller group worked to create the lessons and pilot teach them on every continent, both to new translators and to experienced translation consultants and advisors. Many people have made helpful contributions along the way, more than can be named. As editor, I am indebted to all who have contributed. At the same time, I take responsibility for any errors.

Harriet Hill

Preface

This book is intended to be used in courses or workshops for people involved in communicating Scripture across languages and cultures. The primary audience is Bible translators, but those who review translations and those who develop other Scripture products such as Bible stories or Bible study guides will also find it helpful. The course gives participants an introduction to how communication works from an inference-based perspective and helps them apply these insights to their task of communication Scripture.

The course is designed for people who have (the equivalent of) secondary school education, but those with higher levels of education have also found it beneficial. Each lesson begins with a story which provides the foundation on which the ideas presented in the lesson are built. These should be read aloud. Because we learn best by discovery and experience, the course is participatory, with much of the learning taking place in small and large group exercises and discussions. Work sessions are interspersed throughout the lessons. These are extended exercises that take a full class period. Participants need to have some short texts in their languages available to work with for reference so they can better understand how their language functions.

The course begins with an introductory lesson that helps participants think through reasons for being involved in Bible translation. In the first section of the course, participants learn the basics of how communication functions; in the second section, they learn about the challenges of translating Scripture and the options that are available. The third section focuses on adjusting mismatches between languages and cultures. The fourth section goes into more detail on additional clues texts provide. The final section includes story crafting and special translation issues like names and program issues. Throughout the course, participants study several biblical passages in depth and translate then in a variety of styles, using both oral and written drafting methods.

When the course is taught as a three-week workshop, two or three lessons are covered each day. Most days there are individual assignments. By the middle of the course, assignments include translating Bible passages. The course ends with a test which helps participants internalize all they have learned. A teacher's manual with a suggested timetable, learning objectives, recommended reading, and responses to the exercises is available at www.BtBasics.net.

By the end of the course, participants should be able to begin translating the Bible into their languages. They will need the assistance of more experienced consultants or advisors trained in exegesis who can help them understand the intended meaning of the biblical text. Becoming a skilled translator requires life-long learning. This is only an introduction to the issues involved. Fortunately, translation is very interesting and rewarding work.

Harriet Hill

Introduction

Lesson 1

Why Translate the Bible?

GROUP DISCUSSION

1. Discuss reasons we translate the Bible.
2. Discuss reasons we translate the Bible into local languages.

God comes to us to reach us

In many religions, people try very hard to reach God to be accepted by him. They may consider their way of life too lowly or polluted for God. But the Bible shows that God comes to us rather than expecting us to reach him. Although God is completely holy, he sent his son Jesus to live among us in this world. This did not pollute his divine nature. Instead, Jesus healed the brokenness of the people and the cultures he touched.

God becomes very close and personal to us when we can really understand the Bible. This happens when Scripture is in a language we understand and we have the biblical background information necessary to be able to understand the author's message. God's word is not polluted when it is expressed in our languages. Instead, it allows the Holy Spirit to transform and purify us and our cultures.

GROUP DISCUSSION

Discuss how people in your community feel about God speaking to them in their mother tongue.

> ### If people are ashamed of their language, they will not want to use it to communicate with God.

God wants us to understand him

God wants to communicate with us in a way we can understand. Some religions use various magic rituals and formulas that ordinary people are not meant to understand. They may use a foreign language that is considered holy for prayers and rituals. The fact that most people do not understand it makes it seem magical and powerful. Christianity is not like that.

When Jesus came to earth, he spoke the languages of the people he lived with so they could understand him. He also lived in their Jewish, first-century culture, and communicated in the context of that culture so that people could understand him. For example, he spoke about vineyards and fishing and shepherds, Roman coins, and Old Testament passages because his audience knew about these things. He did not speak in French or talk about computers, rice, or democracy. He used both the language and culture of the people to be able to communicate with them.

GROUP DISCUSSION

1. Look up these Scripture passages. Discuss what they teach about how God wants us to interact with Scripture.

   Luke 24:45   Acts 8:30–35
   2 Timothy 3:16–17   Deuteronomy 6:6–7

2. In your culture, is religion something people expect to understand? Explain.

> **If people do not expect to understand religion, they will not expect to understand the Bible.**

God created the world full of variety

Collect leaves and flowers from different plants. Take time to look at them closely.

Notice how each one is different from the others. Discuss what this teaches us about God's creation.

Nature is full of variety. We know that the variety of languages and cultures will continue to the end of this world because Revelation 7:9 says that people from every language will stand before God's throne at the end of time: "After this I looked and there before me was a great multitude that no one could count, from every nation, tribe, people and language, standing before the throne and in front of the Lamb" (NIV).

The modern world favors things all being the same. For example, rather than each person crafting their own products, most things are produced in factories where every person has to make their part in the same way. Many people in the world today also favor people speaking the same language. They think it is more practical and economical.
No two people or cultures are the same. Each is created by God in its own special

way. Each needs to bring their praise to God in the way that only they can. If people do not praise God in the ways that are particular to their language and culture, no one else can, and the wonder of that special praise will be lacking.

GROUP DISCUSSION

1. Are there ways in which people in your community are shamed for speaking their mother tongue?
2. Are there ways in which people in your community are rewarded for speaking the majority language?
3. Discuss ways in which churches can encourage the use of all the languages in their area.

> ## The diversity of languages and cultures is part of God's plan.

No language or culture is holier than another

When Jesus was born, there were at least four languages used in Israel.

- Latin was the prestigious language of the colonial authorities.
- Greek was the language of education, communication, and trade.
- Aramaic was the language used in the homes of the Jews.
- Hebrew was the language of the Jewish Scriptures, temple worship, and religious studies.

Which do you think Jesus usually used?

At that time, the language most Jewish people spoke at home was Aramaic, and scholars think that Jesus usually used it. He probably spoke Greek and at least read Hebrew as well. You might think that if any language were to be better to use to speak to God, it would have been the language Jesus spoke most often but, apart from a few isolated words and phrases, we do not even have a record of his original words. We only have translations of them. By the time the Gospels were written, the intended audience included many people who did not speak Aramaic or read Hebrew, so the Gospel writers translated what Jesus said into Greek. In fact, the Old Testament had already been translated from Hebrew into Greek in the centuries before Christ, so that Jews living in Greek-speaking lands could understand it.

There were two varieties of Greek the Gospel writers could choose from: sophisticated Greek used in the literature and common Greek spoken by ordinary people. They chose to write in common Greek. This shows that it is the message that is important, not the language that is used. It also shows that God wants to communicate with us in the language we use in our everyday lives and understand best.

On the day of Pentecost, people heard the Good News in many different languages (Acts 2:5–11). Even though the crowd most likely understood Greek, God performed a miracle and they all understood what was said, each in their own mother tongue. This shows that God values the mother tongue, even for people who may know other languages.

As Christianity spread to new regions, the Bible was translated into the languages people spoke in their homes: Syriac, Coptic, Gothic, Armenian, and so forth. Over time, Latin became the language of common people, so the Bible was translated into it so they could understand it. Centuries later, people no longer spoke Latin but the church continued to use the Latin Scriptures because they thought it was a holy, powerful language. Since people could not understand what the priests were saying, the Word was not able to purify their thoughts or influence their lives. As a result, the church was full of superstition and sin. When John Wycliffe decided to translate the Bible into English in the late 1300s, the church leaders said to him, "How can you convey the Word of God in a primitive language like English?" When the Bible was available in a language people could understand, the church grew.

Christianity can be lived out in all cultures. Although God had given laws for the Jews in the Old Testament, the early church decided that non-Jewish Christians did not have to obey those laws except for four they felt were non-negotiable (Acts 15). They needed to live out their faith within their own culture (Rom 14).

No language or culture is holier than another. All are capable of expressing the message of the Bible. If a culture lacks a biblical concept, it can learn that concept, perhaps by connecting it to a similar concept that is known in the culture. This is a question of developing the culture and language, not a question of the capacity of the culture and language.

GROUP DISCUSSION

1. What language do people in your community think the Bible was written in?
2. What translation(s) of the Bible do people use in your churches? Why do they use these translations? Are they able to understand them well?
3. When people have difficulty understanding Scripture, is this because they do not understand the language of the translation, or because they do not understand the cultures of the Bible?
4. Although English used to be considered a barbaric language, it is now considered a language of high status. Discuss the reasons you think people's views of English changed over the centuries.
5. Can you think of examples of people imposing their culture on others, claiming that this is biblical?

Christianity can be expressed in all languages and cultures.

Translation and teaching about biblical cultures is an on-going task of the church

People have been translating Scripture through the centuries. Even before Christ, the Old Testament was translated into Greek so that the Jews who no longer spoke Hebrew or Aramaic could understand it. Translation has continued to be a part of the church's mission from the very beginning. Teaching people about biblical cultures is also an on-going ministry of the church.

Although translators strive to do the best they can to express the meaning of Scripture and help people understand the biblical culture, their work is never complete. No language can fully express God's message, and no translation perfectly reflects the meaning of the original. Translators do their best, realizing that God is able to communicate through imperfect languages and translations. Revision is an expected part of the process.

Translations also need to be revised because languages change over time. Translations that were at one time in the common language become archaic when people no longer speak that way. The language of the King James Version in English was once the way people spoke, but people do not speak English that way anymore and find it difficult to understand. For example, Psalm 88:13 is expressed in the King James Version: "But unto thee have I cried, O Lord; and in the morning shall my prayer prevent thee." English speakers today cannot understand the meaning of this verse from this translation because the meaning of 'prevent' has changed from 'to be ready for' to 'to keep from happening.' In general, translations have to be revised every twenty to twenty-five years to remain in the common language.

GROUP DISCUSSION

1. Does your church see translation as a part of its mission?
2. Does your church see translation as an on-going task?
3. Discuss how you feel about being involved in translating Scripture into your language. Do you have any fears? Joys? Concerns?

Summary

When we understand God's word, it helps us know God and obey him. This involves understanding not only the words of Scripture, but also knowing enough of the biblical context to be able to understand the biblical author's meaning. When we have Scripture in our mother tongue, our ethnic and linguistic identity is affirmed and God enters into the most private parts of our world. Bible translation has been a part of the church's mission from the start and will continue to be in the future as translations continue to need revision and improvement.

Assignment

Imagine a leader in your church or community says to you, "I don't know why you are wasting time translating the Bible into our language. Soon everyone will be able to speak English (or the major language in the area)!" Write a letter to him explaining why you feel translation into your language is important.

The Basics of Communication

Lesson 2

How We Understand Meaning

They're back!?

John Ngu and Peter Rigi were part of the team translating the Bible into the Wizi language. One day an invitation came for them both to attend a conference in the capital city on communicating the message of the Bible by oral means. God made it possible for both of them to attend.

The workshop began and they heard about many interesting things, but during the afternoon break a most extraordinary thing happened! Many of the people at the conference were from the capital city or from the north of the country, but Peter and John were from the south. As they were sitting drinking their tea, a man rushed into the room shouting, "They're back!" All the people from the north and from the city grabbed bowls and brooms and rushed outside to go after them, leaving John and Peter and various other southerners sitting there feeling rather confused. Finally they got up and went outside to find out what was happening. The sky was full of locusts! Some people were trying to get them off the plants and bushes, and some were trying to catch them in bowls.

After five minutes all the locusts left as suddenly as they came, and the conference continued. John whispered to Peter, "Now we know who *they* were."

GROUP DISCUSSION

1. What did the northerners at this conference understand from the announcement, "They're back?"
2. Discuss why John, Peter, and the other southerners were confused.

We look for what seems to be most important

To understand why John and Peter did not understand what was meant by "They're back!" while others in the room did, let us look at how communication works.

Our environment is full of information. Look out the window. What do you see at first glance? Now look again carefully. What else is out there that you did not notice at first? Do you smell anything? Hear anything?

There is too much information in our environment for us to pay attention to it all. Our minds select certain things and disregard others. The first time you looked out the window, you noticed the things that seemed the most important to you right now. When you looked again carefully, you noticed much more.

When we are in church and a person is preaching, we generally pay attention to what he or she is saying, not the kind of shoes he is wearing. We expect the message to be the most important thing to give our attention to. If, however, we are planning to buy new shoes, we may give attention to the preacher's shoes, as any information about shoes will seem important. We are not aware of it, but we are continually making choices like this.

> ## People cannot pay attention to everything.
> ## They give their attention to what they consider
> ## most important and ignore the rest.

GROUP DISCUSSION

1. What do you give your attention to?
   a. What did you give your attention to in this room prior to this exercise?
   b. What else is in this room that you did not notice the first time? List at least four things.
   c. Suggest another circumstance that might have led you to notice these things. For example, if you were feeling thirsty, you might notice that there are some glasses at the back of the room.
2. Discuss whether or not people in your audience are willing to give their attention to Scripture. If not, discuss possible reasons.

Speakers claim to have something worth paying attention to

By communicating, people claim that they have something important for their audience to understand. This is true whether they are communicating with words or by actions. They are claiming their communication to be more important than anything else in the environment and that it will be worth the audience's effort to give their attention to understand it.

When someone addresses us, we no longer give our attention to other things, but we search for the meaning of the words they used, and we try to work out why they said this to us. For example, when the northerners in the story said, "They're back," everyone understood 1) that the locusts were back and 2) that the speaker meant that they should run outside quickly to collect some to eat.

People say less than they mean

What do you see in this photo?

Do you call it a papaya tree?
Does it touch the ground?
How do you know?
Does it have roots?
Does the picture show them?
How do you know it has roots?

We are always trying to make sense of things. What we see is only part of what we understand about the world around us. Automatically, it brings to mind certain things we already know. We combine what we see with what we know to understand what it is we are looking at.

What information do we supply to make sense of this photo?

When we speak, we also say less than we mean. We count on our hearers to supply things they already know. It can include things in our environment we see, smell, hear, or feel, what has just been said, things from our culture and society, from our personal experience, and so forth. We refer to this information as *context*. For example, at the conference in our story, if Peter gets to the classroom and realizes he did not bring a pen to take notes with, he may say:

> Context is information that the speaker thinks we already know before we hear (that part of) a text, and that we use to understand what the speaker means.

Peter: I need a pen.
John: I have an extra one.

What exactly did Peter say? What did he mean? Was it a statement of fact or a question? What context did John use to understand what Peter meant?

What exactly did John say? What did he mean? What does "one" refer to? Is he only stating a fact or was he also making an offer? How do you know? What context did Peter use to understand what John said?

What people say only points to what they mean. Our minds supply the context.

GROUP DISCUSSION

1. Discuss the information Jesus expected his audience to know about the relationship between Jews and Samaritans to understand the story of the Good Samaritan (Lk 10:30–37).

2. Read this passage from the story of the flood:

    > After forty days Noah opened the window he had made in the ark and sent out a raven, and it kept flying back and forth until the water had dried up from the earth (Gen 8:6–7 NIV).

    In Southeast Asia, one group thought ravens had mystical powers that could dry up water by flying back and forth. Discuss how this context might affect how they understand this passage.

3. Often people have misunderstood Scripture because they used the wrong context. Discuss any situations like this that you can think of.

We work out the meaning

Understanding what people mean involves working out the clues they provide in what they say and supplying information they think we already know. For example, when Peter said, "I need a pen," John understood that Peter needed this to take notes, not for some other purpose. He understood Peter needed a pen that worked, that Peter was really asking to borrow a pen, and so forth. Since this context is not spelled out in words, we have to work out the information speakers intend us to use to understand their message. In this course, we will be exploring how we do this.

How do hearers know when they have understood the speaker's meaning correctly? Speakers want to be understood. They do not want to tire out their audience unnecessarily, so they try to make the meaning they intend the easiest one for their audience to work out. This allows hearers to take the first meaning that makes sense as the intended one. If speakers wanted them to understand something else, they would have expressed themselves differently.

This is not to say that all communication is successful. Speakers vary in their ability to communicate but, as much as they are able, they try to make their message as easy to understand as possible.

We are very intent on finding meaning. Even if someone says something that is incorrect or unclear, we try to understand something from what they say. In our search for meaning, we may even correct errors in what is said without realizing it. For example, if John said, "I think I have a pen in my *box*," as he looked for one in his *bag*, Peter would still understand what he meant.

> ## We figure out what is meant from what is said by using context.

Summary

We cannot pay attention to everything in our environment. Our minds pay attention to the things we think will be the most important to us and ignore the rest. When we speak, we are claiming to have something important for our audience to know. We do not say everything we mean; what we say only points to what we mean. The audience is guided by these clues to supply the context needed to understand the meaning. Hearers try to make sense of what is said. Since speakers try to be understood, hearers can take the first meaning that makes sense as the intended one.

> **So what?**
>
> **Translators need to communicate Scripture in such a way that people give their attention to it.**

Assignment

1. Listen to conversations around you. Write down an exchange between two people. Analyze what each one said and what they meant. List the context each one expected the other to supply.
2. Think of a Bible passage that is often misunderstood by people in your church. Explain why it is misunderstood. Write down the reference of the passage and the heading.
3. Read Matthew 12:1–2:

    At that time Jesus went through the grain fields on the Sabbath. His disciples were hungry and began to pick some heads of grain and eat them. ² When the Pharisees saw this, they said to him, "Look! Your disciples are doing what is unlawful on the Sabbath" (NIV).

    Now read this information:

    12:1. Jewish law based on Deuteronomy 23:25 (cf. Ruth 2:2–3) provided for the poor to eat food as they passed through a field. The issue here is thus not that the disciples took someone's grain but that they picked it on the Sabbath; later rabbinic law specifically designated this as one of thirty-nine kinds of work forbidden on the Sabbath.[1]

    what is unlawful on the Sabbath: According to Jewish tradition (in the Mishnah), harvesting (which is what Jesus' disciples technically were doing) was forbidden on the Sabbath (see Ex 34:21 NIV Study Bible).

---

[1] Keener, Craig S. 1993. *The IVP Bible Background Commentary: New Testament.* Downers Grove, Ill.: InterVarsity.

a. Is any of this information different than what you expected?
b. Explain how this information affects your understanding of this passage.
c. Tell how much of this information an average member of your audience would know.

Work Session A: Preparing Texts

Figure 1. Scripture on scrolls

Figure 2. Original manuscript

The Bible was originally written on scrolls as in the photo on the left, rather than in books as we know them today. The Old Testament was written mainly in Hebrew and the New Testament in Greek. The New Testament was written without spaces between words, capitalization, punctuation, titles, chapter numbers, or verse numbers, as in the photo on the right. It would have looked something like this if it had been written in English:

nowoneofthephariseesinvitedjesustohavedinnerwithhimsohewenttothephar
seeshouseandreclinedatthetablewhenawomanwhohadlivedasinfullifeintha
townlearnedthatjesuswaseatingatthephariseeshousesshebroughtanalabaste
jarofperfume

Can you recognize the passage?

When scholars inserted spaces between words, chapter and verse numbers, punctuation and capitalization, they had to make many decisions about what the text meant. For example, in the last line, *houseshebrought*, did the 's' belong to the pronoun to form *she*, or was it the plural of *house* to form *houses*? All Scripture had to be interpreted in this way so we can read it.

E<small>XERCISES</small>

1. Try to understand the meaning communicated by the text below. Insert the punctuation you feel would help make it easier to understand.

   once upon a time the dog and cat were friends they shared everything and went together into the bush to catch and eat small animals one day the dog said to the cat I have collected together a lot of money and I am going to buy a truck that way we can take the meat we do not eat to the market and get lots of money to help our families what a good idea said the cat the next day dog arranged to go and find out who was selling trucks so he

came to the cat and asked him to look after his money while he was away
the cat agreed

2. You brought several texts in your language to the workshop. Check
through your texts and make sure you understand them. If you have
not done so already, make a word-for-word translation of your text into
English. There may be some words you are not able to translate. Leave a
blank under these words. (See Appendix 2.)

Read the text aloud. Where you make longer pauses, put a paragraph
break. You can use this symbol: ¶. Check to be sure periods and commas
are included in the appropriate places.

Make two photocopies of each of your texts once you are satisfied with the
punctuation and back-translation.

Work Session B: Translating the Creation Story

Think of a specific group of people in your community—for example, youth, women, non-Christians, or children. Translate this Bible story into your mother tongue for them to the best of your ability. It is taken from Ken Taylor's Favorite Bible Stories. After you have finished, put it away. We will look at it again later in the course.

God creates a beautiful world

A long time ago, God created the world out of nothing. It did not look then like it does today. At that time there were no people, no animals, no birds, no trees or flowers. Everything was dark and silent. Then God created light. He called the light "Day" and the darkness he called "Night". This happened the first day of creation. The second day, God created the heavens.

The third day, he created the oceans, lakes, and dry ground. Then he created grass and covered the ground with all kinds of flowers, bushes, and trees. The fourth day, God placed the sun, the moon, and the stars in the sky.

The fifth day, God created all kinds of marvelous fish in the sea, big and small. He made the birds as well – ducks and geese that swim, eagles and doves that live in the forests and in the fields.

The sixth day, he created the animals, rabbits, elephants, and even bees. He made everything! And finally he created people.

And God was very pleased with his work. He said, "Everything is so beautiful and good!"

The seventh day, when he had finished everything, God rested. It was a quiet day, different from all the others, a day of rest.

Lesson 3

How We Know When We Have Understood

Which bus?

As soon as they could, Peter and John decided to visit some friends from their village who lived in the capital city where the conference was being held. They had only been to the capital a couple of times before and were not too sure of how to get to their friend's house. During one of the breaks, Peter talked about this with Samson, who also came from the south. Samson told Peter which bus to take.

As they were preparing to leave, Peter told John, "The bus we need stops right in front of the supermarket." John agreed, "Yes, I've seen a bus stop there. This will be easy."

As they were leaving the building, they ran into the conference hostess, Mary, and greeted her. They mentioned that they were going to visit friends in Makri, and were off to catch the bus in front of the supermarket. She said, "Oh, that's not the bus you need at all. You'll never get to Makri that way. The bus you need stops by the mosque." Peter looked at John and said, "Fine help Samson is!"

Then Mary said, "Actually, our driver is just about to go to Makri to do some shopping; he can take you." Peter and John were very glad to hear this. In fact, the driver took them right to their friend's house and they had a very relaxing evening there.

GROUP DISCUSSION

1. In the first paragraph John said, "Yes, I've seen a bus stop there. This will be easy." Discuss how this comment affected or changed Peter's thoughts about which bus they should take.
2. In the second paragraph Mary said, "Oh, that's not the bus you need at all. You'll never get to Makri that way." Discuss how this comment changed Peter's thoughts about how to get to Makri.

3. In the third paragraph Mary said, "Actually, our driver is just about to go to Makri to do some shopping; he can take you." Discuss how this comment changed Peter's thoughts about their trip.

Making sense

We feel we have understood what someone means when what they say makes sense to us. Peter and John felt they understood what each other meant when they were talking about how to get to Makri. Even when Peter said, "Fine help Samson is!" John understood that he meant the exact opposite—that Samson had not been helpful at all. But how did he know this? People do not always mean the opposite of what they say. John could not see into Peter's mind, and what he said only pointed to what he meant.

For communication to "make sense," it needs to connect with what we already know. It also has to change what we know in certain ways. We refer to these changes in our thoughts as *cognitive benefits*, because we benefit from having more correct thoughts about our world. The better our thoughts are, the better we do in life. We consider something relevant if it brings us cognitive benefits.

> *Cognitive benefits are changes in our thoughts that result from incoming information. We consider something relevant if it brings us cognitive benefits.*

If Mary had told John and Peter, "When you get off the bus, go towards my aunt's house," they would not have been able to understand what she meant because they did not know where Mary's aunt lived. Communication that is not connected with what we already know is not relevant because we cannot supply a context in which to process it and so are not able to understand what the speaker means.

If Mary had told John and Peter, "You're in the capital city," they would not have found this to be very relevant because this would not change their thoughts in any way.

Things may change our thoughts a lot or a little. The more changes we experience from a communication, the more relevant that communication is to us.

Group Discussion

1. In the story at the beginning of the lesson, which of these comments changed Peter's thoughts the least?
    John: Yes, I've seen a bus stop there.
    Mary: Oh, that's not the bus you need at all.
    Mary: Actually, our driver is just about to go to Makri to do some shopping.

2. Imagine the afternoon class of this workshop starts at 2:00 and you know this is the case. If the leader tells you, "Class starts at 2:00," is this relevant to you? Explain your answer.

3. Imagine you're at a workshop in Manila and hear the statements below. Decide which statement would be the most relevant to you, and which would be the least relevant. Say which thoughts the most relevant statement would change.
   a. The building you are in is on fire.
   b. A building in the neighborhood is on fire.
   c. A building in Tokyo is on fire.

> ## Relevant communication connects with our thoughts and changes them in some way.
> ## The more the changes, the more relevant it is to us.

Making enough sense

We expect different amounts of cognitive benefits in different situations. For example, we will look for more cognitive benefits from a lecture than from a conversation with a cashier at a store. Our search for meaning is satisfied when we have experienced enough cognitive benefits to satisfy our expectations.

Cognitive benefits help us know when we have understood what people are saying. We assume they want to be understood, and that they make it as easy as possible for us to understand what they mean. This allows us to take the path of least effort to find an interpretation that leads to enough cognitive benefits. Once we have experienced enough benefits to satisfy our expectations, we stop processing. The feeling we experience is similar to when we feel full after eating. We are no longer interested in processing the communication any more.

> ## The Basic Comprehension Procedure
>
> To understand meaning, we:
> 1) take the path of least effort
> 2) consider possible interpretations in the order they come to mind
> 3) stop when we get enough cognitive benefits to satisfy our expectations.

GROUP DISCUSSION

1. Read the scene below:

    You are downtown shopping and notice a friend across the street. You
    wave a greeting, but he keeps beckoning you. Finally you wait for a
    break in the traffic and cross the street to see what he wants. When you
    get there, he simply says, "It's a nice morning!" and walks away.

    Using what you have just learned, explain why you walked across the
    street, what you felt after you got there, and why you felt that way.

2. John wants to travel from Kathmandu to New Delhi. Which route would he
    take? Why? Explain *taking the path of least effort* using these two pictures.

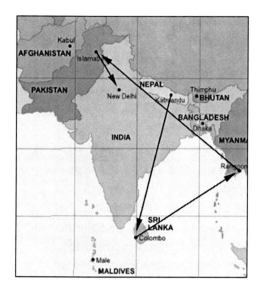 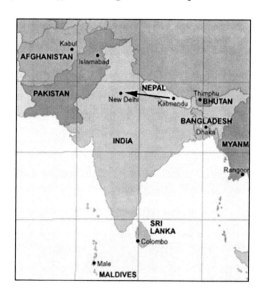

3. Use the three pictures below to explain the process of how we understand
    what someone is communicating to us.

Kinds of cognitive benefits

Three kinds of cognitive benefits are possible. For communication to be *relevant*, it has to have at least one cognitive effect, but it can have several. Let us look at these three kinds.

1. *Strengthening Thoughts*

When John agreed with Peter about catching the bus in front of the supermarket, this served to strengthen Peter's thought that this was the bus they needed. John even gave evidence to support his comment: he had seen the bus there. Peter was quite convinced that this was the bus they should take. The process went something like this:

> Strengthening is a kind of cognitive benefit that increases our belief that a thought we already have is true.

> Peter thought they should take the bus that stopped in front of the supermarket.
> John agreed.
> John said he saw a bus stop there.

STRENGTHENING: Peter was even more sure that this was the bus to take.

GROUP DISCUSSION

1. The first day of the conference, John thought the class session started at 8:30, but he was not sure. While he was chatting with Samson at breakfast, Samson looked at his watch, saw that it was 8:25, and said, "We only have five minutes to make it to the session!" Discuss how this comment affected John's thought about the time the class started.

2. John 9:8–9 says:
   > His neighbors and those who had formerly seen him begging asked, "Isn't this the same man who used to sit and beg?" Some claimed that he was. Others said, "No, he only looks like him." But he himself insisted, "I am the man" (NIV).

   Discuss how the man intended to affect the belief of those who thought he was the blind man when he said, "I am the man."

2. *Eliminating Thoughts*

In the story, Mary's comment eliminated John and Peter's thought that the bus they needed was the one that stopped in front of the supermarket. John and Peter believed that Mary knew what she was talking about. They knew she was familiar with the city's bus system. Their thought about catching the bus in front of the supermarket was based on much weaker sources: a person who was new to the city and John's

> Eliminating is a kind of cognitive benefit in which a thought is contradicted and erased by a stronger, incoming thought.

observation of a bus stopping there. The process went something like this:
>Peter and John are sure their bus stops in front of the supermarket.
>Mary says it is not that bus.
>Mary lives in the city and knows the bus system.
>John saw a bus, but it could have been any bus.

ELIMINATING: Peter and John no longer think this is the bus they need.

Thoughts we hold more strongly overpower those we hold weakly. Since Mary was a resident of the city, Peter and John trusted that the information she gave was correct. If a stranger to the city told them a different way, his or her report would not be strong enough to overpower what Peter and John had learned from Mary.

GROUP DISCUSSION

1. Look at John 9:8–9 again. Discuss how the blind beggar intended to affect the thoughts of the people who thought he only looked like the blind beggar.
2. John 20:24–25 says:
   > Now Thomas (called Didymus), one of the Twelve, was not with the disciples when Jesus came. So the other disciples told him, "We have seen the Lord!" But he said to them, "Unless I see the nail marks in his hands and put my finger where the nails were, and put my hand into his side, I will not believe it" (NIV).

   Thomas refused to believe the disciples' report that Jesus had risen from the dead. Discuss why you think their word did not overpower and eliminate his belief that Jesus was dead.
3. When Mary Magdalene was at Jesus' tomb after his death (Jn 20:10–17), a man appeared to her. She thought he was the gardener. She asked him where they had taken Jesus. He replied by saying her name, "Mary." Discuss how this changed her belief that he was the gardener. Try to trace her thought process.

3. *Forming New Implications*

Mary gave Peter and John two new bits of information: that their driver was just about to go to Makri and that he could take them. This new information changed their thoughts about going to Makri significantly: they could trust the driver to know the way, they would save the money for the bus fare, the journey would probably be quicker with no risk of getting lost, and so forth. These new thoughts resulted from combining Mary's words with things that Peter and John already knew. We refer to these as *new implications*. The process went something like this:

> New implications are thoughts that result from new information combining with things we already know.

Peter and John wanted to go to Makri.
Mary told them that the driver was about to go there and could take them.
People employed as drivers know the city.
Since it was a shopping trip for the guesthouse, it was already paid for.
Small cars go faster than buses which stop frequently.
And so forth…

NEW IMPLICATIONS:
- They'll go with the driver.
- The driver knows the way to Makri.
- They can keep the money for the bus fare.
- They can get there quicker than on the bus.
- And so forth.

If instead Mary had said to them, "The price of butter has gone up again," Peter and John would probably have been quite confused because although this information was new to them, it would not connect with any of the information they had just been thinking about. New implications always involve the combination of what people already know and the new information they are given. This is the most common kind of cognitive benefit.

> **We feel cognitive benefits when our thoughts are: 1) strengthened, 2) eliminated, or 3) combined with new information to form new implications.**

Summary

Relevant communication has to relate to what we already know and changes it in some way. When it does, we feel we have understood what the speaker was trying to communicate—it "makes sense." We have experienced enough cognitive benefits to satisfy our expectations. The more cognitive benefits we experience, the more relevant the communication is. Cognitive benefits come about in three ways: they can 1) strengthen thoughts we have, 2) eliminate thoughts we have, or 3) combine with new information to form new implications.

So what?

> **Audiences need to experience enough cognitive benefits from Scripture to satisfy their expectations.**

Assignment

1. In Acts 2:13–16, some people accuse the disciples of being drunk. What changes is Peter trying to make in their thoughts: strengthen them, eliminate them, and/or form new implications?

    > ¹³ Some, however, made fun of them and said, "They have had too much wine." ¹⁴ Then Peter stood up with the Eleven, raised his voice and addressed the crowd: "Fellow Jews and all of you who live in Jerusalem, let me explain this to you; listen carefully to what I say. ¹⁵ These men are not drunk, as you suppose. It's only nine in the morning! ¹⁶ No, this is what was spoken by the prophet Joel:…" (NIV).

2. Tell how the phrases in italics strengthen a thought the audience already had, eliminate a thought, and/or form new implications. Consider anything already said to that point as part of their knowledge. Remember, the same communication can have more than one kind of cognitive benefit.
    a. Before John left for the conference, he thought that he had to find the money to pay for his transportation to the capital. One day the week before he was to leave, his senior pastor came to tell him, "A gift has been given for your transportation." *"And what's more,"* the pastor said, *"I have it right here with me. Here it is."*
    b. On the first day of the course, Peter thought he knew that the afternoon session began at 2:00 p.m. *Straight after lunch, the leader announced, "Today the afternoon session will begin at 3 p.m."*
    c. Matthew 2:13 Now when they had departed, behold, an angel of the Lord appeared to Joseph in a dream and said, "Rise, take the child and his mother, and flee to Egypt, and remain there till I tell you; *for Herod is about to search for the child, to destroy him"* (RSV).
    d. Matthew 5:17b–18 I have not come to do away with them [the laws], but to make their teachings come true. *Remember that as long as heaven and earth last, not the least point nor the smallest detail of the Law will be done away with—not until the end of all things* (TEV).
    e. Matthew 28:5-6 "The angel said to the women, "Do not be afraid, for I know that you are looking for Jesus, who was crucified. *He is not here*. He has risen, just as he said" (NIV).

Lesson 4

Processing Effort, Benefits, and Relevance

The Amazing Dr. Mumford

Everyone at the conference was looking forward to the visit of a distinguished professor from Oxford, Dr. Mumford. He was an expert in oral communication. Peter and John felt very honored to be at a conference with such important speakers and dressed in their best clothes that day. They were looking forward to understanding how to reach their people better with the gospel and were sure Dr. Mumford's lecture would help them do so.

After a long introduction that listed all of his accomplishments, Dr. Mumford began his lecture. John and Peter had never heard anyone with an accent like his, and they had to strain to make out what he was saying. Besides, he seemed to swallow his words, so John and Peter had to pay close attention. But that wasn't all that made it difficult. Dr. Mumford used long words they had never heard before, like "aggregative" and "mnemonics." When Dr. Mumford started talking about the Homeric tradition and Milman Parry's discovery, John and Peter were completely lost. They felt like they were drowning in a flood of new information. Before long, Peter noticed John's head nodding.

Everyone clapped loudly for Dr. Mumford when he finished his speech, and he was escorted to the dining room where he enjoyed lunch with the conference leaders and then left.

In the afternoon session, the conference leader Mr. Jones asked, "What did you understand from Dr. Mumford's lecture?" There was silence in the room. Mr. Jones realized that no one understood much, so he gave a summary of Dr. Mumford's lecture in a way the group could understand, leaving out the parts that were not relevant to them. What had seemed so difficult to understand suddenly came within reach. Everyone was happy to understand at least something of what Dr. Mumford had tried to communicate.

GROUP DISCUSSION

1. Discuss what made Dr. Mumford's speech so difficult for John and Peter to understand.

2. Discuss what Mr. Jones did to help the conference participants understand what Dr. Mumford has said.
3. A lecture can be easy for some people to understand but very difficult for others. Discuss why this is so.

Effort and benefits determine relevance

We have seen that the more communication changes our thoughts, the more relevant it is to us. In other words, the more cognitive benefits we get, the more relevant it is. For communication to be relevant, the cognitive benefits need to be greater than the effort it takes to get them.

Relevance is determined by the difference between effort and cognitive benefits.

Cognitive benefits are gains. When we receive enough of these, we stop processing. We refer to the amount of effort we need to make in order to understand communi-cation as the *processing effort*. Speakers guide hearers to their intended meaning by keeping the processing costs as low as possible. This allows hearers to take the path of least effort and assume it will lead them to the intended meaning.

Even if a communication requires a lot of processing effort, it may still be relevant. As long as people expect the benefits to be greater than the effort they exert, they will continue to consider the communication relevant and make the effort to understand it. For example, students may consider their most difficult course to be the most relevant one.

Processing effort is the effort it takes us to understand something.

If the effort we have to make to understand communication is greater than the benefits we receive from it, the communication will not be very relevant to us. The pain has to be worth the gain or we may stop listening. John probably fell asleep during Dr. Mumford's lecture because of the very high processing costs and low cognitive benefits. If he tried very hard, he could follow some parts of Dr. Mumford's lecture. Other parts of the lecture he could not understand no matter how much he tried because he was lacking context. John did not benefit from the important things Dr. Mumford had to say because the processing effort was beyond what he was able or willing to pay. When Mr. Jones explained Dr. Mumford's lecture in a way that was related to what the conference participants already knew, John was able to follow.

Processing effort is different for each person. Something that is quite simple for one audience to understand can be difficult for another that lacks the intended context. Dr. Mumford's students at Oxford would most likely have found his lecture easy to understand. They were familiar with Dr. Mumford's variety of English, his vocabulary, and the ideas and people he referred to.

For communication to be relevant, benefits must be greater than effort.

GROUP DISCUSSION

1. Give an example of a time you made a lot of effort to understand something because you expected to benefit a lot from it.
2. Some audiences will not give their attention to Scripture when it is available in print, but respond enthusiastically when it is available in audio form. Explain why this is the case, using what you've learned in this lesson.

Speakers are only as exact as necessary

Every bit of information speakers give requires the audience to make an effort to process it. To keep processing costs as low as possible, speakers are only as exact as they think necessary to satisfy their audiences' expectations of relevance. If an audience's expectations of relevance are satisfied with approximate information, they will not find more details to be relevant. For example, the first day of the conference, if Peter asked John, "When did you arrive?" John may reply, "10:00." In fact, John may have arrived at 10:13 or 10:13 and 20 seconds, but Peter does not want or need to process all of that detail to satisfy his expectations. He only wanted a general idea of the time John arrived, and would not think John had lied when he said 10:00. When people are launching space missiles, however, time is calculated very precisely. Speakers keep processing costs as low as possible by only being as exact as necessary to meet their audience's expectations of relevance.

GROUP DISCUSSION

Describe a situation in which each of these sentences would be relevant. Explain why, using what you've learned in this lesson.

1. The sweater cost $30.00.
2. The sweater cost $32.45.

Extra effort should lead to extra benefits

Speakers want to be understood. They do not intentionally tire out their audience unnecessarily by asking them to exert effort for no benefits. If they express themselves in ways that require more effort to understand, the audience can rightly look for more cognitive benefits than a simpler expression would have given. For example, the workshop leader could say to Peter:

1. Class starts exactly at 2:00 p.m.
2. Class starts exactly at 2:00 p.m. and not a minute later!

The second sentence requires more effort to process, so Peter will look for more meaning to justify this extra processing cost. He may realize that the workshop leader thinks that starting on time is very important, will not tolerate people being even one minute late, intends to be there himself at that time, and so forth.

When reading Scripture, if the biblical author could have said something more simply, we need to ask why he did not do so. Our interpretation needs to account for what he was trying to communicate by the more costly expression.

GROUP DISCUSSION

The second sentence in each of the pairs below takes more effort to process, even if it is the simple repetition of a word or words. Discuss the extra benefits a hearer might receive that would make it worth the extra effort.

1. The journey was long.
    The journey was very, very long.

2. Holy is the Lord God Almighty.
    Holy, holy, holy is the Lord God Almighty (Rev 4:8b).

3. I will never leave you.
    Never will I leave you; never will I forsake you (Heb 13:5b).

4. Do your best to improve your faith. You can do this by adding goodness, understanding, self-control, patience, devotion to God, concern for others, and love (2 Pet 1:5–7 CEV).

5. Make every effort to add to your faith, goodness; and to goodness, knowledge; and to knowledge, self-control; and to self-control, perseverance; and to perseverance, godliness; and to godliness, brotherly kindness; and to brotherly kindness, love (2 Pet 1:5-7 NIV).

Reasons for communication failure

Communication is not always successful. There are at least three reasons for communication failure.

Expectations are not high enough or too high

Audiences stop processing communication when they think they have received enough cognitive benefits. If their expectations of cognitive benefits are too low, they may be satisfied that they have understood the speaker's meaning too quickly. For example, students may read assigned chapters quickly, satisfied that they have understood. When they take a test on the material, they may realize they did not understand enough of the author's meaning.

If their expectations of cognitive benefits are too high, audiences continue to search for more meaning than the author intended. This may lead to interpretations of the text that go beyond the author's intent. For example, in the story of the Good Samaritan, someone may want to find special meaning in the oil, the wine, and the two coins given to the innkeeper.

Expectations are filled, but not in the intended way

A context may come to an audience's mind, but it may not be the one the speaker intended. For example, the Yalunka of Guinea, West Africa believe that witches are not hungry during the day because they eat the souls of others during the night. What might they understand when they hear that "John [the Baptist] came neither eating nor drinking, and they say, 'He has a demon'?" (Mt 11:18).

If an unintended context leads to cognitive benefits, audiences will think that they have understood and not realize that they have actually misunderstood. Sooner or later, something in the text may help them realize they have misunderstood, but this may go undetected for a long time.

Extra effort, no extra benefits

Every effort should be rewarded with cognitive benefits. If people make extra effort to process a communication and do not experience more benefits, they may lose interest and stop processing. Several factors may lead to this.

- The speaker does not know the language well or is influenced by another language. We often refer to this kind of communication as "unnatural." Translations that are unnatural often lead to communication failure, as people have to exert extra effort to understand them but are not rewarded with extra cognitive benefits.
- The speaker uses expressions that the hearer finds difficult to understand.
- The audience lacks the intended context and invests a lot of effort to try to find it. This will make the logic of the communication seem complex.
- The audience knows the intended context but it does not come to mind easily.
- There is too much information (both old and new) for the person to be able to process it.

> Unnatural communication requires audiences to increase their processing effort with no increase in cognitive benefits.

GROUP DISCUSSION

1. A young man in an English class wrote, "From the day I entered your fabulous course, my days have been passed with learning English."
   - Discuss why you think he expressed himself in this way.

- Discuss whether you got extra benefits that made processing the complexity of the sentence worth the effort.
- Suggest how he could have said this more simply.

2. Which of these translations of Luke 4:7 seems more natural to you? Explain exactly what makes you to feel this way.

> "If thou therefore wilt worship me, all shall be thine" (KJV).
> "I will give it all to you if you will bow down and worship me" (NLT).

3. Read Hebrews 7:4–6.

> [4] Just think how great he was: Even the patriarch Abraham gave him a tenth of the plunder! [5] Now the law requires the descendants of Levi who become priests to collect a tenth from the people—that is, their brothers—even though their brothers are descended from Abraham. [6] This man, however, did not trace his descent from Levi, yet he collected a tenth from Abraham and blessed him who had the promises (NIV).

- Discuss whether you find parts of this text difficult to understand and explain why.

Some factors that lead to communication failure:
- **Expectations are not high enough or too high**
- **Expectations are filled but not in the intended way**
- **Extra effort, no extra benefits.**

Summary

Processing effort is the negative factor affecting relevance. Speakers express themselves in ways that require the least effort possible for their audiences to understand their meaning. Benefits are the positive factor and must be greater than the effort for communication to be relevant. Speakers only increase processing effort if they intend a corresponding increase in cognitive benefits. Whenever speakers express themselves in more complex ways, hearers look for benefits which a simpler expression would not have communicated. Communication can fail for various reasons: 1) hearers expectations are too low or too high, or 2) they may get cognitive benefits without realizing they have used an unintended context and misunderstood the speaker's meaning, or 3) they may make extra effort without receiving extra cognitive benefits.

So what? | For Scripture to be understood, translators need to ensure that audiences are able to experience enough benefits without unnecessary processing effort.

Assignment

1. Many Scripture passages involve a lot of new information, especially for people who do not know much about the Bible. Read Acts 18:1–3:

    > After this Paul left Athens and went to Corinth. There he found a Jew named Aquila, a native of Pontus, who had recently come from Italy with his wife Priscilla, because Claudius had ordered all Jews to leave Rome. Paul went to see them, and, because he was of the same trade, he stayed with them, and they worked together—by trade they were tentmakers (NRSV).

    Use any Bible helps available to you to understand the author's meaning.

    Prepare two lists of information communicated by this text that would be new for people in your church. In the first, list anything expressed in words in the text that is new to your audience. In the second, list anything from the context that would be new for your audience. Would this text be easy or difficult for your audience to understand? Why?

2. Compare these translations of Acts 1:18. List some things that might make translations of this verse unnecessarily difficult for your audience to follow, that is, things that increase processing effort without adding benefits.

    > KJV: Now this man purchased a field with the reward of iniquity; and falling headlong, he burst asunder in the midst, and all his bowels gushed out.

    > NIV: With the reward he got for his wickedness, Judas bought a field; there he fell headlong, his body burst open and all his intestines spilled out.

    > TEV: With the money that Judas got for his evil act he bought a field, where he fell to his death; he burst open and all his insides spilled out.

    > God's Word for the Nations: With the money he received from the wrong he had done, he bought a piece of land where he fell headfirst to his death. His body split open, and all his internal organs came out.

Work Session C: Identifying Context

1. In your language groups, think about foreigners in your country. What things do they do that appear odd or out of place? What things do they misunderstand? Make a list of at least ten things. Tell what kinds of contextual information they are missing that would help them understand and fit in better.

2. List all the ways you can think of to greet someone. Then explain the situations in which each greeting is used. What is communicated if your greeting is not the appropriate one for the context? For example, "Hey" is appropriate for young people greeting their friends. If students greet their professor this way, they would communicate disrespect.

3. In language groups, choose one of the letters you wrote to the church leader to convince him or her of the value of Bible translation. Imagine that a non-Christian reads it. Identify parts of the letter that he would find hard to understand because he does not have the right context. Glue or tape the letter in the center of a large flip-chart paper. Underline the problem areas and write the needed context on the large paper. Draw a line to connect the explanation with the underlined part of the text. Share one example from your letter with the whole group.

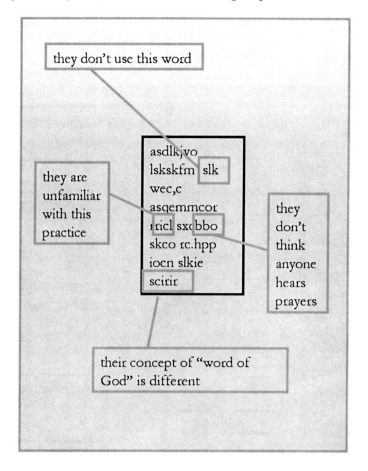

Work Session D: Verbal Sketch #1

Figure 3. Horse in three versions

1. What is the difference between the first two illustrations of the horse?

2. Does the second illustration get across the main idea of the first?

3. Does it have all of the details of the first?

4. Does the third illustration get across the idea of the first one? If not, what is wrong?

When artists sketch, they have to capture the main features of their subject as quickly as possible. Once they have the big picture mapped out, they can begin working on as many of the details as necessary.

Translating is like making a sketch with words. What is really important is that you get the major features of the original communication in place so that people can understand the main thrust of the text right away. Then you can work on filling in the details. If you start with the details, you may well end up with a text like the third illustration.

EXERCISES

1. Imagine you only have one minute to tell someone the main ideas the speaker is trying to get across. Make an oral verbal sketch of the following text in English. Limit yourself to four short sentences. Avoid details that are less important. When you are satisfied with your sketch, write it down.

   [26]They sailed to the region of the Gerasenes, which is across the lake from Galilee. [27]When Jesus stepped ashore, he was met by a

demon-possessed man from the town. For a long time this man had not worn clothes or lived in a house, but had lived in the tombs. [28]When he saw Jesus, he cried out and fell at his feet, shouting at the top of his voice, "What do you want with me, Jesus, Son of the Most High God? I beg you, don't torture me!" [29]For Jesus had commanded the evil spirit to come out of the man. Many times it had seized him, and though he was chained hand and foot and kept under guard, he had broken his chains and had been driven by the demon into solitary places.

[30]Jesus asked him, "What is your name?"

"Legion," he replied, because many demons had gone into him. [31]And they begged him repeatedly not to order them to go into the Abyss. [32]A large herd of pigs was feeding there on the hillside. The demons begged Jesus to let them go into them, and he gave them permission. [33]When the demons came out of the man, they went into the pigs, and the herd rushed down the steep bank into the lake and was drowned. [34]When those tending the pigs saw what had happened, they ran off and reported this in the town and countryside, [35]and the people went out to see what had happened. When they came to Jesus, they found the man from whom the demons had gone out, sitting at Jesus' feet, dressed and in his right mind; and they were afraid. [36]Those who had seen it told the people how the demon-possessed man had been cured. [37]Then all the people of the region of the Gerasenes asked Jesus to leave them, because they were overcome with fear. So he got into the boat and left.

[38]The man from whom the demons had gone out begged to go with him, but Jesus sent him away, saying, [39]"Return home and tell how much God has done for you." So the man went away and told all over town how much Jesus had done for him (Lk 8:26–39 NIV).

2. Now imagine you have 45 seconds. Do a three-sentence verbal sketch.
3. Now imagine you have 30 seconds. Do a two-sentence verbal sketch.
4. Now imagine you have 15 seconds. Do a one-sentence verbal sketch.
5. Share your verbal sketches with your small group.

Lesson 5

How We Select Context

Birgita's done it again!

Peter's uncle lived in a village near the capital city. He heard that Peter was in the city and so he sent a letter to him with one of the mini-bus drivers. As Peter read it he made exclamations of shock and concern, and finally he shook his head and sighed. John didn't know Peter's family and wondered what in the world Peter's uncle had written to him to get such a response. That evening he asked Peter about the letter. Peter smiled to himself and said, "I'll read it to you." This was what the letter said after the opening greetings:

> I need to tell you what has happened to Birgita. You know all about the fuss there was about her two years ago, well she's done it again! It seems quite incredible that she did not learn her lesson the first time. This time, however, Eric has taken a different line with her. He's washed his hands of the whole affair and has left her to sort it out. As a result, she's decided to visit old Veronica and you know where she lives! I cannot imagine what will happen when she finally gets there—or even if she will ever get there.

GROUP DISCUSSION

1. Discuss what questions John might have after hearing this letter.
2. Discuss why you think John has these questions.

Meaning depends on context

If people process a text using different contexts, they will understand different things. For example, if I am busy working indoors, and I see you walking up and call out, "The door is open," what do I mean? If I am at the zoo looking at the lions, and the zookeeper calls out the same thing, what does he mean? The context hearers supply affects what they understand.

39

Speakers have certain thoughts they intend to communicate. In the example above, the speaker either meant "Come in" or "Run for your life." Hearers need to use the context the speaker intended to understand what the speaker is communicating. Hearers are not free to use just any context they wish and claim they understood what the speaker was saying.

Text plus context leads to the intended meaning.

GROUP DISCUSSION

1. Coffee was always available at John and Peter's conference. In the evening, Peter asked John, "Would you like some coffee?" John replied, "Oh, coffee keeps me awake." Should Peter bring John coffee or not?
    *   Think of a context in which Peter would understand that John did not want coffee.
    *   Think of another context in which Peter would understand that John did want coffee.
2. Read the following passage.

    On Herod's birthday the daughter of Herodias danced in front of the whole group. Herod was so pleased that he promised her, "I swear that I will give you anything you ask for!" At her mother's suggestion she asked him, "Give me here and now the head of John the Baptist on a plate!" The king was sad, but because of the promise he had made in front of all his guests he gave orders that her wish be granted. So he had John beheaded in prison. The head was brought in on a plate and given to the girl, who took it to her mother (Mt 14:6–11 TEV).

    In some cultures, people cut off the heads of their enemies and eat their brains to gain spiritual power. What might people from these cultures understand from this passage, especially if they knew that John was an enemy of Herodias?

How do we know the intended context?

Our minds are full of information that we know and believe to be true. We cannot possibly think of everything we know at once. Speakers only intend that we use some of what we know to understand what they mean. Our knowledge is like water in a well. *Contextual information* is the bits of information that come to mind from everything we know— from memory as well as from what we see, smell, hear, taste, feel—as we try to understand a communication. All of the contextual

Contextual information is the bits of information that come to mind from everything we know as we try to understand a communication. Together, all the bits of contextual information make up the context for that part of the text.

information together forms the context we use to understand what someone has said. It is like the bucketful of water we draw from the well.

The context for a communication

Everything we know

Figure 4. Context is like the bucket of water from the well

We choose the context we think the speaker intends very quickly, without even being aware of how our mind is working. The context we select must be:

1. Thoughts that come to mind quickly.

2. Thoughts we think we share with the speaker.

3. Thoughts that lead to enough cognitive benefits.

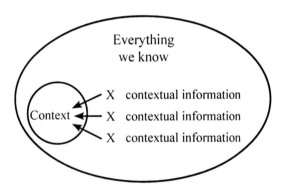

Figure 5. Context is part of everything we know

We think of these things all at once, not in order. Sometimes we are not able to think of any context at all or, at other times, we may think of a context the speaker did not intend. In either of these cases, we will not understand the intended meaning. Now we will look at each of these factors in detail.

The intended contextual information comes to mind quickly

When someone speaks to us, some information comes to mind quickly. It is what we find first as we follow the path of least effort to understand what the speaker is communicating. It is a good candidate for the intended context.

Information we have used *recently* comes to mind most quickly, for example, things we have talked about in the previous part of the conversation. Information we use *frequently* also comes to mind quickly. For example, in this course, when we say 'translation,' our minds think of Bible translation, because that is what we think about most frequently. We do not think about the many other kinds of translations that are possible.

GROUP DISCUSSION

1. What information comes to your mind first when you hear *rice*? Explain why this is so.
2. What information comes to your mind first when you hear "2:00"? Explain why this is so.

The intended contextual information must be thoughts we think we share with the speaker

The only information that comes to mind to serve as context is information hearers think they share with the speaker. For example, if my friend tells me, "John isn't feeling well," I only think of the people called John that I think we both know. I may have a cousin named John. If my friend does not know him, I know she could not be talking about that John and must be referring to another. The first *John* that comes to mind is one that I think we both know.

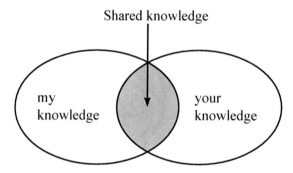

Figure 6. Where we look for context

Exercise

Write down:
1. one thing that you have in common with everyone in this room.
2. one thing you only have in common with the people you work with.
3. one thing you only have in common with the people you live with.

Share what you have written.

The intended contextual information leads to enough cognitive benefits

For us to feel that communication is relevant, it has to change what we know in some way. We continue searching until our expectations of cognitive benefits are satisfied. As soon as we find information we already have that combines with the text that leads to enough cognitive benefits, we assume that we have selected the context the speaker intended. For example, John overheard Samson saying, "2:37 is terrible!" John assumed Samson was talking about 2:37 that afternoon, and could not understand what would be so terrible about it. Finally Peter explained to him that 2:37 was the name of a brand new, cheap airline that Samson had used. Then John felt satisfied that he understood what Samson was talking about.

> Context must:
>   1) come to mind quickly
>   2) be information we think we share
>   3) lead to enough cognitive benefits
>   to satisfy our expectations.

Contextual mismatches and secondary communication

The letter from Peter's uncle was intended for Peter, and he was able to understand it without difficulty. The uncle did not repeat things he thought Peter already knew, like what Birgita did two years ago. We refer to Peter as the primary recipient of the letter. We refer to communication like this between the uncle and Peter as *primary communication*.

The letter was not written to John. We refer to him as a secondary recipient of the letter. The communication that went on between the uncle and John is referred to as *secondary communication*.

John did not know many of the details of Peter's family life, and so he was not able to understand the uncle's letter. His context did not match Peter's. When the context an audience supplies does not match the one the speaker intends, we refer to this as a *contextual mismatch*.

Contextual mismatches occur from time to time in primary communication. In secondary communication, they can be frequent. If Peter wanted John to understand his uncle's letter, he would need to identify the contextual mismatches John was experiencing and address them so that the intended context

Primary communication is addressed to an audience directly. In secondary communication, a second audience is trying to understand a communication designed for another audience.

A contextual mismatch happens when the context intended by the speaker does not match the context the audience supplies.

came to John's mind. Then John could understand the uncle's letter like Peter did.

God intended Scripture to speak to people of all time and in all places, but the biblical authors wrote to specific audiences in specific times and places. When we read or hear Scripture, we are a secondary audience, listening in on something originally addressed to someone else.

Summary

To understand the meaning the speaker intended, we need to use the context the speaker intended. Without thinking about it consciously, we select the intended context out of all the information we know. We look for: 1) information that comes to mind quickly, 2) information that we think we share with the speaker, and 3) information that leads to enough cognitive benefits. In primary communication, the intended context usually comes to mind. In secondary communication, audiences are much more likely to have difficulty identifying the intended context and need to be alert for contextual mismatches that might lead to misunderstanding.

> **So what?**
>
> ## Translators need to be alert for contextual mismatches that prevent their audience from understanding Scripture.

Assignment

Read Matthew 22:15–22:

> [15] The Pharisees went off and made a plan to trap Jesus with questions.
> [16] Then they sent to him some of their disciples and some members of Herod's party. "Teacher," they said, "we know that you tell the truth. You teach the truth about God's will for people, without worrying about what others think, because you pay no attention to anyone's status. [17] Tell us, then, what do you think? Is it against our Law to pay taxes to the Roman Emperor, or not?" [18] Jesus, however, was aware of their evil plan, and so he said, "You hypocrites! Why are you trying to trap me? [19] Show me the coin for paying the tax!" They brought him the coin, [20] and he asked them, "Whose face and name are these?" [21]"The Emperor's," they answered. So Jesus said to them, "Well, then, pay to the Emperor what belongs to the Emperor, and pay to God what belongs to God." [22] When they heard this, they were amazed; and they left him and went away (TEV).

Now read this information about this text (adapted from the NIV Study Bible, the CEV Learning Bible, and Keener 1993):

Rome ruled over Palestine like a colonial power. The Pharisees were completely opposed to Roman rule, while the members of Herod's party supported the Roman rule and wanted Herod to be king in Jerusalem. The Pharisees did not usually do things together with the members of Herod's party. Now, however, the Pharisees

Figure 7. Inscription on Roman coin

enlisted their help to trap Jesus in his words. The coin they had to use to pay taxes had an image of the emperor on it and an inscription, such as "Tiberius Caesar Augustus, son of the divine Augustus." The Jews were opposed to images of any sort, because of the second commandment prohibiting graven images, so they did not like these coins. Earlier in this chapter, Jesus had been gaining popularity with the people and attacking the religious leaders, and they did not like this at all. After trying to put Jesus off guard with flattery, they asked their question: "Is it right to pay taxes to Caesar or not?" If he said "No," the members of Herod's party would report him to the Roman governor and he would be punished for being disloyal to the government. If he said "Yes," the Pharisees would denounce him to the people as cooperating with the Roman government and so being disloyal to their Jewish nation. They thought either way he would lose popularity and lose the possibility of claiming to be the Messiah.

Now discuss these topics:

1. Make a list of at least four bits of contextual information audiences need to know to understand this passage.
2. Explain how your understanding of this passage changed after reading more of the intended context.
3. Discuss how much of this information you think an average member of your church would know. Has the passage ever been misunderstood due to lack of contextual information? If so, how?

Lesson 6

Communicating with Concepts

A walk through the woods

One week-end at the conference, Samuel invited John to go to visit his brother. His brother lived in a village not too far away, but the quickest way to get there was to walk through a forest. John came from the south of the country where all of the forests belonged to someone and where there were many paths between the trees. There were a few small animals that lived in the woods, but nothing that could hurt anyone. John was looking forward to a pleasant walk through the woods on their way to Samuel's brother's house. Samuel asked John if he had any rubber boots. John did not know what rubber boots had to do with a walk in the forest. He did not have any rubber boots, but Samuel managed to find an extra pair.

Samuel and John took a bus that dropped them off at the edge of the forest. "We've got to be careful now," Samuel said. John thought to himself, "Careful? Why do we have to be careful?" As they entered the forest, John realized that this forest was completely different from the forests he knew back home. The trees were very close together, and there were no real paths to be seen. As they battled their way through the thick undergrowth, John realized that he could get lost very easily, so he made sure he kept very close to Samuel. The ground was so wet his feet sunk into the mud, and he was happy Samuel had given him the rubber boots to wear. After a few minutes Samuel started singing and whistling loudly. John was surprised at this, but Samuel explained that this was to keep the wild animals away. Suddenly John felt afraid of what might happen to them, so he started singing, too.

To his great relief, after twenty minutes Samuel told John that they were nearly out of the forest. But at that very moment they heard a large animal coming through the undergrowth behind them. John turned to look and got a glimpse of what looked like a large cat. "Run!" shouted Samuel and they ran at top speed to get out of the forest area as fast as they could. "Pheew!" said John, "Your forest is certainly different from ours! Could we go home by a different route?"

GROUP DISCUSSION

1. Why was John confused when Samuel asked him if he had rubber boots to wear in the forest?
2. What information came to mind for John when he heard the word *forest?*
3. What information came to mind for Samuel when he used the word *forest?*

What is a concept?

Our thoughts are made up of concepts. They are ideas in our minds about things, processes, qualities, or relationships. A concept can come to mind when we see or sense the thing, process, quality or relationship, or it can come to mind when we hear a word or phrase that represents it. For example, these words bring certain concepts to mind:

> *A concept is an idea about a thing, process, quality, or relationship.*

*   Camel
*   Peel
*   Pneumonia
*   Operate
*   Beautiful
*   Before

Concepts are not always represented by words. They can be brought to mind by phrases. For example:

*   The sensation of biting aluminum foil
*   Dried ears of corn tied together by their husks
*   The sound of fingernails scratching a black board
*   People whose eyes are too close together
*   To replant a field that has been damage by animals
*   Son of Man

Concepts are the building blocks of thoughts in our minds. For example, "Bells rang loudly" brings several concepts to mind: BELL, RING, and LOUDLY. [1]

Figure 8. Concepts are the building blocks of thoughts

---

[1] When we talk about the word or expression that represents a concept in this book, we write it in italics. When we talk about the concept itself, we write it in small capital letters.

The information in our minds is organized into networks. A network is a system which links things together. When one part is activated, things linked to it are activated as well. A spider web is an example of a network. Each part of the web is connected to the rest. When a fly lands on one part of a spider web, it makes the whole thing move a bit.

The networks of information in our minds serve to organize our thoughts and make it easier for information to come to mind when we need it. When a concept comes to mind, information linked to it comes to mind, too. For example, when John heard the word *forest*, he thought of a place with trees, plants, and footpaths. This information varies from person to person. For Samuel, *forest* brought to mind different information. The information we link to a concept changes over time as we have different experiences with the concept. John would never think of forests as always being pleasant again!

Concepts are entry points to networks of information in our minds.

The same information can be linked to more than one concept. For example, much of the information linked to FOREST is also linked to GARDEN, but not all. For example, forests are very large and have many more trees than a garden. Gardens have flowerbeds, but forests do not. As a result, when we think about forests, ideas about gardens are not far off.

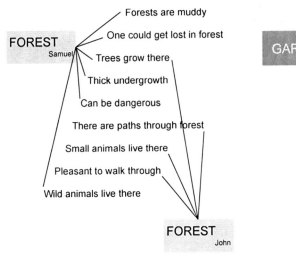

Figure 9. John and Samuel's concept of FOREST

Figure 10. Information linked to more than one concept

We can use different concepts to refer to the same thing or person. For example, John can refer to Peter in a variety of ways. He can introduce him as his friend, a Bible translator, a church leader, a father, and so forth. In each case, John is referring to the same person, but calls to mind different information about him. For example, when John uses the concept BIBLE TRANSLATOR, this brings to mind that Peter must know a good deal about the Bible, languages, and communication, that he works at a computer, that he works patiently in a quiet place, and so forth. FRIEND brings to mind the fact that John likes to spend time with Peter, that they care about each other, that they can call on each other when they need help. Speakers use the word that brings to mind the thoughts they intend to communicate about the person or thing.

EXERCISES

1. Write down all of the ideas the concept CHAMELEON brings to your mind.
    a. In the large group, compare this information:
        •   How much of the information is similar?
        •   How much is different?
        •   Which bits of information are really necessary to know the concept?
        •   Which information is used to categorize chameleons? That is, what information tells us what kind of thing a chameleon is?

2. Write down the first three ideas that come to your mind when you hear: owl, spider, crescent moon, guinea pig. Compare your responses.

3. Think of three ways to refer to your mother. Describe the information that comes to mind with each word or expression.
4. An elderly lady was very sure that the American President McKinley was assassinated in 1901, but when asked if he is dead, she said she did not know. Do you feel she knows the concept ASSASSINATE? Explain your point of view.

How we access information

We have said that as we search for meaning, we take the path of least effort and process until we find enough cognitive benefits to satisfy our expectations of relevance. We do all this without thinking about it. When a concept is communicated to us, the information linked to it comes into our minds automatically. We consider it as we process the communication, starting with the information that takes the least effort to activate. The process goes something like this:

1. We use the most accessible information associated with the concept expressed in the utterance first. This information comes to mind most rapidly and so it has the lowest processing costs. If it leads to enough cognitive benefits, we are satisfied and stop our search for meaning. If not, we use the next most accessible information associated with the concept expressed in the utterance. If we have tried all of the information associated with a concept and still have not gotten enough cognitive benefits, we continue our search.

2. We consider other concepts linked to that information. This process may be repeated more than once. Once we feel we have understood, we stop processing.

3. If we invest a lot of effort and still do not feel we have understood the speaker's meaning, at some point we may give up. When this happens, we feel we simply cannot understand what the speaker means.

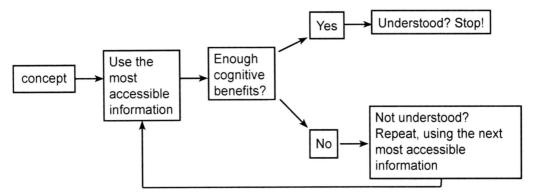

Figure 11. How we access information associated with concepts

For example, imagine Peter is having a serious problem. It is time for him to marry, but he is not in a position to do so. He and John have been discussing the situation, and finally Peter says, "I'm going to Bukoko. I'm sure I'll find a solution." The information John associates with the concept BUKOKO may not lead directly to cognitive benefits: it is a small village, remote, renowned for its quarrelsome inhabitants, Peter's uncle lives there. His mind might then search further in the concept of MATERNAL UNCLE and access the information that they care for their nephews and intervene on their

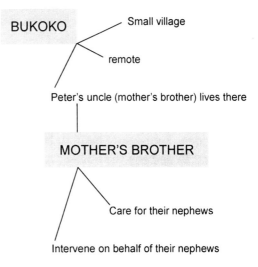

Figure 12. Searching for meaning in the concept network

behalf, regardless of the size of the problem. John had to search in the information associated with the concept MATERNAL UNCLE that was associated with the concept BUKOKO before he was able to understand what Peter meant.

Differences between languages

Translation is challenging because it is not simply a matter of substituting words in the receptor language for words in the source language. Concepts between two languages are rarely identical. The expression one language uses to indicate a concept can use more words or fewer words than the expression used in another language. For example, the Ngbaka have one word for the concept FATHER'S BROTHER (*nya*) and another for the concept MOTHER'S BROTHER (*fele*), but they do not have a word for a concept that combines them both. Conversely, English has one word for the concept UNCLE which combines both FATHER'S BROTHER and MOTHER'S BROTHER, but it does not have a distinct word for each concept. Much of the information associated with these concepts differs between cultures as well.

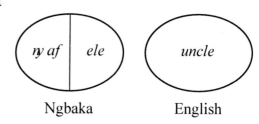

Ngbaka   English

Figure 13. Difference in concepts between languages

If a concept is used frequently, it is usually expressed in a word, but not always. We can know a concept without having a specific word to express it. For example, both Ngbaka and English speakers have concepts for FATHER'S BROTHER, MOTHER'S BROTHER, and UNCLE, but they do not have single words to express each one.

On the other hand, one word can represent more than one concept. For example, the word *running* in English expresses different concepts in these sentences:

> She was RUNNING with all her might to get away from the lion.

> The water was RUNNING all night.

In the first sentence, running means moving very quickly. In the second, it means flowing. In French, two different words are used for these two concepts: *courrir* and *couler*. Translators need to be sure they understand the concepts words are referring to and use the correct one in their language.

Languages can also differ in the word categories they use to express certain concepts. One language might be able to express a certain concept with a noun when another language might express it with a verb. For example, 'the *creation* of the world' (Rom 1:20) might need to be expressed in some languages as 'when the world *was created*'. Or '*the coming* of the Lord' (1 Thes 4:15) as '... the Lord *comes*'.

> Differences between languages:
> - The concepts they have.
> - The number of words they use to represent a concept.
> - The information they associate with a concept.
> - Whether they express a concept with a noun or a verb.

1. Think of two concepts expressed by each of the words in this list:
   a. to take off
   b. leaf
   c. to beat
2. Think of a word in your language that English uses two or more words to express. For example, Hebrew *tsoon* is expressed by *sheep* and *goats* in English.
3. Think of a word in English that your language uses two or more words to express. For example, English *uncle* is expressed by *nya* and *fele* in Ngbaka.
4. Underline the nouns in the following verses that can be expressed as a verb:
   a. Luke 2:47 … all who heard him were amazed at his understanding and his answers.
   b. Luke 4:18 … to proclaim release to the captives and recovering of sight to the blind, …
   c. Acts 16:26 … suddenly there was a great earthquake, …
5. Rewrite the following sentences, making the italicized nouns into verbs:
   a. 2 Timothy 4:21 Eubulus sends *greetings* to you.…
   b. Hebrews 4:6 … those who formerly received the good news failed to enter because of *disobedience,* …
   c. Hebrews 9:6 These *preparations* having thus been made, …

Summary

Concepts are ideas about things, processes, qualities, or relations. They are the building blocks of our thoughts. A concept can come to mind when we see or sense that thing, process, quality, or relationship. It can also be brought to mind when we hear a word or phrase that represents it. Whole bundles of information are linked to a concept. Some of this information is shared widely by members of a group, while other information varies with individuals and time. When a word is used, some of the information linked to that concept is activated. Our minds use the information that is activated and search until we find a context that leads to enough cognitive benefits. Different languages have different ways of grouping information into concepts, making translation a challenging task.

	Translators need to understand how our minds store and access concepts as they try to communicate across cultures.
So what?	

Assignment

1. Make a list of information you associate with the following words and phrases. Compare you list with another person. How are your concepts similar? How are they different?
    a. horse
    b. white man
    c. village house
    d. staple food (This is the food that you feel you need to eat each day in order to say you have really eaten.)
2. Compare the concept of bread in your language and in Jesus' day.
    *   Describe what bread looked like for the first audience.
    *   Give some of information that was associated with it.
    *   Compare this with the information that comes to mind for your audience.
3. Look at your texts in your language and chose two words that can have more than one meaning.
    *   Give the meaning the speaker intends in this text.
    *   Contrast this with another meaning this word could have that is not intended in this case.
        For example, for the word *burning* in "I'm burning with fever."
        1. The meaning the speaker intended: to have a body temperature that is much higher than normal.
        2. Another possible meaning: to turn into ashes.
        For the word *tulu* in Ngbaka of the Democratic Republic of Congo is *Mi he'de ga tulu we ne losambo* "I wore my large *cloth* to church."
        1. Intended meaning: skirt
        2. Another possible meaning: a tablecloth

Lesson 7

Filling Out What Is Said

News from home

That day, Peter got a phone call from his wife telling him their son, who had just recovered from a serious bout of malaria, had a temperature again and had been taken back to the hospital in the middle of the night. He and John prayed for the situation before going to bed, but all night long, Peter tossed and turned. When they woke up in the morning, he said to John, "I didn't sleep at all! What if my son's fever is worse? How will we pay for medicine? We don't have any money."

John answered, "It's difficult to be away from home when troubles come. Let's continue to pray for healing. God is our rock, especially at times like this."

GROUP DISCUSSION

1. What do you think Peter's wife meant when she said their son had a temperature again? Doesn't everyone have a temperature all the time?
2. When Peter's wife said they took their son to the hospital in the middle of the night, do you think she meant 12:00 a.m. exactly? Could she have taken him at 1:00 a.m.? How do you understand "middle of the night"?
3. What do you think Peter meant when he said, "I didn't sleep at all?" Do you think he didn't sleep, even for a minute, during the night?
4. What do you think Peter meant when he said, "We don't have any money?" Do you think they had nothing at all?
5. What did John mean when he said, "God is our rock?"

What is said serves as a sign post

Speakers use words and expressions to point their audience in the direction of the meaning they want to communicate. For example, fill in the blank in this sentence with the words below:

"Let's go to a _____ for dinner on Friday night,"

- Pub
- Bar

- Restaurant
- Café (coffee shop)

How does each word point you in a different direction as you think about what kind of evening to expect?

Speakers choose the words and expressions they use carefully to get their audience on the right path as they search for the intended meaning, but the audience still has to work out the specific meaning they intend in the context of the communication. One task is to fill out the meaning of what is said so that it is clear. This involves several things:

- determining the meaning of the words in their context.
- determining the meaning of words that have more than one sense.
- supplying parts of sentences that have been omitted.

In this lesson and the next, we will explore how our minds fill out the meaning of what is said.

Speakers may mean more or less than they say

Speakers can use words or expressions to mean more or less than the concepts normally associated with them. For example, when Peter's wife said her son had a temperature, she meant he had a certain sort of temperature, one that was above normal. It would not be relevant for her to mean that her son had a temperature, because everyone has one. Or Peter may refer to Mr. Jones and say, "He's a Brit!" Everyone at the workshop knows Mr. Jones is British, so Peter could not mean what was already obvious. That would not be relevant. He is saying that Mr. Jones is a certain sort of typical Brit, perhaps one that drinks tea at regular intervals. Or Peter might be used to very spicy food and not like the food at the conference center. He may say, "This food is tasteless!" He cannot mean exactly what he says, because all food has some flavor. He means that the food does not have as much flavor as he likes.

Speakers may not intend what they say to be literally true

At times, speakers do not intend what they say to be understood to be literally true. They may intend hearers to access only some of the information associated with the concept. For example, when John says to Peter, "God is our rock," he is not saying God is a kind of stone. He is also not saying God is something slightly more or less than a rock. Peter looks for information that he thinks GOD and ROCK share: they are both solid, immovable, indestructible, something to lean on that will not fall over, and so forth. He does not think of other information associated with ROCK: that of a gem, priceless, used to decorate landscapes, and so forth. Peter accesses a subset of the information stored at the concept ROCK and at the same time broadens the concept to include spirit beings.

When we communicate, we do not stop to classify how the speaker is using words. We simply look for relevance and take the first meaning that satisfies our expectation. We do this automatically. Literal meanings do not come to mind at all when they do not make sense in context.

1. Imagine when Peter returns home, his wife welcomes him warmly with a marvelous meal. A friend stops by to greet him as Peter is finishing the meal, and Peter says, "My wife is an angel." What do you think he means? Did you think he was saying she was invisible and had wings? If not, why not?

2. Imagine a context for the following examples. Explain the intended meaning of the word in italics. How is the meaning different from the literal meaning of the word?
   a. I *burned* my mouth on the sauce.
   b. I don't do *anything* on Sundays!
   c. Trials turn your faith into *gold.*
   d. John, referring to the missionary: "He's a *white* man."
   e. Jesus: "Tell Herod, that *fox,…*"

3. Imagine two ways the following sentences could be understood. Give a context for each.
   a. Don't make as much rice as you did last time.
   b. It won't be the same without you at the party.

Some words or expressions do not have much content on their own

Some words have little content on their own and can mean quite different things in different contexts. For example, what does *big* mean in the examples below?

Mary gave birth to a *big* baby.
The game warden saw a *big* elephant.

In the first example, *big* means perhaps 60 centimeters (24 inches) long and weighing 5 kilos (11 lbs), but in the second example it means more like 4 meters (13 feet) high and weighing 7 tons (over 6000 kilos). Hearers rely heavily on context to know how to fill out the meaning of words like this. Translators need to be sure they understand what these words mean in the original so that they translate them appropriately in their own languages.

1. How much time does *soon* represent in the following examples?
   • The train will be here soon.
   • It will be dark soon.
   • He will be an adult soon.
   • Christ is coming back soon.

2. How much does *expensive* represent in these examples?
   - Tomatoes are expensive today.
   - His new Mercedes was expensive.
   - She always buys expensive clothes.
3. How would you fill out "getting along in years" in the following verse in your culture? How old would you think she would be?

> If anyone thinks he is acting improperly toward the virgin he is engaged to, and if she is *getting along in years* and he feels he ought to marry, he should do as he wants. He is not sinning. They should get married (1 Cor 7:36 NIV).

Some words have almost no content on their own

Some words have almost no content on their own, and hearers have to fill out their meaning completely in the context of the communication. For example, pronouns—*I, you, he, it, we, they*—can be used to represent any number of specific people or things. Words like *here* represent the location of the speaker, and *there* represents a place other than where the speaker is located.

Other parts of language that have very little meaning of their own are words like *of* (or the suffix *'s*) in English. These constructions only give a general indication of a relationship between two nouns (or noun phrases) and let the hearer understand the rest from context. For example, *John's house* (or *the house of John*) could mean any of the following, or more:

The house John owns.

The house John built.

The house John lives in.

The house John drew on a piece of paper.

Hearers understand the relationship between the words *John* and *house* by using the intended context.

These constructions can be difficult to translate in languages that require the relationship between nouns to be expressed more specifically in words. For example, *Jesus of Nazareth* may need to be expressed as Jesus who came from Nazareth. *A city of Galilee* may need to be expressed as *a city located in Galilee*.

Languages may also use *of* constructions where English uses adjectives. For example, in Hebrew, speakers say *a ring of gold* or *a rod of iron,* while in English speakers say *a gold ring* or *an iron rod.* Translators need to understand the author's intended meaning and communicate it in a way their audience can understand at the least processing cost.

EXERCISES

1. What do the following expressions mean? For example, in Matthew 13:35, "Since the foundation *of* the world" means "Since God *founded/created* the world." Look the verses up in their contexts.
    a. Matthew 1:18 the birth of Jesus Christ
    b. Luke 1:11 an angel of the Lord
    c. Acts 11:5 the city of Joppa
    d. Romans 8:39 the love of God
    e. 1 John 5:3 the love of God
    f. Luke 1:44 the city of Andrew and Peter
2. In your language, what construction(s) do speakers use to express concepts like:
    a. *John's car,* or *the car of John*, that is, the car that John possesses
    b. *Bamenda's chief, or the chief of Bamenda*, that is, the chief over the area of Bamenda
3. Translate the following phrases naturally into your language and give an English back-translation.
    a. John 1:44 the city of Andrew and Peter
    b. Luke 4:31 a city of Galilee
    c. Acts 8:27 the Queen of the Ethiopians
    d. Hebrews 2:15 through fear of death
    e. Mark 1:6 Now John wore a garment of camel's hair
    f. Luke 1:5 In the days of Herod, King of Judea
4. What do the words in italics communicate in the sentences below?
    a. Bill is *in* the house.
        Mary is *in* trouble.
    b. Frank sat *under* a tall tree.
        I am not *under* any illusion.
        Do not tell anybody the PIN of your credit card *under* any circumstance.
5. Underline at least six words in the following texts that have special need of being filled out from the context:
    a. John began to feel a bit feverish that afternoon and went to the clinic to see a doctor. He did not want to miss any of the conference, and thought if it was malaria, it would be good to treat it before it got too bad. He explained his symptoms to the nurse at the clinic, and she gave him three pills to take immediately. John did this, and before long, he felt normal again.
    b. Matthew 24:29 Immediately after the tribulation of those days the sun will be darkened, and the moon will not give its light, and the stars will fall from heaven, and the powers of the heavens will be shaken (RSV).

Some words or expressions are associated with more than one concept

Words and expressions can be associated with more than one concept. For example, a little boy heard how Lot's wife looked back and turned into a pillar of salt and said, "My dad looked back once while he was driving and he turned into a palm tree!" This is funny because "turned into" can mean "became" or "changed direction and ran into." Jokes often depend on double meanings like this to be funny. Hearers have to select the intended sense in order to understand the speaker's meaning. Usually context guides them to the intended meaning so smoothly they do not even notice that another sense was possible.

EXERCISE

Think of two ways the words in italics in the examples can be understood. Give a context for each:

1. John referring to his friend: "He *beats* me every time we play cards."
2. He came *back to earth*.
3. Come here, *he won't bite you*!
4. I *hear* you!
5. I love my own *company*.

Often it is not just a word that can have more than one meaning but longer expressions. Read the following two examples:

When John walked into the stable, he *kicked the bucket* that his brother had forgotten to take out of the way.

The gangster *kicked the bucket* at the age of 35. He was killed in a shootout with a rival gang.

In the first example, the words *kicked the bucket* have their normal meaning: someone hit a bucket with his foot. In the second example, however, although the same words are used, they mean someone died. This is not because any of the words are ambiguous but because the words together have a special meaning in this context.

When several words taken together have a special meaning that is different from their normal meaning, the expression is referred to as an *idiom*. Some other idioms in English are *the penny dropped* (he finally realized something), and *she made me climb the wall* (she irritated me). When we come across idioms in a text, our minds automatically look for the meaning that makes the best sense in the context.

> Idioms are expressions in which several words together have a special meaning.

Bible translators need to recognize idioms in Scripture and understand their intended meaning. As usual, they should translate these in a way that leads their audience as close as possible to the intended meaning for the least effort. Sometimes receptor language idioms are the best way to express certain concepts. For example, "I am at peace" might be expressed in a receptor language as "My heart is sitting down." At other times, translators may have a choice between using an idiom and expressing the meaning more directly. Since idioms often convey additional nuances of meaning compared to a more direct expression, translators need to consider the options carefully.

EXERCISES

1. What are some idioms in your language?
2. What do you understand by these expressions in English?
    a. To spill the beans.
    b. To bark up the wrong tree.
    c. To promise the moon.
    d. To put your foot in your mouth.
    e. To hit the hay.
3. What do you understand by the idioms in these biblical passages?
    a. Luke 2:51 … and his mother *kept* all these things *in her heart* (RSV).
    b. John 8:51 … you say, 'If any one keeps my word, he will never *taste death*' (RSV).
    c. Luke 3:8 … *Produce fruit* in keeping with repentance (NIV).
    d. Mark 2:19 … And Jesus said unto them, "Can the *children of the bride chamber* fast, while the bridegroom is with them?" (KJV).

Summary

What people say is only a clue to what they mean. In all communication, hearers have to fill out the meaning of what is said. The words and expressions speakers use serve as the best jumping-off points from which hearers can understand the intended meaning. Words vary in the amount of information they communicate. Some words have more meaning on their own, like *apple* and *duck*. Other words, like *big* and *soon*, have much less meaning on their own. Still other words, like pronouns, have almost no meaning on their own. Idioms are expressions in which several words together have a special meaning. Translators need to recognize them in the biblical text and express their meaning appropriately in the receptor language. In all cases, hearers fill out what is said to discover the intended meaning by using context.

So what? Translators need to use words and expressions that are the best jumping-off points for their audiences to understand the intended meaning.

Assignment

1. List anything in this text that might need to be filled out for your audience. Find at least one word that has more than one possible sense in English.

> Then Ananias went to the house and entered it. Placing his hands on Saul, he said, "Brother Saul, the Lord—Jesus, who appeared to you on the road as you were coming here—has sent me so that you may see again and be filled with the Holy Spirit." Immediately, something like scales fell from Saul's eyes, and he could see again. He got up and was baptized, and after taking some food, he regained his strength (Acts 9:17–19 NIV).

2. Compare these translations of 2 Kings 19:35. What are two ways the KJV could be understood? How have the NIV and TEV removed this confusion?
   a. KJV: And it came to pass that night, that the angel of the LORD went out, and smote in the camp of the Assyrians an hundred fourscore and five thousand: and when *they* arose early in the morning, behold, *they* were all dead corpses.
   b. TEV: That night an angel of the LORD went to the Assyrian camp and killed 185,000 soldiers. At dawn the next day there they lay, all dead!
   c. NIV: That night the angel of the LORD went out and put to death a hundred and eighty-five thousand men in the Assyrian camp. When the people got up the next morning—there were all the dead bodies!

Work Session E: Verbal Sketch #2

Working individually, do a written four-sentence, three-sentence, and two-sentence verbal sketch in English of the following Bible story. You have already worked with this story in Work Session B.

God creates a beautiful world

A long time ago, God created the world out of nothing. It did not look then like it does today. At that time there were no people, no animals, no birds, no trees or flowers. Everything was dark and silent. Then God created light. He called the light "Day" and the darkness he called "Night". This happened the first day of creation. The second day, God created the heavens.

The third day, he created the oceans, lakes, and dry ground. Then he created grass and covered the ground with all kinds of flowers, bushes, and trees. The fourth day, God placed the sun, the moon, and the stars in the sky.

The fifth day, God created all kinds of marvelous fish in the sea, big and small. He made the birds as well – ducks and geese that swim, eagles and doves that live in the forests and in the fields.

The sixth day, he created the animals, rabbits, elephants, and even bees. He made everything! And finally he created people.

And God was very pleased with his work. Everything was so beautiful and good!

The seventh day, when he had finished everything, God rested. It was a quiet day, different from all the others, a day of rest.

Lesson 8

Leaving Parts of Sentences Implicit

Shopping adventures

It was Saturday morning, and John and Peter were setting out to do some shopping. "Only one more Saturday," said Peter, "We'd better go out and buy the things we need to take home." As they sat on the bus, Peter asked John, "What are you going to take home for your wife?" "Cloth for a new outfit. I wouldn't dare arrive home without it!"

As they got off the bus they saw that there was a stall where cloth was being sold, and John walked straight to it. Peter asked him, "Where shall we meet after we've finished?" "At Mary's house over there," he said.

Just as they were both finishing their shopping, all the stall owners grabbed boxes of goods and ran down the road. "What's happening?" asked John. Suddenly police cars appeared around the corner and soon all of the stalls were broken and their parts scattered far and wide. "Wow!" said John as they got on the bus, "I wouldn't like to sell things in this town!"

GROUP DISCUSSION

1. What did John or Peter mean by the following expressions? Write the full meaning on the empty line.

    Only one more Saturday   _____

    Cloth for a new outfit   _____

    ...after we have finished?   _____

    At Mary's house over there   _____

How would they able to understand what each other meant by these phrases? Why do you think they did not state their meaning more fully?

65

2. What context did Peter supply to understand what John meant?
    Peter: "What are you going to take home for your wife?"
    John: "Cloth for a new outfit. I wouldn't dare arrive home without it!"
3. Who do you think broke the stalls and scattered the parts far and wide?
    How do you know this?
    Why did do you think the author did not say this explicitly?

Why don't communicators express everything they mean in words?

Very often when we communicate, we only express part of what we mean in
words. For example, when Peter asked John what he was taking home for his
wife, John said, "Cloth for a new outfit." He could have said, "I am going to take
cloth for a new outfit home for my wife." Peter had to supply this information that
John meant but did not say. Speakers do not always express all the information
necessary to complete their sentences in words. Sometimes they leave parts of
sentences unexpressed.

When the story says, "Cloth was being sold," we
all realize someone had to be selling the cloth
even though this is not stated in words. The verb
"was being sold" allow speakers to talk about an
action without stating explicitly who did it. We
refer to constructions like these as *passives.* Many
languages have passive constructions, but not all.

> *Active sentences: the
> subject does the action.
> Passive sentences: the
> subject has the action
> done to it.*

Information communicators express in words
is referred to as *explicit* information.
Information communicators mean but do not
express in words is referred to as *implicit*
information. Communication can be more or
less explicit. Speakers choose how much they
express explicitly.

> *Explicit information
> is expressed in words.
> Implicit information
> is meant but not
> expressed in words.*

Speakers may not express everything they mean in words for several reasons.
Here are two:

1. Their goal is to guide the audience towards the thoughts they want to share
    without any unnecessary processing effort. One thing that increases processing
    effort is the amount of words. The more words there are, the more effort is
    needed to understand them. For example, if John had said, "I am going to
    take cloth home for a new outfit for my wife," Peter would have needed to
    spend more effort processing the answer to his question without getting any
    more benefit than from the shorter one, "Cloth for a new outfit." One reason
    communicators do not express everything they mean in words is to save the
    audience unnecessary processing effort.

2. They may omit parts of a sentence in order to guide the audience's expectations of relevance. Read the following two sentences, the first a passive and the second an active sentence:

> Finally the gangster was caught.
> Finally the detective caught the gangster.

In the first sentence, the reader's attention is directed entirely to the gangster and what happened to him. In the second sentence, however, the reader's attention is also drawn to the detective. By mentioning the detective explicitly in the second sentence, the speaker increases the processing effort for the audience. As a result, they expect more relevance and so they look for additional cognitive benefits. They may use information linked to the concept DETECTIVE and this may detract from the speaker's intended meaning. One of the main purposes for using passives is to keep the person doing the action out of focus.

When we study the Bible, if we notice that a biblical author has made something explicit that could have been left implicit according to the grammar of the language, we can look for extra cognitive benefits as we search for the intended meaning.

> **Speakers do not express everything they mean in words:**
> - **to save the audience unnecessary processing effort**
> - **to guide the audience's expectations of relevance.**

EXERCISES

1. Compare the two versions of the same event below. How many characters do you think about when you read each story? How has this difference been communicated?
   a. One evening, John went out after dark. Suddenly he was attacked and beaten up very badly. He became unconscious. When he woke up again, his wallet had been taken.
   b. One evening, John went out after dark. Suddenly, a thief attacked him and beat him up very badly. John became unconscious. The thief took his wallet and disappeared.

2. Hebrew of the Old Testament does not require that the subject of sentences be stated explicitly if it is clearly the same subject. However, in Genesis 1:3–5, the author inserted the subject explicitly when God was the subject. Read these verses (below) and discuss what the author communicated by expressing the subject explicitly in this text.

And God said, "Let there be light"; and there was light. [4] And God saw that the light was good; and God separated the light from the darkness. [5] God called the light Day, and the darkness he called Night. And there was evening and there was morning, one day (RSV).

3. Look up the following passages in the Bible. Find the information that has not been expressed explicitly. Why do you think the biblical writer did not express this information in words?

   a. Matthew 3:16 And when Jesus was baptized...
   b. Mark 1:14 Now after John was arrested...

Grammatical differences between languages

The grammar of languages may require that certain kinds of information be expressed explicitly or implicitly. These requirements differ between languages. There are many ways languages can differ, but in this lesson, we will just look at two of them: leaving sentence parts implicit and passives.

Leaving sentence parts implicit

Most languages can leave out some grammatical parts of sentences, but they do not all do it in the same way. For example, English grammar requires an explicit subject in a sentence. For example, you can say the first two sentences below in English, but not the third:

John went home early.
He went home early.
*Went home early.
(The asterisk * indicates that an example is not grammatically correct.)

Even when it is clear from the context who is doing the action, English requires that the person be represented by a noun or pronoun:

John was tired, so he went home early.
John was tired, *so went home early.

Not all languages require a sentence to have an explicit subject. Hebrew and Greek do not, nor does Amharic of Ethiopia. Often when this is the case, an explicit subject is not needed because the verb gives information about the subject, as in this example from Amharic:

begize   wode   bet   heede.
early   to   house   went-he
He went to his house early.

Some languages require that certain things be repeated. Take the verse Titus 3:9, for example: "But avoid stupid controversies, genealogies, dissensions, and quarrels over the law" (RSV). In Amharic, the 'from' has to be repeated before each noun: "From arguments and from recounting genealogies and from strife arising about the law of Moses you-yourself keep away!"

In some languages, a certain verb may require an explicit object while the same verb in other languages may not require this. For example, in English, speakers can simply say *he dreamt*, but for the sentence to be grammatically correct in Ngbaka, speakers have to say "he dreamt a dream."

Likewise, some things that are explicit in Greek or Hebrew need to be omitted in the receptor language. For example, Greek requires the word *the* before Jesus, but in many contexts this would be unnatural in English and it is left out.

In translation, when the grammar of the receptor language requires that something implicit in the original be made explicit, translators are obliged to supply it. Likewise, when the grammar of the receptor language requires that something explicit in the original be omitted, translators are obliged to do so.

> ## The grammar of a language may oblige a translator to make things explicit that are implicit in the original, or visa-versa.

EXERCISES

1. Identify the sentence parts that have been left out in the following examples. Assume that you are translating into a language whose grammar does not allow you to leave these things implicit. Explain how you would you translate these verses.
   a. John 2:10 Every man serves the good wine first, and when men have drunk freely, then the poor wine (RSV).
   b. 1 Corinthians 11:24–25 When he had given thanks, he broke it, and said, "This is my body which is for you. Do this in remembrance of me." In the same way also the cup, after supper, saying… (RSV).
   c. John 4:12 "Are you greater than our father Jacob, who gave us the well, and drank from it himself, and his sons, and his cattle?" (RSV)
   d. Mark 14:17 And when it was evening he came with the twelve (RSV).
   e. John 1:21 They asked him, "What then? Are you Elijah?" He said, "I am not" (RSV).

2. Translate Mark 6:38 into your language. Does your language require you to make any implicit information explicit? If so, what kind of things—subjects, verbs, or objects?

[38] And he said to them, "How many loaves have you? Go and see." And when they had found out, they said, "Five, and two fish."

Passives

Translation problems arise when languages do not have passive constructions, since biblical languages do. For example, Jews in Jesus' day considered the word "God" too holy to pronounce in public. To avoid saying his name, they would say "It was done" rather than "God did this." Everyone understood that a verse like "Ask and it will be given to you" (Mt 7:7) meant "Ask God and he will give it to you."

Sometimes the only way to express the intended meaning of a verse is to make the person doing the action as the subject of the sentence explicit. For example, "It will be given to you," could be translated, "God will give it to you." Or in Acts 4:31 Luke records, "And when they had prayed, the place was shaken where they were assembled together; and they were all filled with the Holy Spirit." The text does not say who shook the place, but most biblical scholars agree it was the Holy Spirit.

In some cases, the context needed to understand the intended meaning is not clear. For example, when translating "Your sins are forgiven," in Mark 2:5 into a language without passives, it is unclear whether Jesus meant "I have forgiven your sins" or "God has forgiven your sins." In cases like these, translators have to research the author's meaning and make the best choice possible.

EXERCISES

1. Think of a context in which the following statements could be made. Say explicitly who might have performed the action of the verbs in each example.
   a. The food was wasted at the picnic.
   b. The mangos were left behind in the store.
   c. I was sent to the office.
   d. He was arrested and thrown into prison.
   e. Jesus said, "All power is given to me under heaven."
2. Imagine you are translating these verses into a language that does not have a passive construction. Determine what the intended meaning is and express it in an active sentence in English.
   a. Acts 4:11 This is the stone which was rejected by you builders… (RSV).
   b. Matthew 24:2 There will not be left here one stone upon another that will not be thrown down (RSV).

Putting it all together

In the last lesson and this one, we have seen how much we have to fill out the text to understand what the speaker has intended to say. Filling out the text involves the following things:

- determining the meaning of the words in the context.
- giving content to words that have little or almost no content on their own.
- identifying the intended sense of words that can have more than one sense, like *turned into*.
- supplying parts of sentences that have been left implicit.

This is one part of the processing our minds do as they search for the speaker's meaning.

Explicitness in translation

Translators need to become familiar with the way their language and biblical languages work and be alert to notice grammatical differences between them. Translators do not make many grammatical mistakes on the sentence level, but problems may arise from three sources:

1. If translators speak another language well and often, they may be influenced by that language and use its structures in the translation.
2. If translators do not understand the meaning of the original text, they may simply translate word-for-word.
3. As translators work with the biblical text in other languages, they may forget what is natural in their own language.

Using constructions that are not common in the receptor language causes additional processing effort which makes audiences look for additional cognitive benefits. If they do not experience them, their expectations of relevance are not fulfilled and they feel the text is unnatural. Whenever this happens, translators need to check if they really understand the meaning of the original and if they are using their language's grammatical structures correctly.

If a translation requires extra processing for no increase in cognitive benefits, it seems unnatural.

When translating, if the grammar of the receptor language requires that something implicit in the original be made explicit, we have no choice but to do so to the best of our abilities, even if it makes some difference in what the audience understands from the text.

In translation, however, we have to juggle many factors and at times, we may choose to make something explicit in a translation which the grammar of the receptor language does not require. When we do so, we need to realize that this will lead our audience to expect extra cognitive benefits—perhaps more than the original author intended. This happens because making things explicit increases processing costs and this raises expectations of additional cognitive benefits, as we saw in the gangster example earlier in this lesson.

**Figure 14. Translation as a
juggling act**

GROUP DISCUSSION

The Chuj language of Guatemala has a passive construction. Acts 4:31 presents a challenge in translation, however: "After they prayed, the place where they were meeting was shaken." They assume that the building was shaken by the devil, because they had experienced something similar that they thought was caused by the devil.[1] Discuss various ways you could correct this misunderstanding and the advantages and disadvantages of each solution.

Summary

Communicators often express only part of their sentences in words. Speakers leave things implicit to save their audience unnecessary processing effort and to guide them to their intended meaning. If they make something explicit that could be left implicit, audiences expect more cognitive benefits. The grammar of a language may require that certain things be made explicit, such as the subject, verb, or object. This differs from language to language. When the grammar of a receptor language requires that things implicit in the biblical text be made explicit, translators must do so to the best of their abilities. When their language's grammar does not require it, translators should proceed with caution so that they do not distort the author's intended meaning.

> **So what?**
>
> Translators need to remember that whenever they make things explicit that could be left implicit, audiences look for extra meaning.

---

[1] Beekman, John and John Callow. 1974. *Translation the Word of God.* Grand Rapids, Mich.: Zondervan, p. 48.

Assignment

1. Fill out the text below with the information the author assumed his readers would supply:

   One day a stranger was noticed in the village. He claimed he wanted to know the way to Botolo. An old man said, "Take the road past the place where the school used to be, and then turn left by Ami's farm. Continue for two miles, then you will see the buildings where coffee used to be stored. After that, you'll see."

2. Fill out the texts below with the information the biblical author expected his readers to supply:

   1 John 4:17…so that we may have confidence in the day of judgment…(NASB).

   1 Corinthians 2:8 None of the rulers of this age understood this, for if they had, they would not have crucified the Lord of glory (RSV).

Work Session F: Filling Out Implicit Information

1. Choose one of the texts you brought in your language.
2. Find any examples of parts of sentences that are left out in your texts. For example, if someone responds to the question, "Where are you going?" with "To town." Put a number by the example, and then on another sheet of paper, write the number and what has been omitted.
3. Find any examples of passives in your texts. Number them and write who is doing the action on the other sheet of paper.
4. Find any examples of constructions like *of* constructions in English. Number them and explain the relationship between the two nouns on the other sheet of paper. For example, A belongs to B, A is from B, and so forth.
5. Find any examples of idioms in your text. Number them and explain what they mean on the other sheet of paper.
6. Find any examples of words that could be understood in two ways, like "He *beats me* every time we play cards." Number them and write the two ways the word could be understood.
7. If time allows, think of a riddle in your language and explain the contextual information needed to understand its meaning. For example, "What am I? What am I? It cries out having a single tooth. The whole town weeps." Answer: The church bell. Contextual information: The bell tolls when someone in the town has died.

Lesson 9

Drawing the Intended Implications

Wonderful Los Angeles!

One night, Peter and John just were not sleepy, and they stayed up late talking. Peter told John about a trip he had made to Los Angeles. It was full of unhappy surprises and confusing moments, which Peter now thought were very funny.

Early on in his visit, he went to a grocery store to buy some candy to bring home to his children. He picked out some kinds he knew they would love. When he went to pay, the clerk asked him, "Paper or plastic?" Peter had no idea what she meant. He knew that sometimes people referred to cash as paper money, and to credit cards as plastic money, so he guessed that she was asking him about how he intended to pay. He held up some dollar bills and said, "Paper." The look in the clerk's eyes let him know that was not what she was asking. She explained, a bit impatiently, "Would you like me to put your things in a paper bag or in a plastic bag?" Peter did not know why she was offering him this choice, but chose paper and hoped no one noticed their conversation. He felt like a fool to not be able to answer this simple question.

Peter went on to tell John about the trouble he had catching his flight home. He had to catch a commuter train to the airport at 8:00 a.m. It took him more time than he expected to pack, say good-by to his hosts, and get to the station. When he got there, he was amazed by how big the train station was, like a small city inside. There were lots of people rushing one way and another. Finally he found the track for his train. A man dressed in uniform looked at him and his luggage, shook his head, and said, "It's 8:05." At first Peter was confused, but then he noticed there was no train in sight, and he remembered that trains leave exactly on time in the U.S. He began to have that sinking feeling—he had missed his train. How would he get to the airport in time?

He had no idea what to do or where to turn. He didn't have enough money to pay for a taxi. The friends he had been visiting didn't have a car, and anyway, they were at work. The airport was too far to walk to, and besides, his bags were so heavy he could hardly carry them.

Just then a whole family came to see their son off. He had hoped to catch the commuter train, too. When they saw that the train had already gone, they said, "Well, we'll just have to drive you to the airport then. We can make it, if we go quickly." Then they noticed Peter with his suitcases, looking very worried. When they found out his situation, they said, "Come with us! No problem!"

Peter was happy to have seen Los Angeles, but he was even happier to be on his way back home.

GROUP DISCUSSION

1. Explain the contextual information Peter would have had to supply to understand what the clerk meant when she said, "Paper or plastic?"
2. Explain the contextual information Peter would have had to supply to understand what the uniformed man at the train station meant when he said, "It's 8:05."

Processing communication

When we process texts, we subconsciously guess what the speaker means. We fill out what was said and take in any other clues from the environment. Our memory supplies a context, and we take the first one that seems to lead to an interpretation that makes sense. From all these inputs, we draw implications and check whether the resulting interpretation meets our expectations of relevance. If it does, we accept this interpretation as the one that the speaker intended. If not, we make adjustments in all or any of the inputs until we find an interpretation that gives enough cognitive benefits to satisfy our expectations. We process this all at once, usually unaware of all that is going on in our minds.

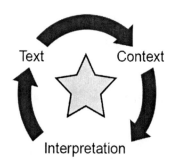

Figure 15. How we process communication

For example, in the story at the beginning of the chapter, the process might go something like this:

The railway official says: The time is 8:05.
    Context: The train to the airport leaves at 8:00 o'clock.
    Context: There is no train at the platform.
    Context: If there is no train at the platform and it's later than the scheduled departure time, then the reason for their not being a train at the platform is that the train has already left.

Contextual information is information hearers know before they hear a part of the text. An implication is information hearers know as a result of processing a part of a text in its context.

The text filled out: The time is 8:05.
Implication: The train to the airport has already left.

What the railway official said is only relevant to Peter if he assumes that the official wanted him to draw this implication. It is not just any new implication that Peter may draw. It is an implication that the railway official intended him to draw. Implications are part of what speakers communicate, even though they are not stated in words. Hearers are not free to understand just any implications and claim they have understood the speaker. If Peter had asked a stranger what time it was and the stranger said, "It's 8:05," this would be quite different. The stranger could trust that Peter thought knowing it was 8:05 would be relevant to him, but the stranger would have no idea how it would be relevant to Peter. That is, he would not have any intended implications in mind when he answered Peter.

GROUP DISCUSSION

1. Trace the thoughts that came to Peter's mind as he processed the clerk's question, "Paper or plastic."
2. Trace the thoughts the clerk intended Peter to have when she asked, "Paper or plastic."

Speakers communicate the meaning of the text, the intended context, and the intended implications.

Processing a Scripture passage

Read Luke 10:13–14 and discuss the questions below in small groups:

How terrible it will be for you, Chorazin! How terrible for you too, Bethsaida! If the miracles which were performed in you had been performed in Tyre and Sidon, the people there would have long ago sat down, put on sackcloth, and sprinkled ashes on themselves, to show that they had turned from their sins! God will show more mercy on the Judgment Day to Tyre and Sidon than to you (TEV).

1. What do you understand from this text?

2. What are Chorazin and Bethsaida?

3. What will be terrible for them?

4. What are Tyre and Sidon?

5. What do these four places have to do with each other?

6. What miracles are being talked about? Who did them? When?

7. What do miracles have to do with turning from sins?

8. Why would people put on sackcloth and sprinkle ashes on their heads?

9. What is the Judgment Day?

10. Why is Jesus saying all this? How was it relevant? That is, what cognitive benefits did it have for the first audience? What thoughts are strengthened? Eliminated? What new thoughts were formed?

Give feedback to the large group. Then have everyone fill in the following sentences:

1. From the text: Jesus thought that something bad would happen to the people of Chorazin and Bethsaida.

   a. Context: Bad things happen to …………………..……………………

   b. Contextual information: Chorazin and Bethsaida are towns where ………live.

   c. Contextual information: Jews considered themselves to be …………

2. From the text: Jesus performed mighty works in these towns.

   a. Contextual information: Mighty works prove ……………………..

   b. Implication: If Jesus performed mighty works, then ………………

   c. Contextual information: Jesus also told people to …………………

   d. Contextual information: God punishes people who ………………

   e. Implication: If the people of Chorazin and Bethsaida did not obey Jesus and repent, then ………………………………………………...……

3. From the text: The people of Tyre and Sidon would have repented if they had seen Jesus' mighty works.

   a. Contextual information: The people of Tyre and Sidon were ……

   b. Contextual information: Jews thought all Gentiles were …………

   c. Contextual information: The cities of Tyre and Sidon were renown for ……………

   d. Text: The people of Chorazin and Bethsaida did not repent when they saw Jesus' miracles, but the people of Tyre and Sidon ………

   e. Contextual information: People who do not repent/obey are more wicked than ……………………..

   f. Implication: The people of Chorazin and Bethsaida (Jews) are even more wicked than …………………………………………………………..

   g. Eliminated: Jews are more godly than ……………

4. From the text: God will show more mercy to the people of Tyre and Sidon on Judgment Day than to the people of Chorazin and Bethsaida (Jews).

    a. Implication: God will show more mercy to ....

    b. Eliminated: God will favor Jews on ....

5. This led to further implications:

    a. Some Gentiles were more righteous than ....

    b. Some Jews would be condemned on ....

Summary

As we process what a speaker is communicating, we make guesses about how the text should be filled out, the intended context, and the intended interpretation. We adjust all of these things until we find an interpretation that yields enough cognitive benefits to fill our expectations.

So what?

Translators need to think about the way their audience will fill out the biblical text, the context they will access, and the implications they will draw from it.

Assignment

Communicate Luke 10:13–14 to your audience in a way that will allow them to understand as much of the meaning as possible. This should not look like what we usually consider a "Bible translation." Instead, feel free to do whatever is necessary for your audience to draw the same implications that Jesus intended his hearers to draw.

Lesson 10

Stronger and Weaker Guidance to Implications

Relaxing on a Saturday afternoon

It was Saturday and John and Peter went to a restaurant in town for lunch. When they had sat down, a man from another table came over and said, "Hello, John! What a surprise to see you here!" It was Eric, John's old school friend who he had not seen for many years. Eric sat down and asked them, "Would you like a beer?" John answered, "No, thanks." Eric ordered some soft drinks for John and Peter and a beer for himself. They chatted together for quite a while, thinking of their school days.

After lunch, John asked Peter, "What shall we do this afternoon?" Peter said, "Oh, I'm very tired." In the end, they just walked back to the conference center. Peter took a nap and then listened to some music. John washed his clothes for the next week.

GROUP DISCUSSION

1. When John answered Eric "No, thanks," what do you think he really meant?
2. What do you think Peter meant when he answered John's question about the afternoon's activities by saying "Oh, I am very tired"?

Speakers can give stronger or weaker guidance to implications

When John said "No, thanks" to Eric's offer, he gave Eric strong guidance to one very specific implication: he did not want Eric to buy him a beer. At other times, speakers want to guide hearers to a range of possible implications. For example, when John asked Peter what he wanted to do that afternoon and Peter responded "I'm tired," John did not get a very specific idea of what Peter wanted to do. Peter only guided John's thoughts in a certain direction. His answer was still relevant to John's question, however, because it gave him some ideas about what Peter might like to do.

> Stronger guidance leads hearers to a specific implication. Weaker guidance allows hearers to understand a range of possible implications.

John used the information he knew about what tired people do not like to do. He found much of that information linked to his concept TIRED. For example, tired people do not want to play football, basketball, or tennis; they do not want to go on a strenuous trip, listen to a lecture, do their washing, clean the house, and so forth. John could understand that Peter would not want to do any of these things.

John's concept of TIRED might also contain information about what kinds of things tired people like to do, for example, tired people want to rest or even go to sleep, listen to music, go for a short walk, chat with friends, and so forth. With this information, John could understand the kinds of things Peter *might* want to do. *Any* implication based on this information, or *any possible combination* of them would lead to enough cognitive benefits.

When speakers give weak guidance to a range of possible implications, none of them are communicated very specifically. This creates an impression in the hearer's mind. Poetry often makes use of this kind of communication. For example, Song of Solomon 4:1b says, "Your hair is like a flock of goats descending from Mount Gilead." Hearers are guided to a wide range of implications, but none of them are communicated very specifically. It may even be difficult to express any of them in words.

Sometimes within the range of possible implications, speakers give stronger guidance to some of them than to others. For example, in Genesis 22:17a, God tells Abraham:

> I will surely bless you and make your descendants as numerous as the stars in the sky and as the sand on the seashore (NIV).

God could have simply said, "I will make your descendents numerous." There must have been some added meaning he intended by adding "as the stars in the sky and as the sand on the seashore." It invited Abraham to consider a range of possible meanings. For example, that his descendents would too many to count, that they would always be there, that they would give light in the night, that they would guide people on their way. The implication that they would be too numerous to count is more strongly communicated, but the others were weakly communicated and Abraham could think about them as well.

Hearers do not stop to think about whether the speaker is providing strong guidance to a specific implication or weaker guidance to a range of implications. They use the same process to understand the speaker's implication in all cases. They look for a relevant interpretation and take the first one that comes to mind as the intended one. All this goes on subconsciously.

Exercises

1. How is the meaning communicated by each set in these examples different?

   Situations: Peter and John spent an evening together in town. During the evening, they ate at a restaurant, went for a boat trip on the river, and then went to a concert at a church. On their way home Peter says:

   a. That was wonderful!
   b. Eating in a restaurant, going for a boat trip, and the concert at the church was wonderful!

2. Compare the pairs of examples below. Mark communication that leads to more specific implications with an S (for stronger guidance). Mark the communication that leads to less specific implications with a W (for weaker guidance). For each weakly communicated example, list three possible implications.

   Situation: An employee wants to know whether it is a good time to approach the boss about an important issue. He asks his colleague, "How's the boss?"

   a. It's the end of the financial year again.
   b. Very irritable.

   Situation: There is a war and the news channel is covering it:

   a. The President says, "Things are becoming rather difficult with the war situation. We'll have to take some action soon."
   b. The news reporter asks, "So you're saying there is no hope of winning and getting the troops back home soon?"

3. Decide in which of these two passages Jesus is giving weaker guidance to a range of possible implications. List some of the implications.

   a. John 20:21 Jesus says to his disciples, "As the Father has sent me, I am sending you" (NIV).
   b. Matthew 28:19 Jesus said to them, "Go and make disciples of all nations, baptizing them in the name of the Father and of the Son and of the Holy Spirit, and teaching them to obey everything I have commanded you" (NIV).

4. List a range of implications you understand from the examples below. Underline any that you think the author intends to communicate more strongly.

    a. Two adults at a restaurant commenting to each other on the behavior of a child at another table: "That child's a pig!"

    b. Psalm 23:1 The Lord is my Shepherd.

Stronger guidance can be implicit

In the story at the beginning of the lesson, John gave strong, explicit guidance to Eric's question about whether they wanted a beer when he said, "No thanks."

Sometimes people communicate what they mean implicitly but still give strong guidance to a very specific implication. Imagine John answered Eric by saying, "We don't drink alcohol." This leaves the answer he intended to communicate implicit. However, most people link the information "beer has alcohol in it" to the concept BEER, and this information would lead straight to the following thought process:

> Would you like a beer?
>   Beer has alcohol in it.
>   John and Peter do not drink alcohol.
> So John and Peter do not want beer.

The conclusion that John and Peter do not want beer is the first interpretation that is relevant because it answers Eric's question. Eric has every right to understand that John meant that they do not want beer. Though John's answer was implicit, what he meant was very clear.

Who takes responsibility for the implications?

When speakers give stronger guidance to specific implications, they take more responsibility for them. Hearers can be sure they have understood what the speaker intended. For example, there was no doubt in Eric's mind that John and Peter did not want a beer.

When speakers provide weaker guidance, hearers take more responsibility for the implications they understand. For example, after Peter said he was tired, John could have said, "So do you want to chat with friends?" John would have to take more responsibility for choosing that implication, because Peter didn't provide any specific guidance to that implication over any of the things people like to do when they're tired.

In any communication, hearers can continue to draw more and more implications. When they do, they take more and more responsibility for them. For example, when Eric understood that John and Peter didn't want to have a beer, he could have gone on to understand that Peter and John probably didn't drink whiskey either, that they didn't watch movies or dance, that they were Baptists, and so forth. The more implications Eric draws, the more responsibility he takes for them.

> ## The stronger the guidance speakers provide, the more they take responsibility for the implication(s) hearers understand.
>
> ## The weaker the guidance speakers provide, the more hearers take responsibility for the implications they understand.

Stronger and weaker guidance are not interchangeable

Weaker guidance to a range of implications is different in nature than stronger guidance to a specific implication. These two ways of communicating have different goals. Even if a person could list the range of intended implications of a line of poetry in words, it would change the nature of the communication because every thought expressed would be communicated specifically. It would also change the audience's role, as they would no longer be free to explore a range of possible implications. Speakers give weaker guidance intentionally because it is the only way they can express the range of implications they want to communicate.

For example, in Luke 9:3, Jesus tells the disciples, "Take nothing for your journey, no staff, nor bag, nor bread, nor money; and do not have two tunics. …" (RSV). One translation help suggests inserting *"because you are to trust God to supply your needs"* after "take no money." This limits the meaning to one strongly communicated implication and eliminates the range Jesus may have intended. It also does not explain why they could not take a staff (walking stick). Keener (1993) finds other reasons Jesus told them this:

> Jesus instructs the disciples to travel light, like some other groups: (1) peasants, who often had only one cloak; (2) traveling philosophers called Cynics; (3) some prophets, like Elijah and John the Baptist. They are to be totally committed to their mission, not tied down with worldly concerns.

EXERCISES

1. Compare the implications you understand from this prayer of St. Augustine with the second version below it. Discuss the changes in the text and the differences they make in the way you understand it.

> All shall be Amen and Alleluia.
> We shall rest and we shall see,
> We shall see and we shall know,
> We shall know and we shall love,
> We shall love and we shall praise.
> Behold our end which is no end.

All shall be agreement and praise. We shall rest, see, know, love, and praise. Let us consider our end which has no end.

2. In the right-hand column of the table below are suggested translations of some Bible verses. Study each of the expressions in italics in their context. Explain how the differences would affect the way an audience understands the text.

Original	Suggested translation
Matthew 4:7 Do not put the Lord your God to the test (NIV).	Do not put the Lord your God to the test *by seeing if God will help you when you do something foolish.*
Luke 9:26 For whoever is ashamed of me and of my words, of him will the Son of man be ashamed when he comes in his glory and the glory of the Father and of the holy angels (RSV).	For whoever is ashamed of me and of my words *because he fears persecution,* of him will the Son of man be ashamed when he comes in his glory and the glory of the Father and of the holy angels.
Matthew 5:4 Blessed are those who mourn... (NIV)	Blessed are those who mourn— *especially about sin and evil, ...*
Matthew 5:29 If your right eye causes you to sin, ... (NIV)	If your right eye causes you to sin *by making you covet or lust,*

Summary

Speakers can give hearers stronger guidance to more specific implications. Alternatively, they can give weaker guidance and allow their audience to discover a range of implications. Within this range, some implications may be communicated more specifically than others. The stronger the guidance speakers provide, the more they take responsibility for the specific implications they communicate. The weaker the guidance speakers provide, the more they let the audience take responsibility for the implications they understand. Even when speakers do not state things explicitly, they can guide hearers to a specific implication. Since strong and weak guidance have different goals, it is not possible to replace one with the other without some changes in the implications.

Translators need to understand the different
goals communicators have when giving
stronger and weaker guidance.

So what?

Assignment

Study each of the expressions in italics in their context. Explain the range of
implications the author is conveying.

1. Psalm 3:3 But thou, O LORD, art a *shield* about me (RSV).
2. Jude 12–13 These are the men who are *hidden reefs* in your love feasts
   when they feast with you without fear, caring for themselves; *clouds
   without water*, carried along by winds; *autumn trees without fruit*, doubly
   dead, uprooted; *wild waves of the sea*, casting up their own shame like
   foam; *wandering stars*, for whom the black darkness has been reserved
   forever (NASB).

The Basics of Bible Translation

Lesson 11

Describing or Retelling

An old man on a bicycle

The noise of a crowd split the early morning air, waking Peter and John up from their sleep. Something bad had happened just below their window. Within seconds, Peter had his clothes on and was racing down the stairs to the street. There he saw what had happened. An old man on a bicycle had been hit by a taxi, and a crowd had formed. Some tried to help stop his bleeding, while others surrounded the taxi driver and shouted at him.

Peter asked a woman who saw the accident what had happened. She said, "The old man on the bicycle was just crossing the intersection in a normal way when out of nowhere this taxi came speeding through and hit him. The taxi knocked him off the bike and into the gutter."

Before long the police came and got the situation under control. Some friends took the old man to the hospital, and the police made a report of the accident and took the taxi driver to the police station for questioning.

Peter went back to his room and told John what had happened. He said, "A woman I asked said an old man on the bicycle was just crossing the intersection when the taxi came speeding through and hit him."

GROUP DISCUSSION

1. Discuss how the content of Peter's report is different from the content of the woman's report.
2. In what other ways was Peter's report different from the woman's?

Two kinds of communication

In the story, the woman was describing things she saw. When we describe things, we take responsibility for the information. The woman claimed to be describing what she saw, and this was exactly what Peter expected.

When Peter got back to his room and told John what happened, he retold what he had heard the woman say. When we retell what someone said earlier, we claim that what we say resembles the original meaning, and our audience expects this. We do not take responsibility for the truth of the information ourselves. If Peter retold something other than what the woman said, even if it was actually the truth about what happened, his communication would not be acceptable because it was not what she originally said.

> *Describing is telling about something.*
> *Retelling is telling again what someone said or thought earlier.*

We can retell things that either we or someone else said earlier, or we can retell what we or someone else thought. We do not always have a particular person in mind. For example, if I say, "Better late than never," I am retelling something that has been said earlier by many people, but I am not thinking of anyone in particular who said it.

Imagine I walk in the room and say, "It's a beautiful day," and then someone else walks in and says, "It's a beautiful day!" Is that person retelling what I said?

Two accounts may resemble each other completely without the one being a retelling of the other. For example, another bystander at the scene of the accident in the story may have described the event in much the same way as the woman did, but without actually knowing what she said. In that case, the two accounts would both be saying the same thing because both happened to describe the same event, not because one was a retelling of the other. The key difference between describing and retelling is the speaker's claim about the origin of the information, not whether they are talking about the same thing nor how similar what they say is.

EXERCISES

1. In the following example, explain the meaning John would have understood if he thought Susan was describing. Then explain the meaning John would have understood if he thought Susan was retelling.

    John asks Susan: What did the student say?
    Susan: I do not know.

2. Underline the parts of these verses where Paul is describing something he experienced or believes and circle the parts where he is retelling what someone had said or thought earlier. Explain how the meaning of the verse changes if you do not recognize when he is retelling.
    a. 1 Timothy 3:1 Here is a trustworthy saying: If anyone sets his heart on being an overseer, he desires a noble task (NIV).
    b. Galatians 2:9–10 James, Peter and John, those reputed to be pillars, gave me and Barnabas the right hand of fellowship when they

recognized the grace given to me. They agreed that we should go to the Gentiles, and they to the Jews. All they asked was that we should continue to remember the poor, the very thing I was eager to do (NIV).

   c. 1 Corinthians 6:12–13 Everything is permissible for me—but not everything is beneficial. Everything is permissible for me—but I will not be mastered by anything. Food for the stomach and the stomach for food—but God will destroy them both. The body is not meant for sexual immorality, but for the Lord, and the Lord for the body (NIV).

> ## The key difference between describing and retelling is the speaker's claim about the origin of the information.

Audiences need to recognize if speakers are describing or retelling

We have seen that we can describe or retell when we communicate. Usually we can understand what the speaker intended to communicate from the context. Compare the following examples:

1. Peter: What did Sally say to Kathie?
   John: She can't go to Bangkok.
2. Peter: We need someone to bring this bag to Bangkok. Do you think Sally can do it?
   John: She can't go to Bangkok.

In the first example, the only relevant interpretation is that John is retelling. In the second example, the only relevant interpretation is that John is describing.

Speakers can also show that they are retelling with explicit expressions like "John said that," or "apparently," or "I heard that." In many languages, speakers only indicate they are retelling when they feel it is necessary to do so. In other languages, speakers are obliged to indicate when they are retelling. For example, retelling in Sissala of Burkina Faso is indicated by a short word. In a number of Ethiopian languages, retelling always ends with a form of the verb "say." Adioukrou of Côte d'Ivoire uses a special set of pronouns for retelling, as in this example:

N'iím   Dabou.
He-went   Dabou.
He went to Dabou (describing).

ín   ím   Dabou.
He (retelling)   went   Dabou
He went to Dabou (retelling what was said or thought earlier).

GROUP DISCUSSION

Does your language require speakers to indicate when they are retelling? If so, how is this done?

Retelling in a relevant way

As in all communication, retellings need to be relevant. Audiences will only give their attention to information they expect to be relevant. If they make the effort to process a communication but do not receive enough cognitive benefits to fulfill their expectations, they will stop processing.

One expectation audiences have is that the meaning they understand from the retelling resembles the meaning the original speaker communicated, but this does not mean they necessarily expect complete resemblance. They expect there to be just enough resemblance to satisfy their expectations of relevance. Speakers adjust their retelling so that this is the case.

> Retellings need to resemble the ideas communicated by the original just enough to satisfy the audience's expectations of relevance.

EXERCISE

Get one person from the group who knows a reasonable amount about computers. He/she will function as the reteller. Now get three other volunteers from the group:
1. A person who knows a lot about computers.
2. A person who does not know much about computers and does not want to learn.
3. A person who does not know much about computers but wants to learn.

Send these volunteers out of the room.
Then tell the reteller:
  I am really having trouble with my email program. I cannot seem to get anything to send. I've tried reinstalling Outlook, but that did not help. I am constantly being disconnected. I think I might have a virus.

Now call the three volunteers into the room one by one, and have the reteller communicate this message to each one.

Discuss how the three retellings were different. Add any ideas below that were not mentioned:

#1: The hearer had high expectations of relevance and high contextual knowledge. The meaning communicated by the retelling resembled the meaning communicated by the original very much. The hearer had both high expectations of relevance and the necessary context to understand this kind of retelling.

#2: The hearer had low expectations and low contextual knowledge. The meaning communicated by the second retelling did not resemble the meaning communicated by the original nearly as much. The hearer lacked the intended context to be able to understand the original communication. He or she also had very low expectations of relevance, and so was not willing to learn new contextual information about computer viruses. The only option the reteller had was to simplify the retelling and communicate less than the original communicated.

#3: The hearer had high expectations but low contextual knowledge. In the third retelling, the hearer had high expectations of relevance, but lacked the context needed to understand it. The reteller had to add a lot of this information to the original telling so that the hearer could understand what the original communicated. This allowed the hearer to understand more of what was originally communicated. However, the retelling was quite different from the original telling.

Whenever the second audience has a different context than the original audience, there will be communication challenges. Retellers have two basic choices:

1. They can adjust their text to their audience's context, by simplifying and/ or amplifying the text. This is the strategy we use most often in ordinary retelling. As we saw in the computer virus retelling, we adjust our retelling to increase the audience's understanding. The disadvantage is that the audience no longer knows what was originally communicated. They only have the reteller's version.

2. They can keep the text similar to the original and help their audience adjust their context outside the text. We use this strategy when someone wants to know as exactly as possible what was originally communicated. For example, if a court case developed around the old man's accident, a lawyer may want to know exactly what was said at the scene of the accident. The audience will only understand this kind of retelling, however, if they know the intended context.

Meaning resemblance

Resemblance is when two things are similar. For example, if a son looks and acts like his father, people may say, "He resembles his father so much!"

In communication, the meaning a speaker communicates by a retelling needs to resemble the meaning the original speaker communicated.

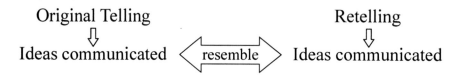

Two things can resemble each other more or less. When the ideas communicated by a text resemble the ideas communicated by the original a lot, we say it has a high degree of *meaning resemblance*.

The meaning that speakers communicate includes what is communicated by the text and the implications they intend the audience to understand. All this requires the audience to use the context the speaker intended. These three things interact.

> *Meaning resemblance is the degree to which a retelling communicates the same ideas as the original communication.*

Speakers may adjust their retellings for their audience to increase comprehension, but this will decrease meaning resemblance between the original and the retelling. For example, a man tells his auto-mechanic friend, "There's a vapor lock in my carburetor." The auto mechanic retells the message to his wife by saying, "His car doesn't work." The wife understands her husband's communication completely, but the meaning she understands is only part of what was originally communicated. The meaning resemblance between the original and the retelling is low.

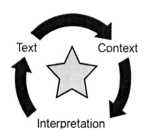

Figure 16. How we process communication

Making what was implicit in the original telling explicit in the retelling lowers the resemblance between the meaning communicated by the retelling and the original because:

- The retelling communicates that the original audience also needed that contextual information supplied. This was not the case. This gives an incorrect perception of the original audience.
- Ideas that are made explicit will make other ideas come to mind. In the computer example above, the passive expression "I'm constantly being disconnected" guides hearers to think about being constantly disconnected. If the reteller made the subject explicit by saying "The internet provider there was constantly disconnecting him," hearers

would be guided to think about the internet provider as well as the experience of being constantly disconnected.

- The reteller may include information that is not correct. If the reteller doesn't understand computer viruses correctly, the audience will only have his version of the original and will be misled by the reteller's misunderstanding.
- When things that were communicated implicitly are now communicated explicitly, this usually gives stronger guidance to the intended interpretation.
- The audience cannot know what the original communicator actually said.

GROUP DISCUSSION

1. Peter overhears a conversation between two Americans. One of them tells the other, "My brother is working in Omaha." That night he and John are talking and Peter tells John about this conversation. He says, "The American's brother is working in Omaha, *a big city in the U.S.*"
   a. Explain why Peter made this adjustment.
   b. Explain how it lowers the meaning resemblance with the original.

2. A student has missed an important lecture, and so he asks his classmate to tell him what the lecturer said. The classmate tells him everything he can remember, and adds some ideas that he thinks will help his friend understand the material better. Unfortunately, the classmate has misunderstood the lecture. What kind of problems will occur due to this adjusted retelling?

3. The story is told of one of the United States' presidents, Calvin Coolidge:

   President Coolidge was known as "Silent Cal." One Sunday, his wife could not go to church with him. When he returned, she asked, "What did the pastor preach about?" He replied, "Sin." She was not satisfied with such a short answer, so she asked, "What did he say about it?" He replied, "He's against it." She rolled her eyes in exasperation.

   Using what you have learned in this lesson, explain why Mrs. Coolidge is not satisfied with her husband's responses.

Translation is a kind of retelling in another language

There are many kinds of retelling. If we look at translation as a whole, it is retelling an original message in a different language. To be relevant, translators need to consider their audience's expectations of relevance and their contextual knowledge. Where there are significant differences between the original

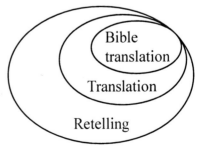

Figure 17. Bible translation, a kind of retelling

and second audiences, *translators of ordinary texts* have all the options available to them. They can 1) adjust the text to their audience's context, either adding needed contextual information and/or leaving out information that is not relevant to their audiences, or 2) they can keep the text as similar as possible to the original communication and adjust their audience's context outside the text so they are able to understand it.

In addition to the challenges of any retelling, translators have the challenge of differences between the languages in question. Due to these differences, translations can rarely attain complete meaning resemblance. They can only get as close to the original meaning as is possible using the structures of the receptor language. For example, in languages that do not have passives, translators may be obliged to supply subjects for verbs even if there is not one in the original text. To communicate successfully, translators need to understand how the language of the original communication works as well as how the receptor language works. Bible translation is a special kind of translation that has additional constraints. We will be looking at these in the next lesson.

Summary

When we communicate, we may be describing events or we may be retelling what was said or thought earlier. When we describe events, we take responsibility for the *truth* of the information. When we retell, we claim that the meaning communicated by our account *resembles* the meaning communicated by the original. Audiences do not always expect it to resemble completely, but rather just enough to satisfy their expectations of relevance.

Where there are differences between the first and second audiences' contexts, measures need to be taken for communication to be successful. Retellers can either 1) adjust their text to their audience's current context, or 2) help the audience adjust their context (outside the text) so it resembles the originally intended context. When we adjust the text to the audience's current context, it helps them understand the communication more easily right away. However, these adjustments change what is communicated in some way, and so they lower the meaning resemblance between the original and the retelling.

As a whole, translation is retelling across languages. It must deal with language as well as contextual differences. Due to differences between languages, translations can rarely give an exact retelling. Bible translation is a special kind of retelling which we will be exploring more in the next chapter.

So what? Bible translators must communicate the ideas communicated by the original in ways that resemble the original enough to satisfy the audience's expectations of relevance.

Assignment

How would you retell what you have learned in this course to these four audiences? In what ways would each account be different?

1. To someone who is a participant at this seminar but was sick yesterday and could not come to class. He needs to prepare for the test coming later this week.
2. To another member of your translation team who is very interested in what you are learning but does not know anything about the course materials.
3. To a former Bible translator who studied communication and Bible translation in the past, but has lost interest in it.
4. To a family member who is not interested in the details of communication and translation.

Work Session G: Communication Chart

How can we determine what a speaker communicated by a text? Let's look at this example from the story at the beginning of Lesson 11. Compare what the old woman said in the story with the way Peter retold it to John.

> The old woman said, "The old man on the bicycle was just crossing the intersection in a normal way when out of nowhere this taxi came speeding through and hit him. The taxi knocked him off the bike and into the gutter."

> Peter's retelling to John: "A woman I asked said the old man on the bicycle was just crossing the intersection when the taxi came speeding through and hit him."

Peter's retelling was not an exact restatement of what the woman said, but the meaning communicated by it resembled the old woman's report enough to satisfy John's expectations of relevance. Discuss these questions:

- What did the woman think Peter wanted to know?
- What did Peter think John wanted to know?
- What differences do you notice between the woman's telling and Peter's retelling?
- Explain why Peter retold what happened in this way.

The chart below is a tool that can help us understand what is communicated by a text. We refer to it as a *communication chart*. Filling it out makes us slow down our minds and reflect on exactly what is communicated by a text. It is only an analytical tool and not a reproduction of how our minds process communication. That is far too complex to chart on paper. Here is how it works:

Text	Communicated Ideas	Context
The original text	1. The ideas that have been communicated by the text itself: the text filled out with the meanings of words specified, the referents of pronouns clarified, missing parts of sentences supplied, and any other clues from the text explained.	The context the speaker intended the audience to use. Contextual information that came to mind but was later eliminated is indicated by putting a line through it.

	2. The implications the speaker intends the hearer to draw from the combination of the text and the context.	

Here is an example of a communication chart of the woman's account of the accident from the story in Lesson 11.

Text	**Communicated Ideas**	**Context**
The woman said to Peter, "The old man on the bicycle was just crossing the intersection in a normal way	The old man was crossing the intersection on a bicycle in a normal way, that is, very carefully. (This eliminates context 1 and 2.)	1. ~~Bicyclists may sometimes not be careful in traffic.~~ 2. ~~Old people may have lost some of their sense of balance and not be able to ride bicycles as well as when they were younger.~~ 3. The normal way for bicyclists to cross intersections is to slow down, look left and right to see if it is safe to cross, and then cross carefully.
when out of nowhere	The old man could not see the taxi before he crossed the intersection.	4. Taxi drivers are careless drivers.
this taxi came speeding through at him.	The taxi came towards him at a high speed. (This strengthens context 4.) The taxi driver was careless. (This is an inference.)	5. The normal behavior for car drivers to cross intersections is to slow down, look, and cross carefully, paying attention to pedestrians and bicyclists. 6. Speeding amounts to dangerous driving. It puts others in danger.

The taxi knocked him off the bike and into the gutter."	The taxi injured the old man by knocking him off the bike into the gutter.	

Once we have understood what the original speaker communicated, we can compare that meaning with the meaning communicated by a retelling. In the story, Peter adjusts his retelling to John's expectations of relevance. He expected that John just wanted to know what all the noise was about that woke him up in the early morning hours. He didn't think John was concerned with who was at fault. The parts of the text Peter left out have a line through them. The parts he modified or added are in italics.

> Peter's report: The woman said that *an* old man on *a* bicycle was just crossing the intersection ~~in a normal way~~ when ~~out of nowhere~~ *a* taxi came speeding through *it* ~~The taxi knocked him off the bike and into the gutter~~ *and hit him.*

Text	Communicated Ideas	Context
Peter's report: A woman I asked said an old man on a bicycle was just crossing the intersection when a taxi came speeding through it and hit him.	• The woman said that: • The old man crossed the intersection on a bicycle. • At the time when the old man crossed the intersection, the taxi came speeding through it towards him. • The taxi hit the old man.	1. Accidents are more likely to occur at intersections. 2. It was hard for drivers to see other traffic at that particular intersection. 3. It's hard for drivers to see other traffic if there is not full daylight.

By comparing these two charts, we can see that the adjustments Peter made in his retelling made the communication more relevant to John. The parts Peter left out would have only increased processing costs without adding the kinds of benefits John was expecting. The parts he simplified provided enough information to satisfy John's expectations. John was not expecting a higher level of meaning resemblance.

EXERCISE

In the story about Birgita in Lesson 5, Peter gave John an exact report of the letter from his uncle. John had difficulty understanding it because he lacked this context:

- Birgita is Peter's cousin.
- Birgita stole money from the church and kept denying that she had done so.
- Last time, her father Eric punished her but replaced the money at his own expense.
- Veronica, Peter's great aunt, is known by the family to be a bit odd but she has taken in other wayward children in the past. She lives 200 miles (around 320 kilometers) away from where Birgita's family live, in a very remote spot.
- Birgita has never lived in a remote rural setting.
- Birgita has never travelled far from home.
- Veronica can be very rough and doesn't always welcome visitors.
- There is no public transport from the nearest town to Veronica's village, just 40 miles (around 65 kilometers) of bush paths.

Fill out the communication chart based on your understanding of the letter. The first two boxes give you some clues.

Text	Communicated Ideas	Context
I need to tell you what happened to Birgita.	I (your uncle) need to tell you (Peter) what has happened to our relative named Birgita.	Peter's uncle is writing to him. Birgita is Peter's cousin.
You know all the fuss there was about her two years ago.	You (Peter) remember how there was a fuss with the family about her stealing money from the church two years ago and how she kept denying that she had stolen the money.	Birgita stole money from the church two years ago and kept denying that she did it.
Well, she's done it again!		
It seems quite incredible that she didn't learn her lesson the first time.		
This time, however, Eric has taken a different line with her. He has washed his hands of the whole affair and has left her to sort it out.		
As a result, she has decided to visit old Veronica,		

and you know where she lives!		
I can't imagine what will happen when she finally gets there		
—or even if she will ever get there.		

Now imagine Peter adjusted the letter to John's context when he retold it. Write a retelling of the letter in English to John. Remember his only interest is to understand why Peter is shocked and concerned. Compare your retelling with the originally communicated meaning. Does it resemble the original meaning enough to fill John's expectations?

Lesson 12

Genre and Translation

Fun night

After a week of serious meetings, the conference leaders organized a fun night. Participants put together short dramas, told jokes and riddles, shared songs, and danced. Towards the end of the program one participant took the stage very seriously and sat on a stool. He opened the manual of his cell phone book and began to read as if he were reading a sermon. He began reading aloud slowly in a quiet voice. "A text message can be up to 160 characters in length. Messages sent or received that are longer than 160 characters will be delivered in multiple segments." His voice became louder as he continued, "Each segment will be billed as a separate message," he said, slamming his hand down on the podium. "Text messages are stored and retried until delivery is successful," another slam on the podium, and in a very loud voice, he shouted, "for up to 72 hours!" Then he was completely silent and looked at them as if letting this truth sink in. Now he pointed his finger at them and continued reading in a pleading voice, "Text Alerts are stored and retried up to 24 hours." On and on he went reading. John laughed so much his sides ached. He could not explain why it was so funny.

GROUP DISCUSSION

Discuss what made this reading so hilarious for John.

Genre can guide our expectations of relevance

The cell phone manual reading was hilarious because the sermon intonation led the group to expect an exhortation from Scripture. These expectations were not fulfilled as, instead of an exhortation, the audience was given technical information about cell phones.

We bring different expectations about how different kinds of communication will be relevant. We expect a sermon to have a certain sort of relevance and a computer manual to have another. We expect the news to have factual information, and riddles to be entertaining. These expectations combine with other clues and guide us to the speaker's meaning.

Cultures develop patterns of speaking that guide audiences to expect certain kinds of communication. These are referred to as *genre.* Sermons, manuals, and songs are genre in English. Another English genre is the limerick. It has a set structure of two eight-syllable lines that rhyme, two five-syllable lines that rhyme, and a final eight-syllable line that rhymes with the first two lines. For example:

> There was a young farmer from Leeds,
> Who ate sixty packets of seeds,
> It soon came to pass,
> He was covered with grass,
> And he could not sit down for the weeds!

Genre are culturally defined kinds of communication that raise audience's expectations for a specific kind of relevance.

When English speakers hear limericks, they expect to be entertained. Of special interest is how the last word will rhyme with the last word of the first two lines.

Genre can be signaled in many ways and often a combination of clues work together to guide the hearer. For example:

- A genre may begin and end with a formulaic expression that is always the same. For example, English folk stories often begin with "Once upon a time" and end with "and they lived happily ever after." When audiences hear these, they expect a story in which things take place that cannot happen in the real world, such as animals talking. They may also expect the story to teach a lesson.
- Certain words can raise the audience's expectations of a certain genre. For example, in Scripture, often the vineyard was used to talk about the male-female love relationship, as in Isaiah 5. When Jewish audiences heard certain passages about vineyards, they expected it to have a symbolic meaning rather than a literal one (for example, see Mt 21:33–45).
- Some communication is labeled as a genre. For example, in Scripture, Jesus spoke in parables. Parables are a genre in which an earthly story tells a heavenly meaning. Often the contents of the story is familiar, but there is a surprise element. Hearers understand that the story is not historical, but look for what it teaches.
- Audiences may recognize statements to be proverbs if their meaning is too obvious to be relevant (for example, "what goes around comes around"), or if they seem unrelated to the topic at hand. For example, while looking at a leaky ceiling, someone might say, "A stitch in time saves nine."

We look for relevance according to the expectations the speaker has led us to have, without classifying the communication into one genre or another. For example, when a speaker gives clues that he is giving a sermon, we expect him to talk about a lesson or a main point and we look for it. When a speaker gives clues that he is going to teach us how to do something, we will look for steps in a process.

Most communication does not fall into genre categories. However, when it does, as in all communication, we take the path of least effort and process the communication until our expectations of relevance are satisfied. Then we stop, because we assume we have understood the intended meaning.

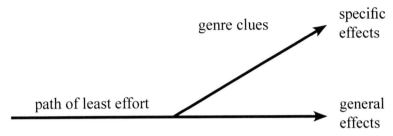

Figure 18. Processing communication marked for genre

GROUP DISCUSSION

1. Discuss some different kinds of genre your culture distinguishes. Explain how speakers indicate these genre.
2. What kinds of expectations do the following texts raise for you? How do you refer to this genre of communication?
   a. Once upon a time, a lion was walking in the forest and fell down a hole. After a while a monkey came past and the lion persuaded him to help him out, but then the lion ate him. So children, learn from this that you should beware of helping strangers.
   b. Mix in a large bowl:
      2 eggs
      2 cups milk
      2 cups flour
   c. Grant of Rights: Licensor hereby grants to Licensee the following: The non-exclusive right and license to convert The Work to a digital format....
   d. Dear John,
      It is been so long since you left, and last week I met a man who was…

3. Within the Bible, there are many genre. Discuss the kinds of expectations the following biblical texts stimulate. What genre do you consider each one to be?

   a. "What shall we say the Kingdom of God is like?" asked Jesus. "What parable shall we use to explain it? It is like this. A man takes a mustard seed, the smallest seed in the world, and plants it in the ground. After a while it grows up and becomes the biggest of all plants. It puts out such large branches that the birds come and make their nests in its shade."
   b. O LORD, rebuke me not in thy anger,
      nor chasten me in thy wrath.

> Be gracious to me, O LORD, for I am languishing;
> LORD, heal me, for my bones are troubled.
> My soul also is sorely troubled.
> But thou, O LORD—how long?

c. Treasures gained by wickedness do not profit,
   but righteousness delivers from death.

d. Out of the eater something to eat; out of the strong, something sweet.

Hearers may be guided by expectations of a certain genre, but not always.

Bible translation as a genre

We use the word *book* to refer to each book of the Bible, but we also say the Bible as a whole is a book. In the same way, within the Bible there are many kinds of genre (love songs, laments, and so forth), but the Bible as a whole can be thought of as a genre that raises certain kinds of expectations. Let us shift now to this big picture and think about the expectations that are raised by the genre "Bible translation".

GROUP DISCUSSION

1. Discuss the expectations the genre *translation* raises in your community. When would people say, "This is a bad translation"? If someone gave a one-page summary of a 500-page book, would you consider it a translation?

2. When do people in your community hear or read translations of communication other than the Bible? Include print translations, dubbing of videos, spontaneous oral interpretations, and so forth.

In the large group, discuss responses. Are there any similar expectations of things that are translated?

3. Now show a variety of Scripture products, including Bibles, story books, and so forth, or have each participant describe a Scripture product they know about. Have the class say what they expect each product to be like, based on the cover and formatting.

When audiences see a Scripture product, the formatting gives them clues about what kind of product it is before they ever read one word of it.

4.	What expectations do Christians in your community bring to a book called a Bible translation? Contrast this with biblical materials that are not called a Bible translation.

Discuss responses in the large group. Are there any similar expectations? Have expectations changed over time?

Bible translation and expectations of meaning resemblance

Most audiences that are aware of the Bible in more than one language expect those Bibles to say similar things. If one translation seems very different than the others, they will feel something is not right, even if they do not understand the issues involved in translation.

Compare the following three retellings of Matthew 4:18–20. Would you call all of these a good Bible translation of this text? If not, why not?

a.	Walking and beside the Sea of Galilee he saw two brothers, Simon, the one being called Peter, and Andrew the brother of him, casting [a] net into the sea; they were for fishermen. And he says to them, come follow me, and I will make you fishermen of men. And immediately leaving the nets they followed him.

b.	One day Jesus saw Simon and Andrew busy at work. He called them to follow him and right away, they left their work and followed him.

c.	As Jesus was walking along the Sea of Galilee, he saw two brothers, Simon called Peter and Andrew his brother. They were throwing their nets into the sea, for they were fishermen. He said to them, "Follow me and I will make you fishers of men." Immediately they left their nets and followed him.

Discuss responses in the large group. Bring out any of the following points that are not already mentioned:
a.	The first retelling does not use normal English and so is very difficult to understand. It simply gives a word in English for every word in Greek. Most people would not consider this to be a good translation.
b.	Most people would not consider the second retelling to be a good translation because the meaning resemblance is not high enough. It leaves out several bits of the original meaning.
c.	Only the last of these three retellings satisfies the expectations raised by the genre *Bible translation* for most people. Of course, to understand the

intended meaning, the audience would still need to have access to the intended context (for example, information about fishing by throwing nets.) Like all genre, Bible translation raises certain expectations but these are defined differently by different societies and they may change over time. When a group first has contact with the Bible, they may not have many expectations at all. Over time, as they learn more about the Bible, their expectations may become more clearly defined. Genre expectations of Bible translation are not defined with exact precision. There are usually some Scripture products people are not completely sure if they consider translation of the Bible or not. For example, English speaking audiences may not be sure if they consider *The Living Bible* or *The Message* a translation of the Bible or a paraphrase.

Although the audience's expectations of the genre "Bible translation" are important, they are a part of the larger body of Christ. The church as a whole shares certain expectations of this genre. Christians believe that Scripture is inspired by the Holy Spirit and that God has promised to speak through it in a way that does not apply to any other literature. Because of this, they believe it is authoritative, that is, they can and should rely on its teaching more than on anything else. These beliefs lead them to want a translation that allows them to understand what the original author communicated as much as possible. They do not expect ideas to be omitted, nor do they expect ideas to be added.

Bible translators share these expectations and take them very seriously, as is clear from these quotes:
- The Bible is the Word of God, inspired by the Holy Spirit. The translator has a very serious responsibility not to change the meaning in any way (Barnwell 1986:12).
- All translators are agreed that their task is to communicate the meaning of the original. There is no discussion on this point (Beekman and Callow 1974:20).
- Translating must aim primarily at 'reproducing the message.' To do anything else is essentially false to one's task as a translator (Nida and Taber 1969:12).

The genre Bible translation raises expectations of a high degree of meaning resemblance.

Because the genre Bible translation raises expectations of a high degree of meaning resemblance, translators are not as free to adjust the text to the audience's context as they can in other retellings, as this may decrease meaning resemblance with the original below levels the audience would accept. If an audience's expectations are not met, they will not accept or use the translation.

The meaning of "shaking off the dust of your feet" (Lk 9:5) is unfamiliar to many audiences. Some have proposed adding "as a sign of God's displeasure and rejection" in the translated text so audiences like these will understand the intended meaning.

- How would adding these words affect the resemblance between the ideas communicated by the original and those communicated by the translation?
- What other ways might a translator help an audience understand this gesture?
- What are the advantages and disadvantages of each solution?
- For whom might each be appropriate?

Summary

Speakers make use of genre to guide their hearers to expect a certain kind of benefit. Some genre are very specific to certain cultures, like the limerick in English. Others are more widely shared, like sermons. Speakers may use genre to guide their audience to expect a certain kind of benefit, but often communication does not fall into neat genre categories. Hearers do not try to classify communication, but simply take the first interpretation that makes sense as the intended one, based on the clues they have been given.

Bible translation is a genre which raises the expectation that the meaning the audience can understand from the translation will have a high degree of resemblance to the meaning the original author intended to communicate. Meaning resemblance is determined by comparing the ideas communicated by the original and the translation. The more the ideas resemble each other, the higher the meaning resemblance.

Bible translation must address language differences, contextual differences, and genre expectations.

Assignment

1. Read Luke 14:7–11. Notice that this is labeled as a parable. Discuss how this affects your understanding of what Jesus intended to communicate.

> [7] When he noticed how the guests picked the places of honor at the table, he told them this parable: [8] "When someone invites you to a wedding feast, do not take the place of honor, for a person more distinguished than you may have been invited. [9] If so, the host who invited both of you will come and say to you, 'Give this man your seat.' Then, humiliated, you will have to take the least important place. [10] But when you are invited, take the lowest place, so that when your host comes, he will say to you, 'Friend, move up to a better place.' Then you will be honored in the

presence of all your fellow guests. [11] For everyone who exalts himself will be humbled, and he who humbles himself will be exalted" (NIV).

2. Make a list of different Scripture products that are available in your community. What kind of expectation is raised by each one? What clues lead people to have those expectations?

Work Session H: Determining Meaning Resemblance

Since meaning resemblance is of particular concern to Bible translators, they need to know how to determine it. They need to be able to compare the meaning communicated by their translation with the originally intended meaning, as well as being able to compare the meaning communicated by other translations with the originally intended meaning.

Unintentional loss of meaning resemblance

Translators may reduce meaning resemblance unintentionally by making errors in the translation process. Before considering a translation complete, they need to compare what is communicated by their translation with what was communicated by the original to catch any mistakes of this sort. For example, discuss the differences between the original and the translation in sentences below:

1. Original: When I get home I will have a cup of tea and a bath.
    Retelling: When I get home I will have a bath.

2. Original: There were four rooms in the house.
    Retelling: There were four rooms in the house and a kitchen outside.

3. Original: My grandfather took all his grandsons back to the village.
    Retelling: My grandfather took all his grandchildren back to the village.

EXERCISES

1. Compare the sentences below and decide what was left out.

    Original: Before half-time, four men were hurt on the football team.
    Retelling: Four men were hurt on the football team.

    Original: They asked us to go to the meeting house and vote for a leader.
    Retelling: They asked us to go and vote for a leader.

2. Compare the sentences below and underline information that was added.

    Original: The old lady was tired and sat down.
    Retelling: The old lady was tired and sat down under a tree.
    Original: When the store owner caught the boy stealing, he punished him.

Retelling: When the store owner caught the boy stealing, he punished him with a stick.

3. The second line in each pair is a back-translation into English of a translation. Circle the place where the back-translation is different from the original and explain how it affects what is communicated.

Original: All I wanted was to find some food to eat.
Retelling: All I wanted was to find some meat to eat.

Original: The child was crying for his aunty to carry him.
Retelling: The child wanted his aunty to carry him.

Original: Before the child's fever got high, her father carried her to the clinic.
Retelling: When the child's fever got high, her father carried her to the clinic.

Original: While the car was stopping, the little boy fell out.
Retelling: When the car stopped, the little boy fell out.

Original: While my husband waited, I did my shopping.
Retelling: My husband was waiting, so I did my shopping.

4. Compare the two versions of these verses from Acts 5. Would your audience understand the same meaning from each version? If not, explain the difference.

Version 1: But a man named Ananias with his wife Sapphira sold a piece of property,
Version 2: But a man named Ananias and a woman called Sapphira sold a piece of property, …

Version 1: and with his wife's knowledge he kept back some of the proceeds,
Version 2: he kept some of the money which he had got from the sale of the property, and his wife knew about this.

Version 1: But Peter said, "Ananias, why has Satan filled your heart to lie to the Holy Spirit?
Version 2: But Peter said, "Ananias, why has Satan made you tell this lie?"

Version 1: And great fear came upon all who heard of it.
Version 2: Everyone who heard what had happened was very afraid.

Version 1: The young men rose and wrapped him up and carried him out
and buried him.

Version 2: Some people wrapped his body in a blanket and carried it out
and buried it in a graveyard.

Comparing existing translations with the originally intended meaning

Translators also need to know how to identify differences in translations they use
in their study of passages as they prepare to translate. They need to know how
to compare the meaning communicated by these translations with the originally
intended meaning. Sometimes these differences seem small, but they may lead
to significant differences in what people understand. Such is the case with 1
Corinthians 6:1. Here is a word-for-word English translation of that verse from
Greek. Pay special attention to the terms *unrighteous ones* and *holy ones*.

Word-for-word English translation: Dares anyone of you a dispute having with
the other, to be judged before the *unrighteous ones* and not before the *holy ones*?

Paul was complaining that the believers in Corinth were taking their disputes to
be settled by the official judges. However, instead of referring to them as *official
judges*, he calls them *unrighteous ones* (*adikos* in Greek). Why does he use this
term? Greek society did not believe in God, and so their judges were considered
unrighteous in God's sight. By referring to them in this way rather than just
saying *official judges*, Paul was deliberately drawing his audience's attention to
(what he felt was) God's view of these judges.

What was the relevance of doing this? Earlier in this book, Paul calls the
Corinthians "those sanctified in Christ Jesus and called to be holy" (1 Cor 1:2).
In this verse (6:1), he refers to them as *holy ones* again. They had been made
holy through Christ's sacrifice for their sins. One important characteristic of *holy
people* is that they obey God. As people who follow God, they should not go to
people who do not care about God (unrighteous people) to judge their disputes.
Not only does this not make sense, it offends God. That may be one reason why
Paul asks how these people dare (*tolmaoo*) do this. As holy people they should be
able to settle their disputes among themselves. The way Paul expresses himself
using the terms *unrighteous* and *holy* makes it very clear that he is wanting them
to consider their relationship to God as they try to solve their disputes.

The table below shows how three English versions have translated these terms.

Original concept	Unrighteous ones	Holy ones
Translation 1	Unrighteous	Saints
Translation 2	Secular courts	Christians
Translation 3	Wicked people	God's holy people

All of the terms are true in some respects: the judges were unrighteous (before God), they served in a secular court system, and they were ungodly. The holy ones were Christians, God's holy people, and saints. However, each term guides the audience in a significantly different direction.

Translation 1

> When any of you has a grievance against another, do you dare take it to court *before the unrighteous* instead of taking it before the *saints*?

> *Unrighteous* brings out the idea of not being right with God, and this makes the contrast between the spiritual state of these judges and God's holy people who are right with God. However, it may not be clear right away that the term here is actually referring to court judges. It is also a term that is not used outside the church in most English-speaking communities today so it may not bring much to mind for many people. *Saints* brings out the idea of holiness. However, some audiences may think Paul is referring to unusually devoted people who have been canonized by the church after they have died. This is not the intended meaning.

Translation 2

> When you have something against another Christian, why do you file a lawsuit and ask a *secular court* to decide the matter, instead of taking it to other *Christians* to decide who is right?

> *Secular court* is easier for audiences today to understand, as they do not have to learn that the courts in Corinth were part of a society that did not acknowledge the God of the Bible. *Christians* is a more common word than *saints* and so easier to understand as well. While the concepts these words encode are true, referring to *secular courts* communicates that they were not part of a religious system, but the idea that they are not justified by God is not communicated very strongly. To refer to *the holy ones* as *Christians* indicates the religion they followed, but does not draw attention to their holiness as strongly as in the original. Much of the contrast Paul makes by saying *unrighteous* and *holy ones* is lost. A reader might wonder why Paul was opposed to secular courts.

> By making these adjustments in the text, the audience could understand the translation more easily in their current context. At the same time, it limits the meaning they could understand from a translation that did not make these adjustments, if they were to learn the intended context.

Translation 3

> When one of you has a complaint against another, how dare you go to court to settle the matter in front of wicked people. Why don't you settle it in front of God's holy people?

Wicked people makes it quite clear that these judges were not in a right relationship with God. In addition, *wicked* is used in ordinary speech by many English-speaking audiences. *God's holy people* captures the idea of holiness and is easily understood by most English-speaking people. This translation allows an audience to understand the meaning Paul was trying to communicate: that holy/godly people should not go to wicked people for wisdom.

EXERCISE

Compare what you understand from the words in italics in these two translations. Which one do you find easier to understand? Which one allows an audience to understand more of the meaning communicated by the original? What context is needed to understand that meaning? What might an audience misunderstand from these translations?

> Luke 11:36b he *reclined-for-a-meal* (original)
>   1. Jesus went to the Pharisee's house *and reclined at the table* (NIV).
>   2. Jesus accepted the invitation and *sat down to eat* (NLT).

Understanding the original using a communication chart

To evaluate the degree of meaning resemblance between translations, we first need to understand what the original author intended to communicate. Study this communication chart of Matthew 13:31–32.

Text	Communicated Ideas	Context
Another parable he placed before them saying,	Jesus told the disciples another parable. The disciples expect this story to be a sort of metaphor that illustrates a larger truth about the Kingdom of God.	Parables are stories that illustrate a greater truth. This parable comes in a series of parables on the theme of the Kingdom of God.
"The Kingdom of the Heaven is like a mustard seed,	The Kingdom of the Heavens is like a mustard seed,	Jews spoke of the mustard seed when speaking of the smallest seed [even though technically it is not]. A mustard seeds is very small. Mt 17:20 faith like a grain of mustard seed.

which [a] man planted in his field,	A man planted the seed in his field. The man expects the seed to grow and produce a crop. The Kingdom of Heaven has been started and grows.	A seed must be planted to grow. A seed must be alive to grow.
which on the one [hand] is indeed smaller than all of the seeds,	Which [as you know] on the one hand is much smaller than all of the seeds The beginning of the Kingdom of Heaven is almost unnoticeable.	The disciples already knew the size of the mustard seed. Jesus repeats this to guide them to reflect on the smallness of the mustard seed. This is underscored even more with the word 'indeed'. One might expect small seeds to produce small crops/plants.
but on [the] other hand, when it grows,	But on the other hand, when it grows,	It takes time for the seed to grow. It grows on its own once planted ~~Small seeds produce small crops/plants.~~
it is the largest of the garden vegetables and it becomes a tree,	It is the largest of all the plants and [most miraculously] turns into a tree. The Kingdom of Heavens is miraculous/beyond any normal expectations in terms of growth and significance.	~~Plants do not become trees.~~

| so that the birds of heaven come and live in its branches. | The reason the tree grows so big is so that 'the birds of the air/ heaven can come and make their home in its branches'.

Although at the time Jesus said the Kingdom of Heaven was incredibly small, Jesus says it will become as significant as the other known world kingdoms (Babylon, Persia, etc.).
It provides a home large enough for all the people of the world to live in it. | Tree/Birds of the air: this metaphor is used to refer to great kingdoms in the Old Testament: see Ezekiel 31:6; 17:23; 31:6; Daniel 4:12, 20–22. |

Comparing translations using a comparison chart

A comparison chart displays different translations verse by verse. This helps us notice differences between translations. As we study a passage, we may start either with a comparison chart or a communication chart. We go back and forth between the two until we are satisfied we have understood the author's intended meaning.

Use the comparison chart below to compare the back translations of Matthew 13:31–32 in three languages with the Greek. What differences do you notice? How do these differences affect the meaning you understand from the text?

Greek	Language 1	Language 2	Language 3	Observations
Another parable he placed before them saying,	Again Jesus sought to make a comparison with the word he spoke to the people. He said:	[31] And Jesus taught again another parable.	[31] After that Yesus again said another parable to the crowd, he said:	

"The Kingdom of the Heavens like is a mustard seed, which [a] man planted in his field,	"I am going to teach you about how the people will multiply, those who will enter God's hand. There in the field of a man was planted a small seed of mustard.	"The increase in size of the ruling of God," he said, "it's like a plant whose seed is very small. A person plants this in his field,	"When God becomes King on earth, it will happen like this story: There was a person who took hawi [mustard greens] seeds, he went and planted it in his small-garden.	
which on the one [hand] is indeed smaller than all of the seeds,	This seed truly is the smallest of all the other seeds.	(reordered)	That seed was very tiny, smaller than other seeds.	
but on [the] other hand, when it grows, it is the largest of the garden vegetables	But when it grows, then it is a larger plant than all the other plants in the plant garden.	and when it sprouts and gets big, it becomes the largest of the vegetable plants.	But when it grew, it was bigger than the other vegetables.	
and it becomes a tree, so that the birds of heaven come and live in its branches.	There in its branches birds make nests.	It's like a tree and the birds can light in it and can build their nests in its branches."	It grew like a tree, with the result that birds came and made their nests in its branches."	

Compare these English translations of Matthew 13:31–32 with the Greek. What differences do you notice? How do these differences affect the meaning you understand from the text?

Greek	Phillips	New Century	The Message	Observations
Another parable he placed before them saying,	Then he put another parable before them:	Then Jesus told another story:	Another story.	
"The Kingdom of the Heavens like is a mustard seed, which [a] man planted in his field,	"the kingdom of Heaven is like a tiny grain of mustard-seed which a man took and sowed in his field.	"The kingdom of heaven is like a mustard seed that a man planted in his field.	"God's kingdom is like a pine nut that a farmer plants.	
which on the one [hand] is indeed smaller than all of the seeds,	As a seed it is the smallest of them all,	That seed is the smallest of all seeds,	It is quite small as seeds go,	
but on [the] other hand, when it grows, it is the largest of the garden vegetables	but it grows to be the biggest of all plants.	but when it grows, it is one of the largest garden plants.	but in the course of years it grows	
and it becomes a tree,	It becomes a tree,	It becomes big enough	into a huge pine tree,	
so that the birds of heaven come and live in its branches.	big enough for birds to come and nest in its branches."	for the wild birds to come and build nests in its branches."	and eagles build nests in it."	

Lesson 13

Appropriate Scripture Products

Land Cruiser, small car, or motorbike?

One night as they were chatting, John told Peter about a car his father once owned when he was young. His father had saved his money for years and finally was able to buy a Land Cruiser. He drove it home and parked it in front of their house. Everyone could see it there, and his father was delighted to have the status of owning such a car. There was a problem,

however. It used a lot of gas (petrol) and the repairs were so expensive that his father did not have enough money to pay for all these things. In fact, his father was a bit nervous driving the car, as he did not know how to drive very well and was afraid he might cause an accident. So the car sat there. Whenever the family needed to go somewhere, they had to walk or take public transportation.

One day John's uncle came over on a shiny new motorbike. He said, "This motorbike is really helping me. It hardly costs anything for the gas, and the repairs are not expensive, either. It's true, it doesn't protect me from the rain like your car does, and I can't take my whole family in it, but since I bought it, my life has changed. I'm able to do errands for my business and make much more money than ever before, and I can visit people from the church more easily, too." John's father looked at him and thought deeply. He realized his Land Cruiser was not meeting his needs. He still wanted a car, but not one that was so expensive to own and use. The next day he put his Land Cruiser up for sale and before long he was able to buy a smaller, more economical car.

John's family was much happier with the smaller car, and found it changed their lives significantly. They could get to places much more quickly and easily than before, so they were able to go out more often. John's father also got a lot more experience driving, and before long he could drive on the main roads or in heavy traffic without any problem.

A couple years later, John's father got a promotion at his job with a salary increase. His work in the church required him to be out in the villages more and more. The roads were so bad he often felt like his little car was being shaken apart. Finally he said to the family, "This little car has served us well, but now that I'm out on the dirt roads so much, I need a more solid car. I think if we get a Land Cruiser now, it would really serve us well." He bought a Land Cruiser a second time. With the changes that had taken place in his life, this time it was just what he needed.

GROUP DISCUSSION

1. Discuss the advantages and costs of owning a Land Cruiser, a small economical car, or a motorbike.
2. How did John's father's needs change over time?
3. How might this apply to Bible translation?

Conflicting expectations

Some people want a translation of the Bible that allows them to understand as much of what the original author communicated as possible, but they do not benefit from it. They may not have access to the intended context, or they may not be interested enough to make the effort to learn it. Whatever the case, without the intended context, a high meaning resemblance translation is like the first time John's father owned a Land Cruiser. It did not help him at all.

Audiences like these may benefit from Scripture products that have been adapted to their context and require less effort to understand. These products may not give them access to all of the meaning communicated by the original, but they will be able understand them and grow in their faith. This is like the uncle's motorbike. It did not provide all the benefits of a Land Cruiser, but it was easy to use and met the uncle's needs.

Over time, audiences' needs may change. At first, a Scripture product that is easier to understand may serve their needs. In the process of using it, they will learn some biblical contextual information. Later, as their interest in Scripture grows, they may want to understand more exactly what the biblical author communicated and may be willing to put more effort into understanding it. This is like Peter's father at the end of the story who had became a good driver and needed a larger vehicle to do his job. At that point, he could drive the Land Cruiser without difficulty and it served his needs better than the small car.

A communication strategy

The goal of communicating Scripture to people is to make it possible for them to engage with it in life-changing ways. To accomplish this goal, we need to broaden our scope and think about the most appropriate communication strategy for an audience rather than thinking only of the genre 'Bible translation'. For some audiences, something that does not claim to be a Bible translation may be more relevant at certain times. An appropriate communication strategy may include a variety of Scripture products: those that claim to be a translation of Scripture and those that claim to be based on Scripture.

> *Scripture products include products that claim to be a translation of Scripture, and those that claim to be based on Scripture.*

Of course, all Scripture products should follow the natural linguistic structure of the language. Word-for-word translations resemble the linguistic form of the original rather than the meaning. They express things in unusual ways, and this requires the audience to exert more effort to understand the meaning without adding any extra benefits. This decreases relevance and so they are to be avoided.

Word-for-word translations raise processing costs without increasing cognitive benefits. This decreases relevance.

Here are three basic approaches to communicating Scripture to an audience. A communication strategy may make use of more than one of them for different needs of their audience.

Approach #1: Scripture products that are easy to understand right away

Approach #1 aims at communicating to an audience in their current context in a relevant way. This is especially appropriate for audiences that are just hearing the Bible for the first time. For example, Tom Headland tells of the Dumagat of the Philippines. For them, the New Testament had so much new information, they suffered from "information overload." They simply could not learn that much at once.[1] Peter Kingston tells a similar story for the Mamainde of Brazil. He lists many pages of information they would have to learn just to be able to understand the book of Mark.[2] Learning biblical contextual information is a process that takes place gradually over time, and for people with no biblical knowledge the effort required to understand may be too much to do all at once.

> *Approach #1 involves adjusting the text to the audience's current context so that they can understand it right away.*

In Approach #1, communicators select passages from the Bible that are especially relevant to their audience. These may be passages that address issues they are particularly interested in, or passages that do not require them to learn much new contextual information.

---

[1] Headland, Thomas. 1981. Information rate, information overload, and communication problems in the Casiguran Dumagot New Testament. *Notes on Translation* 83:18–27.

[2] Kingston, Peter. 1915. The Gospel of Mark: Good news or confusion? *Notes on Translation* 57:22–29.

Wherever there are contextual mismatches between the first and second audiences, they will lead to communication problems. In this approach, these problems are solved by making adjustments in the text so that the audience can understand it easily in their current context. These adjustments increase their immediate understanding. At the same time, they lower the amount an audience could understand from an unadjusted text if they knew the originally intended context.

Where audiences expect the meaning communicated by a Bible translation to have a high degree of resemblance to the original meaning, it is better to refer to these products as *Scripture-based products* rather than Bible translations. In this way, genre expectations about high meaning resemblance are not stimulated, and communicators are free to do what is really necessary to make the message of Scripture immediately relevant to the new audience. They can omit parts of the text that are not relevant at the time, for example the exact type of work the disciples did before Jesus called them, or the exact kind of wood Noah used to build the ark. They can also insert necessary information which the audience is lacking. Developing these products is often referred to as *crafting* rather than translating. Some examples of Scripture-based products are Bible stories, the New Readers Series (UBS), or comic books.

In this approach, communicators take more responsibility for the decisions they make as they try to make the text easy to understand. The more adjustments are made, the less the audience has access to what the original actually said, the more they see the original through the 'translators' glasses'.

As communicators craft these texts, they need to focus on two things:
- that the information they convey agrees with the meaning of the passage.
- that they make enough adjustments to make the passages relevant to the audience in their current context.

GROUP DISCUSSION

1. What advantages does this approach have?
2. Think of a situation in your community where this approach would be helpful.

If not already mentioned, discuss the following advantages of this approach:
- Audiences who are not very interested in Scripture are more likely to engage with this kind of Scripture product.
- Audiences can understand at least something of Scripture without learning much new contextual information.
- Scripture products are often shorter, and so it takes less effort to read or listen to them.

- The selection of highly relevant passages responds to the audience's current interests, so they are motivated to read or listen to them.

We will be learning more about preparing Bible stories in Lesson 21.

Approach #2: Scripture products that aim at high meaning resemblance

Approach #2 aims at offering the audience the possibility of understanding as much of the original intended meaning as possible, given the differences between the original and receptor languages. We have seen that making things explicit in the translation that are implicit in the original changes the meaning resemblance, so this is avoided as much as possible (see Lessons 8 and 11).

> *Approach #2 aims at keeping the ideas communicated by the translation as similar to the ideas communicated by the original as possible. This requires that the audience learn the intended content to be able to understand.*

As in all secondary communication, where there are contextual mismatches between the contexts of the original and secondary audience, there will be communication problems. In this approach, the audience needs to learn the originally intended context to be able to understand the author's intended meaning. This learning may take place over time, so the audience may not understand as much initially from the translation, but as they learn the intended context, their understanding will surpass what they could have understood from a text adjusted to their context. This is because they have access to as close a version of the original evidence—the text—as is possible in their language, rather than an adjusted version of it. Without learning the intended contextual information, however, they will understand less of the ideas communicated by the original from this approach as compared to Approach #1 or #3.

> **An audience may not understand less initially from an Approach #2 translation, but as they learn the intended context, they will understand more than they could have from an Approach #1 or #3 translation.**

This contextual information can be provided in multiple ways: helps accompanying the text, teaching in sermons and Bible studies, courses and Bible schools, films, books, and so forth. The translator can contribute to this process, but helping an audience become biblically literate goes beyond what can be included in a Bible. It involves the larger teaching ministry of the church.

Many audiences find this approach satisfies their expectations of the genre Bible translation.

Some advantages of this approach are:
- Audiences can trust the Scripture product to give them the possibility of as full and accurate a rendering of the original meaning as possible. The more they learn of the original context, the closer they will get to the original meaning. These are the best kind of Scripture products for serious Bible study and theological reflection for people who want to know exactly what the original communicated.
- The Scripture products do not change very much when they are revised.
- The Scripture products tend to be more similar to each other, so readers are less likely to be confused by translations in other languages they know.

Approach #3: Scripture products that are between #1 and #2

Approach #3 aims at providing a Scripture product that has a reasonably high level of meaning resemblance to the original, but that also makes some adjustments in the text to make it somewhat easier for the audience to understand.

In this approach, where there are contextual mismatches, communicators make some adjustments in the text. If the product is expected to fall within the genre Bible translation, they will be quite limited in the adjustments they can make, and the audience will still need to learn quite a bit of context outside the text to understand the intended meaning of many Scripture passages. For example, in the story of the Good Samaritan (Lk 10:33), one translation inserts the word *despised* before *Samaritan* to give the audience a clue of the way they were viewed, as this is important in the story. This helps, but the audience still needs to know who Samaritans were, who despised them, why, how this affected their interactions, and so forth.

> *Approach #3 involves some adjustment of the text to the audience's current context, all the while keeping the degree of meaning resemblance high enough to fulfill the audience's expectations of the genre 'Bible translation.'*

Additional information like this might be supplied in extra-textual helps, teaching, and so forth, as in Approach #2.

One challenge of this approach is to be consistent in the degree of adjustments that are made. The other is to ensure that the combination of the adjustments to the text and the adjustments to the audience's context outside the text are enough to make the Scripture product relevant. One advantage of this approach is that the text is somewhat easier for people to understand immediately. One disadvantage is that the audience cannot tell which parts of the translation have a high degree of resemblance to the original and which parts have been adjusted. Some translations solve this by marking all adjustments in a special way in the text, for example by putting the words in small brackets.

GROUP DISCUSSION

1. Discuss the advantages and disadvantages of adding the words in italics to the translation of these verses. Look up the passages if necessary.
   a. Luke 12:7 "Why, even the hairs of your head are all numbered. Fear not; you are of more value than many sparrows; *therefore your Father will protect you.*"
   b. Luke 5:12 ... a man came along who was covered with leprosy. *Because he was a leper, he was ritually unclean....*"
2. Think of a situation in which Approach #2 would be appropriate as the main Scripture product.

Identifying relevant Scripture products for an audience

Audiences may respond enthusiastically to one kind of Scripture product while showing no interest in others. What may seem like disinterest in Scripture may actually be a problem of inappropriate communication strategies and Scripture products. Factors affecting this decision are:

1. *The audience's current knowledge.* The greater the difference between the audience's current knowledge and that of the first audience, the more *effort* they will have to exert to understand Scripture. The audience's current knowledge is affected by many things: their traditional culture and worldview, their exposure to other cultures, their knowledge of the Bible, the ease with which they entertain new ideas, and so forth. Products that require more effort than their audience is willing or able to make will not communicate successfully. The audience's knowledge changes over time, so it needs to be reassessed regularly.

2. *The audience's expectation of relevance to life.* If people expect a lot of *benefits* from Scripture, they will be motivated to put out more effort to understand it. If they do not expect many benefits, they will not be very motivated to put out much effort.

3. *The audience's expectation of the degree of meaning resemblance.* If the degree of meaning resemblance between the translation and the original is not what an audience expects, they will lose trust in the translation. Once trust is lost, it is very hard to regain.

Many audiences do not have access to biblical languages and so they can only compare their translation with another translation in a language they know. They may expect a word-for-word translation of that text rather than high meaning resemblance to the original. Translators need to help audiences understand that the Bible was originally written in Hebrew and Greek, and that word-for-word translations do not communicate the intended meaning successfully because audiences have to exert a lot of effort, but are not rewarded with more cognitive benefits. Examples comparing word-for-word translations with the originally intended meaning can be convincing.

Responding to the audience's needs, abilities, and expectations is very important for Scripture products to be used. If audiences are given more information than they can process, they will not use the Scripture product, as we have seen in the Dumagat and Mamainde examples. On the other hand, if the degree of meaning resemblance is lower than audiences expect, this will also result in the Scripture product not being used. For example, in the Guarani translation in Brazil, the translators made adjustments to the text so that it was easier for their audience to understand. For example, they said it would be easier for a cow to go through the eye of a needle because the Guarani had never seen a camel. Later when the translation was tested in the churches, people rejected it because the meaning resemblance was lower than they expected. One of the translators laughed and said, "When we wrote that, we didn't know the difference between a cow and a camel!"[3]

Audiences may have conflicting desires: they may want a translation of Scripture that has a high degree of meaning resemblance to the original, but they may not be willing or able to make the effort to learn the intended context. The first question should be the communication question: what kind of communication strategy will lead this audience to engage with Scripture in life-changing ways? Having a Bible translation that looks impressive but no one uses is much like the first Land Cruiser Peter's father owned. It is better to have a simpler Scripture-based product that an audience uses than a translation that they do not use.

Church and/or community leaders need to consider their needs, abilities, and expectations of the audience they intend to reach. Translators can help them understand what successful communication requires. They can explain the advantages, disadvantages, and requirements of different approaches, so these leaders can choose one (or more) that suits their needs.

> ## The relevance of a Bible translation depends on:
> - The audience's current context.
> - Their expectations of relevance.
> - The degree of meaning resemblance they expect.

---

[3] Dooley, Robert A. 1989. Style and acceptability: The Guarani New Testament. *Notes on Translation* 3(1):49–57.

The media factor

When working out an appropriate communication strategy for an audience, translators need to use the kinds of media that correspond to their audience's preferences. Some audiences prefer oral communication and, at least initially, will not use Scripture in print even if they know how to read the language. They may be willing to listen to a recording of a written translation read aloud, however. Many audiences benefit from having oral, audio, and written Scripture products.

Oral and written styles differ so different approaches are needed. For example, someone hearing a passage of Scripture cannot see punctuation, so additional things may need to be made explicit in the text. The text needs to flow well when read aloud. Sentences may need to be a different length or less complicated, with more repetition, since hearers cannot look back and reread the text. Information provided in helps in a printed version needs to be provided in a way that is appropriate to oral media.

GROUP DISCUSSION

1. About what percent of the people in your area know how to read?
2. What media do people prefer: audio, video, or print?
3. Discuss the kind of communication strategy you think would be relevant for your audience. Which approaches would be best and for whom?

EXERCISE

Imagine that you are preparing a communication strategy for the following three groups. What type of overall communication strategy would you expect to be relevant to each audience? Decide on the approach(es) and media. Then list three or four Scripture products you think would be appropriate.

First Group: Six million nomadic people living in east Asia who speak Kubamen. A few of them have now settled in towns. There are ten known Christians in the whole ethnic group. The group mainly follows their traditional religion. The literacy rate is very low, around two percent, and there is very little interest in Christianity. The group is beginning to be interested in violent videos that are coming from another Asian country. There is also some interest in learning English.

Second Group: 100,000 people living in central Africa who speak Bakama. There are churches in every village and almost everyone considers himself or herself to be a Christian. The literacy rate is about forty percent though some literates do not really like reading. The church leaders of the main denominations revere the King James Version in English and feel their translation should be as near to it as possible. Recently, many people have been killed in ethnic conflict and the situation is getting worse.

Third Group: Five hundred people living on an island in the Pacific who speak Shilak. They all consider themselves Christian since the gospel was brought to them in 1850. (The first missionary who came was killed and eaten, but the next group of missionaries was able to tell the people about God's way of salvation.) The language is probably dying out, as no one under the age of twenty speaks it. It is being replaced by a trade language. The elders of the community want to see their language and culture retained. All adults are literate to some degree. Recently electricity came to the area and in its wake, television, radio, and MP3 players.

Summary

Many communication strategies are possible, and translators need to help church or community leaders develop one that will be relevant for them. It may contain more than one approach. Approach #1 aims at Scripture-based products that are easy for an audience to understand in their current context. This requires adjusting the text to their context so that they can understand it. Audiences accept a lower degree of meaning resemblance for the ease of understanding right away. Approach #2 aims at Scripture products that allow for a high degree of meaning resemblance with the original. With these products, an audience may understand less of the intended meaning initially, but over time their understanding will grow as they learn more of the intended context. In the end, audiences have the possibility of understanding as much of the intended meaning as is possible in their language. Approach #3 falls somewhere between these two. The communication strategy that is relevant to an audience depends on their current knowledge of the Bible, on their expectations of relevance to life, and on their expectations of meaning resemblance. The media in which the products are developed is another significant factor affecting their use. Translators can help church and community leaders understand the benefits and limitations of each kind of Scripture product so they can develop an appropriate communication strategy. A variety of Scripture products can be tested in a variety of media— oral, audio, print, video, internet, text messages, and so forth—to see which ones are most relevant to the audience.

> **So what?**
>
> Bible translators need to help communities understand the advantages of a variety of communication strategies so they can choose the kind that is most relevant to them at the time.

Assignment
1. Prepare a presentation for the church leaders in your area, explaining the three different approaches to communicating Scripture.
2. Explain how you would go about developing a communication strategy that would be likely to work best for the people in your community.

Lesson 14

Understanding a Biblical Passage

John and Peter prepare sermons

John and Peter had been going to the same church each Sunday. One week near the end of their course, the pastor asked John to preach on the next Sunday and Peter on the following Sunday. John was going to preach first, and he spent a lot of time in the evenings preparing his sermon. Finally, he asked Peter to listen to it.

He took his reading from Colossians 2:16–17: "Therefore let no one pass judgment on you in questions of food and drink or with regard to a festival or a new moon or a Sabbath. These are only a shadow of what is to come; but the substance belongs to Christ."

He was very excited as he explained to Peter, "I never knew these verses were in the Bible! They mean that we shouldn't keep Sunday special, and that we can eat or drink absolutely anything!" "Wait a minute," said Peter, "I don't think Paul was saying that. You need to look at the whole chapter and understand his argument." "But I found a commentary that said is what it means!" said John. "Well, let's look at other commentaries and see what they say. You can't rely on just one," said Peter.

As they started to look at other commentaries, they found that all of them talked about Paul emphasizing freedom from the Jewish law for non-Jewish believers. This was because a group of people called Judaizers had come and tried to get these non-Jewish believers to obey the Jewish law in all its detail. It did not mean that Paul was telling believers they could be greedy at meals or get drunk. John looked rather disappointed and went away to rewrite his sermon.

Peter had problems the next week. He wanted to prepare his sermon really well, so after choosing the passage, he borrowed a whole stack of commentaries and read each one to find out what it said about the passage he had selected. By Friday, he had a headache and his eyes were bloodshot. John asked him what was wrong. "I've read so many commentaries that now I can't see the forest for the trees!" answered Peter. "Maybe you should put them all away now, and just go back to the passage," suggested John.

In the end, they both preached very good sermons that were much appreciated by the congregation. Later the next week, Peter said to John, "You know, we need to have some help in choosing three or four good basic commentaries. I wonder who could help us. Maybe we should talk to our translation advisor."

GROUP DISCUSSION

What do you think we can learn from John's and Peter's experience?

Using biblical resources

Discuss this statement:

> You cannot translate what you do not understand. Understanding is the heart of translation.

What happens if translators do not understand what they are translating?

To understand a biblical passage, you need to understand the context which the author expected the first audience to have. Many resources are available to help you learn these things, for example:

- Different translations
- Commentaries
- Bible dictionaries (encyclopedias)
- Bible atlas
- Exegetical Summaries (these give short quotes from various commentaries for all of the books of the NT and part of the OT)
- Translator's Notes
- Interlinear Translations
- UBS Handbooks
- Concordance
- Computer programs with helps for translators, such as Translator's Workplace, Paratext, and so forth.
- DVDs that give background information on Jewish culture and the geography of Israel
- Study Bibles, for example the NIV Study Bible, the CEV Learning Bible, and so forth
- Internet websites

EXERCISES

Imagine that you have the following resources in your project library:

- A basic series of commentaries on all the books of the New Testament
- The InterVarsity Fellowship Bible dictionary

- A Bible atlas
- The series of Exegetical Summaries
- A series of DVDs that give background information on Jewish culture and the geography of Israel
- Translator's Workplace
- The NIV Study Bible and the CEV Learning Bible
- Occasional internet access to the web

In the large group, discuss which resources you would turn to first to find the answers to the following questions:

1. When did Paul write the epistle to the Philippians and where was he at that time?
2. How far is it from Nazareth to Jerusalem?
3. When the New Testament talks about John the Baptist being in the desert, what did it look like?
4. In John 3 after verse 14, where do most commentaries think the words of Jesus end and the words of John begin?
5. What is the meaning of *phylactery*?
6. What would be a suitable application for church leaders of 1 Corinthians 8?

In small groups:

1. Find the answer to one of the questions above.
2. List the kinds of resources that are available in your translation project to study biblical passages.

Get the big picture of a passage

The first step in understanding a passage is to place it within the larger context of the book of the Bible in which it is found. Read an introduction of the book where the passage is found. We will be working on Luke 7:36–50.

Browse the section headings in the book that come before the passage. Note what that leads up to this passage.

EXERCISES

1. Find out who wrote the gospel of Luke, to whom, in what situation, and for what purpose.
2. Look at the section headings in Luke 6–8. What topics come before Luke 7:36–50? What topics come after? How does this passage fit the chapter and book? Why do you think Luke included it at this point?

Compare the passage in several versions/languages

Read the passage (Lk 7:36–50) and try to understand the author's meaning. Then read it in several versions, and in more than one language, if possible. Compare them.

EXERCISE

Divide the verses of Luke 7:36–50 among the small groups. Have each group compare the meaning that is communicated by each translation of their verses with the meaning of the original. Are there differences? How do they affect the meaning you understand from the text?

Go through the whole passage together as a large group, with feedback from each small group on their verse(s).

Back-translation of the Greek	NIV **Jesus Anointed by a Sinful Woman**	NLT **Jesus Anointed by a Sinful Woman**	Observations
[36] Someone was asking him (to eat with him) - one of the Pharisees that he should eat with him …and having-entered the house of the Pharisee …he reclined-for-a-meal	[36] Now one of the Pharisees invited Jesus to have dinner with him, so he went to the Pharisee's house and reclined at the table.	[36] One of the Pharisees asked Jesus to come to his home for a meal, so Jesus accepted the invitation and sat down to eat.	
[37] and look, a woman who was in the town a sinner and having-learned that he was reclining-for-a-meal in the house of the Pharisee bringing an alabaster jar of perfume	[37] When a woman who had lived a sinful life in that town learned that Jesus was eating at the Pharisee's house, she brought an alabaster jar of perfume,	[37] A certain immoral woman heard he was there and brought a beautiful jar filled with expensive perfume.	

[38] and having stepped behind him by his feet as she was crying with the tears she began to wet his feet and with the hair of her head she was drying and she was kissing his feet and she was anointing	[38] and as she stood behind him at his feet weeping, she began to wet his feet with her tears. Then she wiped them with her hair, kissed them and poured perfume on them.	[38] Then she knelt behind him at his feet, weeping. Her tears fell on his feet, and she wiped them off with her hair. Then she kept kissing his feet and putting perfume on them.	
[39] And having-seen the Pharisee who-had-invited him said within himself saying, If this was prophet, he-would-have-known who and what-sort-of woman who is touching him she-is sinner	[39] When the Pharisee who had invited him saw this, he said to himself, "If this man were a prophet, he would know who is touching him and what kind of woman she is—that she is a sinner."	[39] When the Pharisee who was the host saw what was happening and who the woman was, he said to himself, "This proves that Jesus is no prophet. If God had really sent him, he would know what kind of woman is touching him. She's a sinner!"	
[40] And answering Jesus said to him: "Simon, I have to-you something to-say:" He (but), "Teacher, speak" said.	[40] Jesus answered him, "Simon, I have something to tell you." "Tell me, teacher," he said.	[40] Then Jesus spoke up and answered his thoughts. "Simon," he said to the Pharisee, "I have something to say to you." "All right, Teacher," Simon replied, "go ahead."	

[41] A moneylender had two debtors. One owed him five hundred denari, but the other fifty.	[41] "Two men owed money to a certain moneylender. One owed him five hundred denari, and the other fifty.	[41] Then Jesus told him this story: "A man loaned money to two people— five hundred pieces of silver to one and fifty pieces to the other.	
[42] When both couldn't pay back, he cancelled [the debt of] both. So who of them both will love him most?"	[42] Neither of them had the money to pay him back, so he canceled the debts of both. Now which of them will love him more?"	[42] But neither of them could repay him, so he kindly forgave them both, canceling their debts. Who do you suppose loved him more after that?"	
[43] Answering Simon said: "I suppose the one to whom the bigger [debt] was cancelled." But he said to him: "You have judged correctly."	[43] Simon replied, "I suppose the one who had the bigger debt canceled." "You have judged correctly," Jesus said.	[43] Simon answered, "I suppose the one for whom he canceled the larger debt." "That's right," Jesus said.	
[44] And turning to the woman he said to Simon: "Do you see this woman? When I came into your house, you have not given me water over my feet. But she, with her tears she has wet my feet and with her hair has dried them.	[44] Then he turned toward the woman and said to Simon, "Do you see this woman? I came into your house. You did not give me any water for my feet, but she wet my feet with her tears and wiped them with her hair.	[44] Then he turned to the woman and said to Simon, "Look at this woman kneeling here. When I entered your home, you didn't offer me water to wash the dust from my feet, but she has washed them with her tears and wiped them with her hair.	

45 A kiss you have not given me. But she, from the time I entered, did not stop to kiss my feet.	45 You did not give me a kiss, but *this woman*, from the time I entered, has not stopped kissing my feet.	45 You didn't give me a kiss of greeting, but she has kissed my feet again and again from the time I first came in.	
46 You have not anointed my head with oil. But she has anointed my feet with perfume.	46 You did not put oil on my head, but she has poured perfume on my feet.	46 You neglected the courtesy of olive oil to anoint my head, but she has anointed my feet with rare perfume.	
47 For this reason I tell you, her sins which were many will be forgiven, so she has loved much. But to whom less is forgiven, he will love less."	47 Therefore, I tell you, her many sins have been forgiven—for she loved much. But he who has been forgiven little loves little."	47 I tell you, her sins—and they are many—have been forgiven, so she has shown me much love. But a person who is forgiven little shows only little love."	
48 But he said to her: "Your sins are forgiven"	48 Then Jesus said to her, "Your sins are forgiven."	48 Then Jesus said to the woman, "Your sins are forgiven."	
49 and the ones reclining said among themselves: "Who is he that he even forgives sins?"	49 The other guests began to say among themselves, "Who is this who even forgives sins?"	49 The men at the table said among themselves, "Who does this man think he is, going around forgiving sins?"	
50 But he said to the woman: "Your faith has saved you. Go in peace."	50 Jesus said to the woman, "Your faith has saved you; go in peace."	50 And Jesus said to the woman, "Your faith has saved you; go in peace."	

Act out the story

In small groups, prepare to act out the story for the large group. This will help you experience the passage. Try to imagine how each character felt and get the main point of the story across with feeling rather than getting every word of the text exactly correct. (Remember the lessons on verbal sketching.) Do not read the text. It is okay if some details are missing or incorrect.

Compare the ways different groups acted out the story. Notice any differences and note down any questions the skits raise about the meaning of the passage.

Study the passage using helps

1. Read through any helps you have available on the passage. Notes based on the IVP Bible Background Commentary are provided at the end of this chapter, but use any other helps you have as well. A communication chart like the one you used to analyze retellings is provided below. Record the things you want to remember when you translate this passage on this chart.

   a. The first column is a back-translation of the Greek that lets the structure of the Greek language show through as much as possible (word order, verb forms, and so forth). These structures provide clues to the reader so pay attention to them. Try to find the meaning the author intended to communicate by requiring his audience to make the extra effort to process any unusual structures.

   b. In the second column, write the ideas that have been communicated. This includes filling out the text: identifying who pronouns refer to, parts of sentences that are left out, ambiguous expressions, and so forth. It also includes the implications the author intended his audience to draw and other cognitive benefits.

   c. In the third column, list the contextual information the author intended the audience to use. Pay particular attention to contextual information your audience may be lacking.

2. Write down any questions you cannot answer in a notebook reserved for questions to ask your consultant.

Text	Communicated ideas	Contextual information
7:36 Someone was asking him (to eat with him) - one of the Pharisees that he should eat with him … and having-entered the house of the Pharisee … he reclined-for-a-meal	One of the group of Pharisees was asking Jesus to eat at a dinner party with him and so then Jesus entered the Pharisee's house and then lay-down-for-a-meal on the couch/cushion with his head near the table and feet stretched out away from the table. An invitation to a formal meal indicated that the Pharisee at least pretended to honor Jesus. Jesus accepted the Pharisee's invitation.	Invitations to dinner parties were a way to honor someone, and several guests were invited. The guests might become clients of the host and be obliged to repay the host (patron) with public honor and support in the future. At these meals, guests would lie on their side on divans/cushions and eat from low tables, head towards the tables, feet stretched away. They wore sandals and removed them before lying down to eat. Uninvited people could come and watch the meal from the sides.
7:37–38 and look, a woman who was in the town a sinner and having-learned that he was reclining-for-a-meal in the house of the Pharisee bringing an alabaster jar of perfume and having stepped behind him by his feet as she was crying with the tears she began to wet his feet and with the hair of her head she was drying and she was kissing his feet and she was anointing		

7:39 And having-seen the Pharisee who-had-invited him said within himself saying, If this was prophet, he-would-have-known who and what-sort-of woman who is touching him she-is sinner		
7:40 And answering Jesus said to him: "Simon, I have to-you something to-say:" He (but), "Teacher, speak" said. 7:41 A moneylender had two debtors. One owed him five hundred denari, but the other fifty. 7:42 When both couldn't pay back, he cancelled [the debt of] both. So who of them both will love him most?" 7:43 Answering Simon said: "I suppose the one to whom the bigger [debt] was cancelled." 7:44a But he said to him: "You have judged correctly."		

7:44 and turning to the woman he said to Simon: "Do you see this woman? When I came into your house, you have not given me water over my feet. But she, with her tears she has wet my feet and with her hair has dried them. 7:45 A kiss you have not given me. But she, from the time I entered, did not stop to kiss my feet. 7:46 You have not anointed my head with oil. But she has anointed my feet with perfume.		
7:47 For this reason I tell you, her sins which were many have been forgiven, so she has loved much. But to whom less is forgiven, he will love less."		

7:48 But he said to her: "Your sins are forgiven" 7:49 and the ones reclining said among themselves: "Who is he that he even forgives sins?" 7:50 But he said to the woman: "Your faith has saved you. Go in peace."		

So what?

You cannot translate what you do not understand. Understanding is the heart of translation.

Helps based on the IVP Bible Background Commentary[1]

Luke 7:36–50 The Pharisee and the Loose Woman

Jesus shocked people by reaching out to people who were rejected by society. For example, he associated with the disliked Romans (7:1–10), the poor (7:11–17) and those considered "sinners" by the religious leaders (7:36–50). Since the classical Greek period, formal meals had become a setting for moral instruction.

7:36 It was considered a good thing to invite a teacher over for dinner, especially if the teacher was a stranger to the town or had just taught at the synagogue. That they are "reclining" rather than sitting indicates that they are using couches rather than chairs and that this is a banquet, perhaps in honor of the famous guest teacher.

7:37 That this woman is a "sinner" may mean that she is a prostitute, or at least a woman known to be immoral. If the Pharisee is well-to-do, he may have a servant as a porter to check visitors at the door; but religious people often opened their homes for the poor, and the woman manages to get in. In banquets where uninvited people could enter, they were to remain quiet and away from the couches, observing the discussions of host and guests. Alabaster was considered the most appropriate container for perfume.

7:38 Jewish people did not consider perfume sinful, but because this woman is

[1] Keener, Craig S. 1993. *The IVP Bible background commentary: New Testament.* Downers Grove, Ill.: InterVarsity.

a "sinner" and uses the perfume as a tool of her trade, Jesus' acceptance of the gift of perfuming would offend religious people. That she stands "behind him" and anoints his feet instead of his head has to do with the posture of guests reclining on the couches; he would have had his left arm on the table and his feet away from the table toward the wall.

7:39 Adult women who were religious were expected to be married and thus would have their heads covered; any woman with her hair exposed to public view would be considered an immoral woman. That the host thought that Jesus might be a prophet at all suggests great respect, because Jewish people generally believed that prophets ceased after the Old Testament period.

7:40–42 Some scholars have argued that Aramaic does not have a way of saying "be grateful", and this is why Luke wrote "Which will love him more?" rather than, as we might expect, "Which will be more grateful?" Although the law said that debts should be forgiven in the seventh year, experts in the law had found a way to get around that law. Those who could not pay could be imprisoned, temporarily made a slave, or have some of their possessions taken away; but this creditor goes beyond the letter of the law and shows mercy.

7:43–46 People welcomed guests into their homes by providing water for the feet (though well-to-do householders left the washing to servants). Oil for the dry skin on one's head would also be a thoughtful act. An affectionate or respectful greeting would be a kiss.

7:47–50 Although the priests could tell someone he was forgiven after he had made a sin offering, Jesus says that her sins are forgiven without requiring her to make an offering in the temple. When Jesus said this, he contradicted the way the Pharisees taught. Most Jews would have seen Jesus' response to the woman as strange at best.

Adjusting Mismatches in Translation

Lesson 15

Identifying Mismatches in Secondary Communication

A difficult request

Peter and John were having breakfast one morning when Peter received a thick envelope from Pastor Anthony. Peter tucked it away as it looked like he would need a good bit of time to read it.

That evening, they were relaxing after supper and Peter opened the envelope. "Hmm," said Peter as he read the letter. "He's giving me a hard job here. Pastor Anthony has never learned our language, but he's very concerned about the situation with Birgita. He's written me this letter in English but now he needs me to translate it in Bingolan so she'll really understand what he's trying to say." Peter got some sheets of paper and settled down to the job.

Peter started writing, but after a few minutes he crossed out what he was writing and tried again. "Having problems?" asked John. "Well," said Peter, "I keep having to remember that this letter is addressed to Birgita, not me. When I read, 'You should be sure to come and see me as soon as possible,' for one minute I thought he meant that I should go and see him! Then I realized of course he is speaking to Birgita.

"Then I have another sort of problem. He has quite different ideas from mine, and I've got to think of what he was thinking when he wrote the letter. Listen to this for example, 'I know that Veronica has special powers. Remember that these can be dangerous and say your prayers every day.'

"You see my problem? What does he mean by *special powers*? There are two or three words we could use for this in Bingolan, but I've got to work out which one Pastor Anthony means.

"Yes, it is very difficult," John commented. "You have to try and decide what he was thinking when he wrote the letter, and that is very hard! Maybe you should try to phone him?"

GROUP DISCUSSION

Discuss reasons you think Peter was having trouble translating Pastor Anthony's letter to Birgita into Bingolan.

More cautious processing of secondary communication

In Lesson 5, we said that primary communication is addressed to an audience directly, but in secondary communication, a second audience is listening in on communication designed for another audience.

In primary communication, we generally take the first meaning that gives enough cognitive benefits to be the intended meaning. However, if we sense that a speaker does not know our context, we use the context we think the speaker thought we would use, rather than our actual context to process the text. For example, you may tell me, "Class starts at 2:00." If I think that you do not know that I already know this, I'll understand that you are simply telling me this because you think I do not know it and need to know it. I will interpret what you said using the context you thought I had rather than my actual context. (This is quite different than when we both know that I know when class starts. In that case, I will look for additional meaning, such as "be sure not to be late this time.")

When we recognize we are in a secondary communication situation, we follow the comprehension procedure in this more cautious way. Rather than using the first context that comes to our minds, we think of what the speaker or author thought would have come to mind for the first audience.

We can check if we are understanding the intended meaning by asking ourselves if the first audience would have used the context we used. If not, we may have misunderstood what the author meant, because using a different context leads to a different meaning. After understanding what the author intended the first audience to understand, we can go on to process how this information is relevant to us in our context.

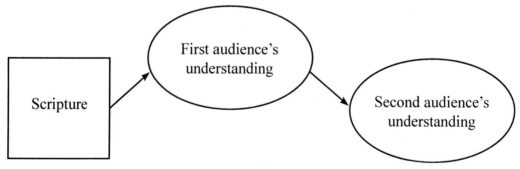

Figure 19. Understanding Scripture

We are able to think about what a speaker may be thinking because God created us with the ability to have thoughts about thoughts. We are not limited by our own thoughts or experiences. All people have this ability, regardless of their race, culture, or education.

> ## All people are able to have thoughts about thoughts beyond their experience.
>
> ## We use this ability to understand Scripture.

GROUP DISCUSSION

Think of one passage in the Bible which you think people in your area often misunderstand. Tell how they misunderstand it and give the correct interpretation.

Kinds of mismatches

Communication can fail due to various kinds of mismatches between the first and second audience. In the same way a doctor needs to find out what a patient is suffering from before prescribing medicine, communicators need to understand the kind of mismatch that has caused the miscommunication. Each kind of mismatch requires a different kind of solution.

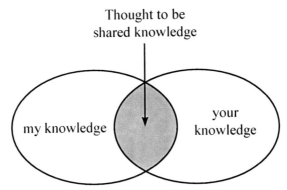

Figure 20. Where we look for context

In Lesson 5 we saw that we look for context in the information that we think we share with our communication partner. For example, if you say, "John's not feeling well," I will only think of people named John that I think we both know. I will not think of my brother John if I do not think you know him.

We guess what our partner knows, but sometimes we get it wrong. We may think we share some thoughts that we do not actually share, or we may think we do not share certain thoughts when actually we do share them. This gives four basic kinds of outcomes to our search for shared concepts and context.

Table 1. Context possibilities

	Hearers Think Concept or Context Is Shared	**Hearers Do Not Think Concept or Context Is Shared**
Concept or Context Is Actually Shared	1. Intended Concept/ Context "Birgita"	2. Unrecognized Concept/ Context "Aha! You're talking about Kilonzo!"
Concept or Context Is Not Actually Shared	3. Unintended Concept/ Context "I think of Birgita Kindiki, when actually he intended Birgita Kilonzo"	4. Unknown Concept/ Context "I don't know anyone named Birgita."

We only access concepts or context we think we share, so we only access Boxes 1 and 3.

Box 1: Intended Concepts and Contexts

Hearers may share and think they share concepts or the intended context with their communication partner. In this case, they understand the meaning without difficulty. For example, if Peter's uncle refers to Birgita and John knows her, he will understand who Peter is referring to.

Between cultures, some concepts are basic to human experience and are widely shared by people around the world, like sleeping, eating, dying, and so forth. These ideas are not shared in an identical way by everyone, but if they are widely shared and adequately similar, the audience can understand the communication without difficulty.

Things do not have to be a part of the traditional culture to be known. People acquire new ideas through exposure to other cultures and institutions, like the church, school, radio, and so forth. For example, many people know that some people consider pork unclean, but they may have this from Islam rather than from their traditional culture.

GROUP DISCUSSION

> Think of three biblical concepts that are easy for people in your language group to understand.

Box 2: Unrecognized Concepts and Contexts

Hearers may share concepts or contexts with a speaker, but not realize they share them. In this case, they will not think of that information when they try to understand the communication. For example, if Peter tells John about Birgita, but John knows her by the name "Kilonzo," although he knows the person Peter is referring to, he does not realize that he does.

This happens when audiences listen to Scripture. They may think a word refers to something they do not know about when actually they do know about it. For example, traditional societies may think they did not know about good or bad angels before the arrival of Christianity. In fact, angels are spirit beings, and often traditional people are very familiar with spirit beings.

For example, a Sudanese woman was listening to a presenter talk about spirits and how some spirits disobeyed God and were cast out of heaven. The woman was not understanding anything the presenter was saying until someone whispered to her "divinities." In fact, she knew all about divinities. Once the link between spirits and divinities was made, all of the knowledge she had about divinities came to mind.

The Adioukrou experience a similar mismatch. First-century Jewish ideas about angels are quite similar to the Adioukrou concept of ELMIS (spirit beings, divinities). Both were thought to serve God and care for the earth, to have areas of expertise and people to watch over, to have taboos, and so forth. *Elmis* is not used for angels (or demons) in Adioukrou Scripture, and so they think they did not know anything about angels before Christianity arrived. When they hear the term used for angels, they do not access what they know about *elmis*.

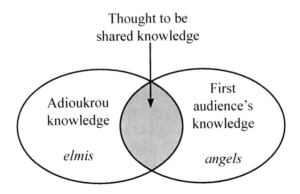

Figure 21. Unrecognized context

This is the most difficult kind of mismatch to uncover. People may not recognize the similarity between local concepts and those found in the Bible because they do not know much about the biblical culture. For many centuries, the center of Christianity was in the West, so much of the way we understand the Bible today is influenced by a Western worldview. In fact, biblical cultures are often more similar to traditional cultures than to Western cultures. When people from traditional cultures study biblical cultures directly without passing through the Western filter, they may find they share many more concepts with the biblical author than they realized.

GROUP DISCUSSION

Try to think of something your audience shares with one of the biblical authors that they do not realize they do. Explain your example.

Box 3: Unintended Concepts and Contexts

Hearers may think they share concepts or contexts with a speaker when, in fact, they do not. For example, if John knew another Birgita, Birgita Kindiki, while Peter's uncle was talking about Birgita Kilonzo, he will think the story is about a completely different person. He may think he has understood what the uncle was communicating when, in fact, he has misunderstood.

Some concepts that seem to be similar at first may, in fact, have very different information associated with them. For example, for Jews, circumcision was a mark of ethnic identity but it is done for hygienic reasons in Western cultures today. In Genesis 34, where the Israelites used circumcision to weaken their enemies so they could attack them, these differences might not be significant, but in Galatians 5:2–6 where Paul writes about the Christians not needing to be circumcised, they are very significant.

If an unintended context leads to enough cognitive benefits, the audience will assume it has understood the intended meaning without even realizing there is a problem. For example, when Jesus gave the bread to Judas at the Last Supper and immediately the devil (or Satan) entered him, people in some cultures may understand that Jesus gave Judas witchcraft by means of this enchanted food. Actually, giving food to a guest like this was a sign of special affection in Jewish culture. If nothing contradicts an interpretation, people may not be aware of the problem for some time. Sooner or later there is usually something in a text that causes people to think again, but this may not happen for some time.

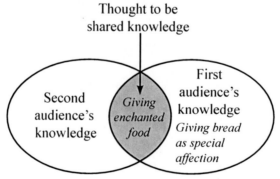

Figure 22. Unintended context

Another unintended context problem is when context comes to mind that distracts the audience from the main meaning of the passage. For example, in the story of the four men taking their friend to Jesus in Mark 2:1–5, the friends climb on the roof and remove part of it so they can lower their friend down through the hole to see Jesus. In many places, houses do not have flat roofs, nor can they be taken apart easily. People may be so distracted by exactly how the friends were able to do this that they miss the main meaning of the story.

EXERCISES

1. Traditionally for the Adioukrou of Côte d'Ivoire, the first meaning associated with the concept ADULTERY *(nfaci)* was having sexual relations outdoors, even between spouses. A less serious form of adultery was for a man to have sexual relations with a woman who was married to another man. Adultery did not include a man having sexual relations with an unmarried woman. Discuss the possible outcomes of using *nfaci* for adultery in Scripture.

2. Think of a word used in your church or community that leads people to wrong meaning. Find a passage where this concept occurs and identify the context that gets them off on the wrong path.

3. Think of one concept that shares certain information with a concept in the Bible, but has other information that is quite different. If possible, give a Bible passage where the difference would be significant and another where it would not be.

Box 4: Unknown Concepts and Contexts

Hearers may not know concepts or contexts and may be quite aware of the fact they do not. For example, John may not know anyone named Birgita. No matter how much he tries, he cannot think of anyone by that name. Or he may not know what Birgita did two years ago. He may exert a lot of effort without receiving any benefits.

In Scripture, many concepts specific to the Jewish culture fall into this category. People who have not had contact with the Bible would never have heard of the Sanhedrin, a synagogue, a Messiah, the Passover, and so forth. Money and the systems used for weighing and measuring things in the Bible were also specific to that time. Abstract ideas like *grace* or *to redeem* may also be unknown. Biblical authors expected their audiences to know these ideas and so they did not explain them.

The Old Testament provides some information that helps audiences understand the New Testament, but cultures change over time. What came to mind for New Testament audiences may have been quite different than what is recorded in the Old Testament. For example, when the Israelites lost the temple in Jerusalem and their independence as a nation in 586 B.C., the way they celebrated the

Passover was quite different than the Passover prior to that time. Knowing the Old Testament helps people understand the New, but it is not enough.

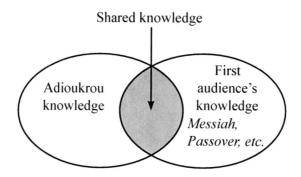

Figure 23. Unknown context

Identify any unknown concepts or contextual information for your audience in Luke 7:36–50.

Summary

In secondary communication situations, there are a lot of differences in concepts and contexts and these can lead to communication problems. Rather than taking the first meaning that leads to cognitive benefits as the intended one, audiences need to think about the context that would have come to mind for the first audience and the implications they would have drawn. Mismatches occur when: 1) audiences do not recognize a concept or context they share with the first audience, and therefore do not use it to understand the intended meaning, 2) audiences access an unintended context and do not realize they have misunderstood, or 3) audiences do not share any context with the author and cannot understand anything from the communication. These will lead to miscommunication.

> **So what?**
>
> **Translators need to be able to identify the kinds of contextual mismatches their audience experiences to be able to adjust them.**

Assignment

Read this summary of the story in the book of Ruth, or read the whole story in your Bible. Think about contextual mismatches for your audience.

- Box 2: See if you can find something in Ruth that is similar in your culture but is not recognized to be shared with the original audience by some readers.

- Box 3: See if there is anything in the book that the readers may think they understand but in fact do not.
- Box 4: Find some aspect of the Jewish culture in the book of Ruth that your audience doesn't know about.

The book of Ruth tells the story of a woman named Ruth who lived in a country near Israel called Moab. At that time, there was a famine in Israel, and a Jewish couple, Elimelech and Naomi, and their two sons went to live in Moab so that they could find food. While there, the husband died and the two sons married Moabite women. After ten years, both sons died as well. This left Naomi and her two daughter-in-laws, Ruth and Orpah. Naomi heard that the famine was over in Israel and decided to go back, and Ruth and Orpah followed her. Naomi encouraged them to stay in Moab because she was too old to give them other sons as husbands. Oprah turned back, but Ruth went with Naomi and adopted Naomi's land and God as her own.

When they got to Israel, people were surprised to see Naomi. She told them not to call her Naomi (which means pleasant), but to call her Marah (which means bitter), because God had made her life bitter. Naomi and Ruth needed to find food. It was barley harvest time, so Ruth went to glean barley in the field of one of Naomi's rich relatives, Boaz. (Poor people were allowed to pick up the sheaves of grain that the harvesters had missed.) Boaz noticed Ruth and was very kind to her because he was impressed with how loyal she had been to Naomi. He told his workers not to hurt her, but to give her water to drink and to leave extra grain behind for her. He even invited her to eat with him and his men and told her to glean only in his fields.

Naomi decided it was time to find a husband for Ruth and counseled her to go to Boaz in the night after he has feasted and lift the covers and lie down at his feet. Israel practiced the levirate marriage: if a man died, one of his brothers was expected to marry his widow. This meant Elimelech's family was expected to supply another husband for Ruth. Ruth reminded Boaz of this, and he was pleased that she had come to him even though he was an older man. But there was another relative who was closer to Naomi who had first choice. So Boaz arranged a meeting at the city gate with other respected men of the village. He brought up the issue of Elimelech's land. The closer relative first wanted to buy it, but Boaz reminded him that he had to take Ruth as wife if he bought the land, so he changed his mind. Boaz quickly agreed to buy the land and to take Ruth as his wife. The relative gave him a sandal as a sign that he had given Boaz his rights to the land.

Before long, Ruth had a son and Naomi blessed God for his goodness to her. The baby was named Obed, and he was the great-grandfather of King David.

Lesson 16

Cultural Research

An extraordinary story

John grew up in a Christian home in a large town. His father was a business man who was also a deacon in the local Baptist church. Peter, on the other hand, had become a Christian through a group of Christians he had met at university. He had grown up in a polygamous household in a small village. His father and his four wives had all followed African traditional religious practices.

One day, some of Peter's relatives came to visit him at the conference. Unfortunately, Peter had malaria and was in bed with a high fever, so he asked John to entertain his relatives for the evening.

After they had all greeted each other and had heard the news about Peter, John gave them something to drink and eat. After that, he explained he would like to share a Bible story he had prepared at the conference with them. They agreed, although a little unwillingly, and John told them the story of the paralytic and the four friends. When he got to the end, there was a stupefied silence. Finally the senior man of the group spoke, "What an extraordinary story!" John took this as a sign that they liked it very much. He taught them a song he had made based on the story. After that, they left to go home, somewhat to John's relief!

Peter recovered quickly from his fever and the following Saturday was able to go and visit his relatives. When he came back, he was chuckling as he told John that his relatives thought that the four friends in the story had magically removed the pointed roof of a grass hut and flown their friend inside! They concluded that these friends must have had special powers and maybe this was why the paralytic was healed. "You really need to know more about our culture," said Peter. "We are learning a lot about Jewish culture but if we don't know what the ordinary people believe already, then we don't know what they need to know to understand the Bible." "I guess you are right," said John.

GROUP DISCUSSION

1. Why did Peter's relatives misunderstand this Bible story?
2. Why was John unaware of their problem?

What is culture?

To be able to adjust mismatches, translators need to understand the culture of the first and second audiences of Scripture. First, let's agree on what culture is.

In what ways are each of these statements true?

1. Every person is like all other people.
2. Every person is like some other people.
3. Every person is like no other person.

> *Culture is the ideas, beliefs, and practices that are long-lasting and widely shared by a group of people.*

The first statement is about what is true for all people. It does not cause much of a problem in translation. We all share some knowledge about eating, sickness, death, and so forth. The third statement is about individuals. Since the Bible is translated for groups, individual differences are not of particular interest to translators. The second statement is about the cultural level. Cultures guide people to eat, sleep, marry, and bury in certain ways. It is this cultural level that is most interesting to translators, as translations are prepared for people groups that share a culture. Differences between the first and second audiences need to be addressed for successful communication to take place.

These levels are not strictly defined. Information may change levels over time. Some things may start out on the individual level but gradually become widely-shared and long-lasting, at which point they have become cultural.

Within a culture, people share things in an approximate way. There is variation, but things are similar enough to be considered the same thing. Translators should expect to find similar thoughts and actions, not identical ones.

EXERCISE

Think of one thing you share with all people, one thing you share with some people, and one thing that you do not share with anyone.

Who needs to do cultural research?

Sometimes those translating into their own language feel they do not need to research their culture, but their knowledge of their culture may be superficial. They may have grown up in a Christian family separate from their culture, or in an urban area, or away from their cultural homeland. As a result, they may not know their culture well. Even those who grew up in the culture may not know all the parts of the culture and worldview. They may know their culture well, but have never thought about it reflectively, just like people can speak a language fluently without thinking about it. Translation calls for reflecting on the culture and comparing it with the first audience's culture.

GROUP DISCUSSION

What are some beliefs that might block translators from studying their culture?

Discuss answers in the large group, adding any below that have not been mentioned:

1. They may feel the traditional culture is a wasteland that has nothing of value.
2. They may fear that by studying the traditional culture, especially the traditional religion, they may put themselves in danger of spiritual attack.
3. They may fear that studying the traditional religion may be understood as a desire to practice it.
4. They may want to finish their translation quickly and so may not want to take time for cultural research.

To research the audience's culture, translators need to see it as valuable, full of treasures and insights that can help their translations touch their audience deeply. For example, very often people from traditional religions have experienced what it is like to offer a sacrifice, to remove impurity, and so forth. People from Western cultures can only imagine these things.

Ways of researching culture

Use a variety of methods to do cultural research:

- Library or internet research. Use Bible dictionaries and other topically arranged materials to study biblical cultures.
- Observe the culture in daily life, and especially at special events like funerals, sacrifices, and so forth. Discuss what you have observed with people to understand what things mean.
- Interview individuals. Select people who are likely to know a lot about the topic in question. For example, interview a local chief about the traditional political structure, a shaman about healing, and so forth. Know what you want to understand and have some questions in mind, but let the conversation take you where it will.
- Group discussions. Call a group together, give them a question or two on the topic you are interested in, and listen to them interact. Often they will correct and build on each other's comments, challenging and tempering extreme views.
- Study the stories, folk tales, proverbs, songs, and so forth of the culture.

Always take notes of what you learn or observe. You may want to make recordings of some interviews or group discussions so you can listen to them later or even transcribe (parts of) them.

When you have finished researching a topic, write a summary of it. This will serve as a record of your findings that you can refer back to later. Translation consultants may be interested in these reports.

Comparing first and second audiences' cultures

Begin cultural research by studying the culture of the first audience of Scripture. These cultures no longer exist, so we are limited to library research. Although we cannot know everything about them, a lot of information is available. Some of it can be found in the Bible itself, but much of it cannot be found there because the biblical authors assumed their audience already knew it. Even where the New Testament refers to things introduced in the Old Testament, the Jewish culture had changed over time and was quite different in the New Testament period. New Testament readers need to know how the first audience of the New Testament understood the Old Testament passages. Outside of the Bible itself, more information about the cultures in the Bible is available than most of us have time to read, and scholars continue to uncover more all the time.

Understanding the first audience's culture does not mean that it is right or that we should pattern our lives after it. It is not holier than other cultures and it is often challenged in Scripture. The reason we need to understand it is to be able to have a better idea about what came to mind for the first audience as they heard the biblical text.

Once you understand the first audience's culture, you can then research similar areas in your audience's culture. There may be more research published on your culture or on a neighboring culture than you realize, so be sure to check any universities, seminaries, or Bible schools for dissertations or theses that have been done on relevant topics. These often include a lot of very careful research which can save you a lot of time and effort. More and more information is appearing on the internet all the time, so use search programs to see what you can find. Check out any missionary or church archives for relevant research as well.

Usually library research helps, but does not completely answer a translator's questions, and you have to do field research as well: group discussions, interviews, observation, and so forth.

To be sure that the information you are getting is true, try to get information from more than one source. For example, if you read something about biblical cultures in one commentary, see if any other commentary or book says the same thing. If only one author says it, you need to consider carefully whether or not it is true. If several authors say the same thing, it is more likely to be true. In research on your audience, compare what you learn in a group discussion, with what you observe and with what you learn in individual interviews or from other groups. Where you notice contradictions in the information you are receiving, do more research.

In most areas of life, we are encouraged to judge whether things are true or not as we encounter them. When we are trying to understand a culture, we need to do just the opposite. We need to suspend judgment until we think we have understood how the culture functions. Although it can be quite difficult, preaching, teaching, and correcting must be laid aside for a time. If you start correcting people, they will most likely stop telling you what they think.

Jesus provides a model for us when he appeared to the disciples on the road to Emmaus. He listened to them as they walked along until he understood them. Only then did he correct their thoughts (Lu 24).

> ## Research involves suspending judgment until you understand how the culture works.

EXERCISE

Do a role play of someone using good research methods to gather cultural data in an interview and another role play of someone using bad methods.

Identifying topics to study

Studying culture can be a full-time, life-long task, and translators have limited time to give to it. How can you know which topics are most relevant to research?

Passage-level research

As you studied biblical passages using the communication chart in Work Session G, you noted down the context that the text brought to mind for the first audience and the ideas that were communicated. Compare this with your audience. Do you anticipate any contextual mismatches? Test your hunches with your audience to see if they're correct. Read the passage to them and see what they understand and the context that comes to mind for them. You may be surprised. They may know things you did not expect them to know, and things you expected them to know they may not know. Other things may come up you never expected at all. It is not possible to predict how people's minds work with complete certainty.

Theme-based research

As you study passages, certain themes will emerge that frequently lead to contextual mismatches. For example, here are some themes that emerge from John 13:
- ideas about hospitality and greeting guests.

- roles of slaves and teachers.
- ideas about witchcraft and clairvoyance.

Themes may fall into these main areas of culture:

- the economic system
- the life cycle (birth, becoming an adult, marriage, death, and so forth)
- the social system (including family relationships)
- the political system
- the religious system

Research on themes can inform sets of key word choices. For example, work on all of the terms for religious leaders at once in each culture. Once you understand how each culture works, compare them. Each culture is different, and cultural research might uncover more differences than you originally imagined. Translation is about using terms that are only partially similar and then adjusting mismatches. Find the best matches possible for the whole group of terms at the same time, because if you use one word for prophet, you cannot use it for healer.

Since all of culture is interrelated, if you study marriages, you will also learn about family relationships, economics, and political structures. Your understanding of the way the culture functions as a whole will increase. As your knowledge of the cultures grows, your ability to identify and adjust contextual mismatches will grow, too.

When studying your audience's culture, always use local words for key words so that you can be free to understand the concept within the local system. If you refer to it using English words, you will think of the English concept that word is linked to, and this may lead you astray. For example, two Africans were arguing about demons one day when they discovered they were each thinking of very different concepts when using the English word *demons*.

EXERCISE

Identify some themes you might want to research that emerge from Luke 7:36–50. Group these concepts into themes. Do you need to study them more in the biblical culture? In your audience's culture? Both?

Give feedback to the large group.

> Study the first audience's culture.
> Study your audience's culture.
> Compare: same or different?

Summary

Since cultural context plays such an important role in communication, all translators need to understand the cultures of the first and second audiences of Scripture. Of special interest are the differences between these cultures which affect the way people understand Scripture passages. Translators can use a variety of means to study both of these audiences. Based on the study of biblical passages as described in Lesson 14, translators can compare their cultures with the first audience's and identify themes that need more in-depth research. This thematic research will help translators spot contextual mismatches in other passages. After comparing the two cultures, translators are well-placed to adjust the contextual mismatches they have identified so that their audience can understand the biblical author's intended meaning.

So what? Translators need to compare the first and secondary audiences' cultures, and address differences that affect their audience's understanding of Scripture.

Assignment

Read this passage from Genesis 15. Then answer these questions:

1. What would be similar between this culture and yours?
2. What would be different?
3. List some cultural themes to research that emerge from this passage.

[7]Then he said to him, "I am the LORD who brought you from Ur of the Chaldeans, to give you this land to possess." [8]But he said, "O Lord GOD, how am I to know that I shall possess it?" [9]He said to him, "Bring me a heifer three years old, a female goat three years old, a ram three years old, a turtledove, and a young pigeon." [10]He brought him all these and cut them in two, laying each half over against the other; but he did not cut the birds in two. [11]And when birds of prey came down on the carcasses, Abram drove them away. [12]As the sun was going down, a deep sleep fell upon Abram, and a deep and terrifying darkness descended upon him. [13]Then the LORD said to Abram, "Know this for certain, that your offspring shall be aliens in a land that is not theirs, and shall be slaves there, and they shall be oppressed for four hundred years; [14]but I will bring judgment on the nation that they serve, and afterward they shall come out with great possessions. [15]As for yourself, you shall go to your ancestors in peace; you shall be buried in a good old age. [16]And they shall come back here in the fourth generation; for the iniquity of the Amorites is not yet complete."
[17]When the sun had gone down and it was dark, a smoking fire pot and a flaming torch passed between these pieces. [18]On that day the LORD made

a covenant with Abram, saying, "To your descendants I give this land, from the river of Egypt to the great river, the river Euphrates, [19]the land of the Kenites, the Kenizzites, the Kadmonites, [20]the Hittites, the Perizzites, the Rephaim, [21]the Amorites, the Canaanites, the Girgashites, and the Jebusites" (NRSV).

Work Session I: Spirit World Research

Interview someone in the class from another culture using one or two of the sections below. Find out the local term for each spirit being and use that term (not the English term) as you explore the concept.

1. God
   a. Is there a concept of a high God? What word is used to refer to this God?
   b. How do people describe God? Was he perceived to be the creator? Is he moral?
   c. What is his relationship to other spirit beings (divinities, ancestors)?
   d. What is his relationship to people? Does he judge people? Do people ask him for help?
   e. Is this term used for God in Scripture?
2. Spirits, divinities, gods, genies
   a. Are there any beings that are spirits (without physical bodies)? What kinds are there? What word is used to refer to each kind?
   b. How would you describe each kind? Were they thought to be good, bad, or sometimes helpful/ sometimes harmful? Did they punish people for doing wrong?
   c. How do people relate to them? Do they offer sacrifices to them? When? Why? Can they enter into people? How?
   d. How did they relate to God and other spirit beings?
   e. Are any of these terms used in Scripture? For what?
3. Spirits of the ancestors
   a. Do people's spirits continue to be a part of the community after death? Do all people become ancestors?
   b. How would you describe ancestor spirits? Do they punish people for doing wrong? Were they considered to be helpful and good?
   c. How do they relate to people? Are the honored and appreciated or resented? Do people sacrifice to them?
   d. How do ancestors relate to God? To divinities?
   e. Are any of the terms used in Scripture? For what?
4. The invisible parts of people
   a. What are the invisible parts of people? (soul, spirit that animates people while they are alive, and departs at death, and so forth)
   b. How do you refer to each part?
   c. What is the function of each part?
   d. Are any of these terms used in Scripture? For what? What is used for the Spirit of God/Holy Spirit?
5. Spiritual powers
   a. Are there spiritual powers and forces? (They do not have bodies and are not independent beings, witchcraft, manna, magic, psychic powers

that people can use to do good or evil.) What word is used to refer to each kind?

    b.   How do people get these powers?

    c.   Can people use them for good or only evil? Can people protect themselves from these powers?

    d.   Are any of these terms used in Scripture for anything?

Assignment

Write a two-page description of spirit beings in your culture. Give the name for each, a short description, and whether or not it is used in the church. Then indicate the terms used for God, angels, devil, demons, and the Spirit of God/Holy Spirit in your church.

Work Session J: Communicating Luke 7:36–50

Review your notes on Luke 7:36–50. When you feel you understand the passage well, begin working on translating the text for your audience. Translate it in a way that aims at a high degree of meaning resemblance with the original. Explain your strategy for adjusting your audience's context. Prepare any extra-textual helps that may be appropriate.

Follow these steps:
1. Think of an average member of your audience who you hope will use your translation.
2. Review your notes on the passage.
3. Prepare an oral translation of the text.
    - Close all of your books and Bibles, do a verbal sketch of the passage in a few sentences.
    - Have each person in the group tell the whole story in the receptor language in turn while the others listen. Give each other feedback about what you liked about the way they told the story and what you feel could be improved.
    - When you feel you are telling the text well, choose one person to tell it, and make a recording of it. Listen to the recording. If you are not satisfied, try to discover why and then tell the story again.
    - Have each person in the group transcribe this recording. Leave three blank lines betwcen every line of text.
4. Compare your translation with your communication chart of Luke 7:36–50. Will your audience be able to understand the same meaning as the original audience?
    a. Ideas communicated:
        - Has any of the intended meaning gone *missing*?
        - Has any information been *added* that the original text did not communicate?
        - Is any of the information different than the original? If so, how?
    b. Where there are problems, are they due to the way the text has been translated?
    c. Where there are problems, are they due to contextual mismatches? Ask these questions:
        - Is any of the context unrecognized? Are there local terms that could be used? (Box 2)
        - Are they likely to use an unintended context? If so, where do they get off track? How strongly do they hold this information? How can they get back on the right track? (Box 3)
        - Is any of the context unknown? How can they learn this information? (Box 4)

5. Revise your translation to correct any errors you found.
6. Read the text aloud. Is it difficult to read at any point? If so, why? Make any revisions that are needed.

Lesson 17

Expressing Concepts in Another Language

Who was Naomi?

One evening during the seminar, the participants gathered for a Bible study. Since the book of Ruth is very short, everyone agreed to read through the whole book in advance. Samuel was leading the Bible study. There were twenty people at the Bible study, so he first divided them into four small groups and gave them these questions to discuss:

- What happened to Naomi in this story?
- Why do you think these things happened to her?
- What does this teach us about God?

After twenty minutes, Samuel gathered them back together in the large group to discuss their answers. Samuel asked them what had happened to Naomi, and they recounted the events in order. "That's very good," said Samuel. "Now, why do you think these things happened to her?"

Samson was very eager to answer. He said, "These things happened to her because she was a witch. That's very clear. All these bad things happened to her family members but she survived? What do you think? She ate her husband's soul, and then the souls of her two sons. She was no doubt the cause of her daughter-in-laws' sterility, too. And then she left Moab during the harvest! No one would leave a crop standing in the field unless they had big trouble. She had to get out of Moab quickly—that much was clear. Maybe the witches there were stronger than she was, and were going to eat her soul! This teaches me that witchcraft is a gift of God. It can protect you even when everyone else suffers."

Samuel took a deep breath and said a prayer. He realized it would be a long night.

GROUP DISCUSSION

1. Do you agree with the way Samson understood what happened to Naomi?
2. Discuss why Samson misunderstood what happened to Naomi. Notice that 'witch' was never mentioned in the text.

Conceptual adjustment is possible

Translation is not a matter of substituting words in the receptor language for words in the original language. Each culture and language divides information into concepts differently. Even though translators may not be able to find concepts in the receptor language that provide all of the information that was linked to concepts for the first audience, they need not despair. Our minds are designed to learn new things. They can set up a "file" for a new concept even if they do not have much information linked to it initially. This serves as a place where information about the concept can be collected over time and gradually the concept can be built up.

Our minds can also learn new things by modifying the information linked to concepts we already know. We can eliminate, strengthen, or add to the information linked to a concept. Modifying an existing concept takes less time than introducing a new one, as the concept is already established in the network, and it brings some context to the hearer's mind. Setting up totally new concepts is like building a new house. Modifying the information linked an existing concept is like knocking out a wall.

After identifying contextual mismatches, communicators need to move their audience from Box 2, 3, or 4 to Box 1. Each box calls for a different solution. All of them require linking the new information to what the audience already knows so that they have some context to process the new information.

Table 2. Adjusting conceptual mismatches

	Hearers Think Concept Is Shared	**Hearers Do Not Think Concept Is Shared**
Concept Is Actually Shared	1. Intended Concept	2. Unrecognized Concept
Concept Is Not Actually Shared	3. Unintended Concept	4. Unknown Concept

Some concepts that occur frequently in Scripture are very important for the message of the gospel, for example, God, SIN, LOVE, KINGDOM OF GOD, MESSIAH, and so forth. These are sometimes referred to as *key biblical concepts*. Translators need to give extra attention to these concepts and help their audiences understand them correctly.

Key biblical concepts are concepts that occur frequently in Scripture and are very important for the message of the Gospel.

Box 2: Helping audiences *recognize* concepts they already know

When audiences share a concept with the biblical author but do not recognize that they do, the solution is quite simple. Translators can simply use the local word for the concept in the translation. When the audience hears the term, the information linked to that concept will come to their audience's mind and give them a starting point for processing the text. For example, the Adioukrou word for the spirit beings they interact with is *elmis*. If it had been used for *angels* in the Adioukrou translation, the audience would recognize that, in fact, they already know much of what an angel is. Hearing *elmis* used in Scripture would then modify the information they link to the concept and over time, their concept ELMIS would resemble the biblical concept of angels more and more.

Even if the first and second audience's concepts are somewhat different, using the local word is often more successful because initially, it relates to what they already know and so is more relevant. In the long term, it leads to a more accurate understanding of the biblical text because it exerts an influence over their existing knowledge. If the local word *elmis* is not used, the audience will understand that whatever angels are, they are not *elmis*. If they were, their word *elmis* would have been used.

Although the solution is simple, there are some challenges:
- Without an understanding of the first audience's context, similarities that exist may not be recognized.
- When audiences already have a term they've been using, they may resist changing it, especially if they are not convinced their local term is similar to the biblical one.

When other terms have been used for biblical concepts, using local terms may seem scandalous at first.

GROUP DISCUSSION

Think again of the concept you identified in Lesson 15 that your audience shares with the biblical author but do not recognize that they do.
1. Discuss what your audience would *understand* if the local word was used for this concept.
2. Discuss how you think people would *react* to using this local term.

Box 3: Helping audiences avoid unintended concepts

If terms used in Scripture lead audiences to think they share a concept with the first audience when they actually do not, translators need to determine where the problem lies. If the word used in Scripture brings a completely different concept to mind for the audience, a new word or expression may be needed.

If the concept that is brought to mind is somewhat similar, it can be corrected over time in a variety of ways: in notes accompanying the translation, in teaching, and so forth.

Jesus spent a lot of time correcting concepts people had. For example, many Jews knew the concept KINGDOM OF GOD but associated all sorts of ideas with it that were not what God intended. Many thought it was the time that God would rule as king and liberate the Jewish nation from Roman rule. Many thought that those who were important in the KINGDOM OF GOD would have positions with lots of power. Jesus told many parables during the three years of his ministry to correct these wrong ideas.

Even if a word leads to misunderstanding initially, it may still be the best option. If it occurs frequently in Scripture and people hear or read Scripture often, over time Scripture will contradict and eliminate the unintended information associated with the word and add intended information to it. Gradually the meaning of the word will be corrected. For example, the Ngbaka church leaders discussed the word to use in their Scripture for ALTAR. Several pastors did not want to use the local word because of its strong association with the traditional religion. Another example is the word used for GOD among the Adioukrou. The information linked to the local concept of GOD was quite different from the concept of GOD of the Bible: he was distant, unconcerned with people, and not always just. In both of these examples, local words were used in Scripture. Each time the word occurred, Scripture contradicted the unintended information associated with it until eventually it was eliminated and replaced by the intended biblical information. In fact, the English word for God was originally a word used to refer to a local German divinity. Now it is widely accepted as the word for the Supreme, Creator God.

A benefit of using local words in translation is that as the concepts are shaped by Scripture, the audience's worldview and culture are changed. This process happened in the early church when some Jews presented Jesus as "Lord" to Greek people rather than presenting him as Messiah (Acts 10:36). Most Greeks had no concept of Messiah. They used the concept LORD for the many gods and divinities they worshipped. When the disciples used this word to refer to Jesus, they ran the risk that the Greeks might think he was just another god among others. In fact, it connected the Gospel with their culture and eventually their culture was transformed. They came to understand Jesus was Lord of Lords.

GROUP DISCUSSION

Think of a word or practice from your traditional culture that has changed its meaning over time as it is been used in the church or Scripture. For example, child dedications, harvest festivals, names for God, and so forth. Discuss what it meant in the past and what it means now.

Translation is risky business.

Box 4: Finding ways to express new concepts

When concepts are unknown, translators have to find creative solutions to express them in the language. Compare local concepts that are similar to the biblical concept and find the local concept that is the most similar.

If the new concept can be linked to a similar concept the audience already knows, some of the information linked to that concept can be associated with the new concept right away. For example, people may not have a concept CAMEL, but if they are told that it is an animal, their concept ANIMAL will be linked to quite a bit of correct information: a living creature that is born, grows, eats, drinks, reproduces, dies, and so forth. Animals are also related to other concepts the same way that camels are. New concepts always differ in some ways from the known ones, so the audience will need to learn the differences as well as the similarities.

1. Use a more general word or expression

Using a more general concept, such as *animal* for *camel*, is often the best choice even if there is not overlap in the information linked to it. For example, if a language does not have the concept SPARROW, translators have to find a way to express *sparrow* when translating "you are worth more than many sparrows" (Mt 10:31b NIV). Since SPARROW is a kind of BIRD, if the receptor language has the concept BIRD, then this can be a good starting point for finding an appropriate receptor expression because whatever is true of birds will also be true of sparrows. In this case, using the more general expression *bird* to translate *sparrow* would be acceptable, even though it does not specify the kind of bird.

2. Modify an existing word or expression

In other cases, translators may need to add information to an expression to get more of the original meaning across. This can be done in the text itself or in a footnote, depending on the kind of Scripture product being prepared. The additional information should help the audience to understand the implications of the passage. For example, when translating "ship" in Acts 21 for people who only know canoes, modifying their word for *canoe* with *big* might help them understand how so many people could travel in one canoe.

Modifications like these may not always be relevant, however. For example in Matthew 10:31b, translating *sparrow* as *small bird* might lead to the added implication that God even cares about small birds. In this passage, however, the fact that sparrows are small birds does not seem to be as important as the fact that they were of little value, and that information is already expressed in the passage which says they were sold very cheaply (10:29). Adding the modifier *small* would increase the accuracy of what was said a little, but not enough to offset the increased effort it takes to process it.

Translators may make up new expressions using words in the local language, but these expressions may not represent local concepts. For example, in the Adioukrou translation, the expression *abŋ eŋuŋ* (spirits-evil) has been used for evil spirits. This is a word-for-word translation of one of the Greek expressions for evil spirits (*pneuma kakos*). While this seems like a good solution, there are significant differences between Greek and Adioukrou. The Greek word *pneuma* can refer to the spirit of a person or to independent spirit beings. Adioukrou uses two words for these concepts: the word *abŋ* (spirit) refers to the spirit of a person that leaves at death, and the word *elmis* refers to independent spirit beings.

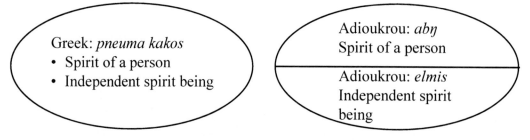

Figure 24. 'Spirit' in Greek and Adioukrou

To add *eŋuŋ* (bad) to *abŋ* (spirit of a person) brings no context to mind that makes sense for the Adioukrou. Even to describe a person with a bad character, they would not use this expression. Nor would they use *abŋ* to describe the kind of independent spirit referred to in the Gospels. They are not able to connect this concept to their world. While it is wonderful to know that Jesus had power over the *abŋ eŋuŋ*, they do not seem to present in the Adioukrou experience. Meanwhile, they face the *elmis* (independent spirit beings) daily. If people are not able to make sense of a modified expression, they will not be able to process it.

3. Use a more specific word or expression

In other cases, translators may have to use more specific expressions to indicate the meaning of an original concept. For example, the Silt'e language of Ethiopia has the word *waaj* for the concept OLDER BROTHER and *maat'a* for YOUNGER BROTHER, but no general word for BROTHER. This can be a problem in translation. For example, Matthew 1:2 talks about "Judah and his brothers." Judah was the fourth son of Jacob by Leah, so he had both older and younger brothers. Translators have to use both of these more specific expressions together to communicate the meaning of the original concept.

4. Use a word from another language

Another solution for translating unknown concepts is to use a word from another language. For example, in some languages a word like *bapitisimo* has been used for BAPTISM. Languages take in new words from other languages all the time, especially for things like radio, video, computer, and so forth. People can certainly learn new concepts. For some hotly debated terms, a borrowed word may be a good solution because it is neutral. Without any further information, however, such words actually have no meaning for the receptors because no information is linked to them. For these expressions to have any meaning, this content must be provided.

Sometimes a borrowed word may only be known by some of the receptors, for example, by those living in towns or speaking another language. In that case, translators have to find out how widely the word is known among the receptor group to judge if it is suitable for use in the translation.

EXERCISES

1. Look up these passages. How would you express the concepts expressed by the terms in italics in these verses in your language? How could you help your audience understand the intended meaning?
   a. Acts 16:24 [the jailer] fastened their feet in the *stocks* (RSV).
   b. Acts 19:29 …they rushed together into the *theatre, …* (RSV).
   c. Acts 27:5 …when we had *sailed* across the *sea…* (RSV).
   d. Acts 27:28 So they *sounded* and found twenty *fathoms;* … (RSV).

2. Look up the following verses and read them in context. Imagine you are translating into a language which has no word for the concepts in italics. Think of a way to express each of the italicized words. Then identify any information your audience will need to understand the passage.
   a. Luke 1:63 And [Zechariah] asked for a *writing tablet, …* (RSV).
   b. Luke 7:2 a *centurion* had a slave who was dear to him (RSV).
   c. John 15:1 My father is the *vinedresser* (RSV).
   d. Acts 8:27 *queen* of the Ethiopians (RSV).
   e. Acts 21:34 He ordered him to be brought into the *barracks* (RSV).

3. What would be a more general word for the following?
   a. bishop
   b. magistrate
   c. car
   d. gun
   e. to devour
   f. to slice

4. Look up the following passages. Imagine you are translating into a language which has no word for the concepts in italics. Re-express each one using a more specific word or words.
   a. Acts 10:12 In it were all kinds of animals and *reptiles…* (RSV).

   b. Luke 10:34 ...he set him on his own *beast*... (RSV).

   c. Matthew 5:29 ...it is better that you lose one of *your members* than that your whole body be thrown into hell (RSV).

   d. Luke 2:41 Now his *parents* went to Jerusalem every year at the feast of the Passover (RSV).

Church involvement

Decisions about important terms need to be made with church leaders. Translators can bring them together to discuss these things and help them understand the issues and options. In the end, however, the decisions belong to them. They may want to use terms similar to those used in a Bible they are familiar with, and this might not be the translator's first choice. After adequate discussion of the advantages and disadvantages of the term, if they still want to use it, their preference rules.

Decisions about certain terms may take years. Church leaders may agree on certain terms, but problems may emerge later with wider use and the decision may need to be reviewed and another word selected.

The choice of some terms is difficult from another perspective. Church traditions often have different words for terms like baptize, Holy Spirit, and so forth. Since most minority languages will only receive one translation, it is extremely important that everyone agree on the terms used in the translation. This can take years, but if agreement is not reached, some of the churches may not use the mother-tongue Scriptures. With patience, prayer, and faith, little by little and with much discussion, solutions can often be found that are acceptable to all. An extra benefit of the translation process is that it can bring churches together in unity.

Language Group Discussion

1. Do you have important terms you need in your translation that have not been decided on yet? Make a list.
2. Discuss how the leaders from all the churches in your area could get together to discuss these terms. Who? Where? When?

Summary

Translators can use different strategies to adjust the different types of conceptual mismatches they may encounter between the first audience of Scripture and their audience. If audiences do not recognize that they share certain concepts with the first audience, translators can help them recognize this by using the local word for the concept. If audiences use unintended concepts to understand a passage, translators need to determine which part of the concept is leading the audience astray and correct that. This may mean using a different word altogether or it may mean modifying the information associated with it. This can be done through notes or teaching, or Scripture itself can modify and correct concepts. Decisions about important terms used in Scripture need to be made with church leaders. This process may take time but is necessary for the translation to be accepted and may lead to more unity among the churches.

So what?

Translators need to find the best way to express concepts in Scripture in the receptor language.

Assignment

1. List five words that have come into your language from another and are now widely shared. For example, they would be known by a middle-aged, uneducated woman who has not traveled much out of her village or town.
2. Think of a word used in sermons in your churches that people do not understand. Suggest two ways to correct this.

Lesson 18

Adjusting Contextual Mismatches

Is Christmas in the Bible?

One day, John and Peter were sitting around with some friends discussing the coming Christmas holidays. One of the group, Gideon, said, "In my church we are told it is wrong to celebrate Christmas." "What!" said the others, "Why wouldn't a Christian want to celebrate the birth of Christ?" "Well," said Gideon, "where in the Bible does it talk about Christmas?" After a lot of discussion, everyone agreed that nowhere in the Bible did it talk about Christmas. "I wonder why we celebrate Christmas on December 25th?" asked Peter. "There is certainly no date given in the Bible." No one really knew the answer and the discussion moved on to other things.

Peter was not satisfied, and the next day he went to the library to find out about the origins of Christmas. He was amazed and shocked when he found out that originally it was a pagan festival. He found out that in the northern countries of the world, people could not farm during the cold period from November to February, and so it was the time for wild festivals with lots of drinking and immoral behavior. He also found out that some traditional gods including Mithras had their festival on December 25th. The sun god was also worshipped at these festivals. When Christianity came to Rome and spread throughout the Roman empire to these northern countries, the early Christians decided to make these festivals Christian. In this way, people could still have festivals and fun together in the winter without the negative effects of drunkenness and immorality.

The next day Peter shared what he had found with his friends. John said, "Wow! I wonder how long it took for people to stop thinking about the pagan gods, and only connect Christmas with Christ." "I should think it took years and years," said Peter.

GROUP DISCUSSION

Discuss the dangers and benefits of transforming a pagan festival into a Christian one.

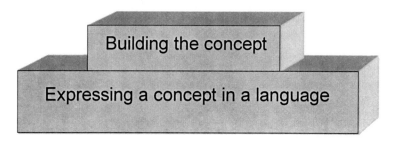

Figure 25: Two steps in communicating concepts cross-culturally

Building concepts

After finding ways to express new concepts in a language, translators need to help build the concepts. For example, when translating *Son of David*, translators need to find a way to express that Jesus was a descendent of David, not his direct son. Should they use the word for son or the word for descendent? The choice may be difficult because there may be several terms to choose from, but this decision is only the first step in communicating the concept. It is like opening a file which then needs information to be added.

GROUP DISCUSSION

Read this text aloud:

> [35] As Jesus approached Jericho, a blind man was sitting by the roadside begging. [36] When he heard the crowd going by, he asked what was happening. [37] They told him, "Jesus of Nazareth is passing by." [38] He called out, "Jesus, Son of David, have mercy on me!" [39] Those who led the way rebuked him and told him to be quiet, but he shouted all the more, "Son of David, have mercy on me!" (Lk 18:35–39 NIV).

What did the blind man mean when he called Jesus "the Son of David?"

Report back to the large group. Add any of the information below that is not already mentioned.

- David was the most honored king in the history of Israel.
- The Son of David was a remote descendant of David. David had lived about 1000 years before Christ.
- King David had received a special promise that his family would continue to rule Israel for all times.
- The Son of David would put all things right.
- In Jesus' day, the Jews were ruled by a foreign nation, the Romans, and they were waiting and praying that this special descendant of David would come and liberate them and end their suffering.

- David's son Solomon was known as a very powerful healer and exorcist.
- The Son of David would heal people from their sickness and ailments.
- Most of the Jewish religious leaders did not recognize Jesus to be the Son of David.
- It is similar to the concept of the Messiah in Hebrew or Christ in Greek.

Lots of information came to mind for the first audience when they heard the expression, "Son of David." If audiences do not know this information, this is a contextual mismatch. Without the intended context, they will not understand much of the intended meaning of this passage even if the words are expressed in their language.

Building contexts

Translators need to find terms that provide the best signposts and the build the concepts so they resemble the concepts of the first audience. No matter how many contextual mismatches exist between the first and the secondary audience of Scripture, they can be adjusted in time if people are motivated to learn and the new information is available to them. Our brains can only absorb a certain amount of new information at a time, so this is a process that takes time, and one that benefits from repeated input from numerous sources. Translators help can supply some of it with their Scripture products. They can also help communities network with organizations that provide these materials.

New information must be bridged to what people already know or they will not be able to absorb it. The bridge between the known and the new has to be complete for people to be able to use it, just like a car cannot cross over a river on a bridge that only goes half way.

Contextual bridges need to be tested to be sure they actually connect the new context to the audience's known world. If audiences cannot explain how the new context relates to their world, the bridge is not yet complete. For example, what would an audience need to already know to understand a note like this, linked to the last supper Jesus had with his disciples in John 13:1:

> During the feast of Passover, the Jews anticipated that God would send a Messiah to deliver them from the suffering that the Romans were inflicting on them.

They would have to know the concepts of Passover, Messiah, and the Roman rule. If they did not, this note would actually have a negative effect. It would increase their processing effort without leading to increased cognitive benefits.

If an audience lacks information associated with a concept that only occurs a few times in Scripture, translators can provide that information in appropriate ways where the concept occurs rather than spending time building up the concepts more fully. For example, the concept ALABASTER JAR only occurs four times in the New Testament, so information about it can be provided each time it occurs. If an audience lacks information associated with a concept that occurs frequently, they need to learn it. For example, the concepts VINE and VINEYARD occur quite frequently throughout the Old and New Testament, and audiences need to know about these.

EXERCISES

1. What would audiences already have to know for these notes to be relevant to them?
    a. *A note linked to Matthew 4:1* Jews of Jesus' day thought that the desert was the place where evil spirits lived. Often, God had his servants go there to be tested, so that he could know the thoughts of their hearts, and see if they would obey his commandments or not (Deut 8:2). Here is something to remember: the Israelites, Moses, and Elijah all passed through this kind of testing in the desert. If God's prophets passed through this testing in the desert, then it was not surprising that the Spirit led Jesus into the desert to have a similar kind of testing before he began his ministry.
    b. *A note linked to Luke 11:15* The people who criticized Jesus are the Pharisees (Mt 12:24). They came to Jesus to find something that they could accuse him of and arrest him.
2. Find the context necessary to answer the questions below, using Bible helps. Then explain this context to your audience in a way that bridges to what they already know. Do not worry about how you will deliver this information to your audience yet.
    a. In Luke 19:7, when Jesus went to eat with Zaccheus, why were the people scandalized?
    b. In Acts 22:21, the Jews listened quietly to Paul's speech until he said, "The Lord said to me, 'Go! I will send you far away to the Gentiles'." Then they wanted to kill him. Why?

Criteria for contextual adjustment information

When we prepare information that adjusts contextual mismatches, the materials need to be relevant, true, and accepted by the churches. These criteria are different than those we observe when translating where the primary concern is faithfulness to the meaning communicated by the original.

Contextual adjustment information must be relevant

Like all communication, contextual adjustment information that is supplied to an audience needs to be relevant. If it increases processing costs without increasing their understanding of the text, it will work against relevance. To be relevant:
*   It needs to be bridged to what the audience already knows.
*   It needs to help the audience understand the author's meaning better. It is not intended to lead to cognitive benefits on its own.

- It needs to be information the audience does not already know or could not already infer from the text. Reminding audiences of things they already know would be relevant if it takes them less effort to process the information than to recall it from memory.
- It may provide information the text is eliminating or strengthening. For example, when Paul writes a letter from prison to the Philippians to encourage them to rejoice in the Lord, he is contradicting the norm. Usually, prisoners were depressed or even suicidal, and friends wrote letters to encourage them.
- It needs to correspond to the level of understanding the audience expects. If the information requires more energy to process than the audience is willing to exert, it is not relevant to them at that time, even if it has the potential of leading to more benefits.

EXERCISES

1. In Exodus 23:19, when God was giving laws about worship to the Israelites, he said, "You shall not boil a kid in its mother's milk" (NAB).
    a. Read the passage where this verse occurs and explain the cognitive benefits you experience.
    b. One interpretation is found in the Catholic Study Bible:
        Boil a kid in its mother's milk: this was part of a Canaanite ritual; hence it is forbidden here as a pagan ceremony.
    Describe how this information affects the cognitive benefits you experience from this passage.
2. Read Acts 27:9–12:
    When considerable time had passed and the voyage was now dangerous, since even the fast was already over, Paul began to admonish them, [10] and said to them, "Men, I perceive that the voyage will certainly be with damage and great loss, not only of the cargo and the ship, but also of our lives." [11] But the centurion was more persuaded by the pilot and the captain of the ship than by what was being said by Paul. [12] Because the harbor was not suitable for wintering, the majority reached a decision to put out to sea from there, if somehow they could reach Phoenix, a harbor of Crete, facing southwest and northwest, and spend the winter there (NASB).

Look at the following information and decide how relevant each note would be for your audience: very relevant, somewhat relevant, not relevant. Explain your views.
- Verse 9: "The fast" refers to the Day of Atonement, when all Jews fasted. It happened in September or October, and the weather at this time of year made sailing very dangerous.
- Verse 12: Southwest is between the compass points of South and West. Northwest is between the compass points of North and West.

- Verse 12: Phoenix is the name of a magical bird that comes back to life from death.
- Verse 12: The voyage altogether would have been about 40 kilometers.

Contextual adjustment information must be true
- It needs to represent the best biblical scholarship available.
- It needs to be widely accepted, not an extreme view held by only one or two scholars.
- It needs to give the intended context, not the intended interpretation, exhortations, or applications. These kinds of helps may be appropriate for other goals, but not for contextual adjustment.

Contextual adjustment information must be acceptable to all of the churches
Contextual adjustment materials need to be acceptable to all the churches that are served by the Scripture product. This may require omitting things translators think are very important but are not held by all the churches. To be sure the information is acceptable to all the churches, a respected leader from each of the major churches in the area should approve all contextual adjustment material.

> ## Contextual adjustment information must be relevant, true, and acceptable to all the churches.

Supplying contextual adjustment materials

Contextual information can be supplied in a variety of ways: in the text itself, outside the text, or through teaching. The choice depends on the kind of Scripture product being prepared.

1. In-text solution: In Approach #1 (easy to understand right away), the needed contextual adjustment material can be provided in the text, even if it is quite lengthy.

2. Out-of-text solution: In Approach #2 (high meaning resemblance), translators can provide at least some of the needed contextual adjustment material outside the text in extra-textual helps. By separating the contextual adjustment material from the text, audiences are able to tell what the original author wrote and what has been supplied for their benefit. This results in a higher degree of meaning resemblance to the original. Once the audience learns the information, they can ignore it on subsequent readings.

   In Approach #3, communicators can provide some contextual adjustment within the text, but most of it will be provided out of the text. For any adjustment they make in the text, they need to weigh the increase in ease of communication against the decrease in meaning resemblance this change will make.

Some translators indicate added contextual information with italics or brackets. For example, the *despised* Samaritan or the ⌊despised⌋ Samaritan. If a lot of information is provided in this way, it can make reading the text more difficult.

3. Through church teaching: Where there are active churches, much of the contextual adjustment can be taught through Bible studies, sermons, and so forth. In fact, often it is the church leaders who use the extra-textual helps as they prepare to teach and preach.

> ## Contextual adjustment information can be supplied in-text or out-of-text, depending on the kind of Scripture product.

Preparing extra-textual helps

If contextual adjustment information is delivered by means of extra-textual helps, they are best developed as the text is translated, as the one affects the other. Each kind of help can communicate the information for which it is best suited, with all the parts working together to make a highly relevant product.

The media in which the Scripture will be delivered affects the kinds of helps that are prepared. To make helps prepared for oral or aural products separate from the text, record them in a different voice, beginning with something like, "Excuse me, there's something you need to know," or, "You may be wondering who Pharisees are." You cannot interrupt the text too often, so contextual adjustment material for oral products need to be grouped together into larger chunks than in printed Scriptures.

In addition to the content of the helps, translators need to work out ways to express titles and instructions used in helps, such as "see another reference," "introduction," or "glossary."

GROUP DISCUSSION

What kinds of helps can be included as part of a printed Bible? What is the function of each kind? List these on the board.

When all the suggestions are recorded, add any comments listed below that are not already mentioned.

Introductions

Introductions give readers to the sociocultural or historical situation of the first audience, as well as key concepts and themes. They tell who is writing to whom for what purpose, if known. They can be prepared for the Bible, for each testament, for groups of books (for example, the Gospels), for books, for parts of books, or for sections. Examples of introductions are available in Study Bibles.

Section Headings

Section headings give the main point or theme of the section. This increases comprehension significantly as audiences are alerted to the way the passage achieves relevance.

Notes (footnotes or side-notes)

Notes can be used to explain the dynamics particular to a passage. They may include:

- contextual information.
- cross references that supply further information on the passage.
- textual information, such as exegetical and manuscript issues.
- information for applying scripture to life. This is best developed by pastors.
- where the text is adapted to the receptor's context, the original text can be provided in notes.

Illustrations

Illustrations can communicate some things better than hundreds of words. They need to be tested to be sure they are understood. Some audiences may consider illustrations offensive or sacrilegious.

Glossaries

A glossary usually provides explanations of concepts. Terms can be marked in the text by an asterisk the first time they occur in a section. Glossary entries are usually listed in alphabetical order, but they can be grouped into themes as in the CEV Learning Bible:

1. A Few Basics
2. Scriptures, Manuscripts
3. Languages
4. People
5. Prophets
6. Twelve Tribes of Israel
7. Christ's Twelve Apostles
8. Groups of People, Cities, Nations
9. Places
10. Objects
11. Festivals and Holy Days
12. Sacrifice, Temple, Worship
13. Customs
14. God, Jesus, Angels
15. Foreign Gods, Fortunetellers, Evil Spirits
16. Plants, Animals, and Farming
17. Society and Its Leaders
18. Families, Relatives
19. Events
20. Dates
21. The Hebrew Calendar

Maps

Maps can be provided at the back of a book or next to relevant passages. For them to be relevant, audiences need to experience cognitive benefits from them, and they need to be able to relate places on the map to their known world.

Topical Index

A topical index gives references arranged by topic listed in alphabetic order. Here are two examples (see Appendix 4 for more):

Baptism
> Matthew 28:18–20; John 3:22; 4:1–2; Acts 2:37–42; 8:12; 8:36–38; 10:44–48; 16:14–15; 16:31–33; 19:1–7; 22:12–16; Romans 6:1–4; Galatians 3:26–27; Colossians 2:12; 1 Peter 3:20–22.

Where to find help when you are
> Afraid: Psalm 34:4, Matthew 10:28, 2 Timothy 1:7, Hebrews 13:5, 6;
> Anxious: Psalm 46, Matthew 6:19–34, Philippians 4:6, 1 Peter 5:6, 7.

EXERCISES

1. Write two notes for Luke 7:36–47 that will help your audience understand the passage better.
2. Write one glossary item for a word in this passage that occurs in other passages and needs explanation.
3. Write a section heading for the passage.
4. Propose an illustration that would be useful for this story.

Testing materials with target audiences

Translators can anticipate where contextual mismatches are likely to occur and how they can be adjusted for their audience, but they need to check out their hunches. There are always surprises! You may discover additional contextual mismatches that need to be adjusted.

Once prepared, extra-textual helps need to be tested along with the translation. Two questions are key:
> 1) What do you understand from the material?
> 2) How does this affect the way you understand the meaning of the passage?

If people cannot understand the helps, or if they cannot see the relationship between them and the text, revise until they can.

Write three questions you could ask to find out if the helps you wrote for Luke 7:36–45 help your audience understand the passage better.

Teaching people how to use helps

Extra-textual helps are not difficult to use, but people need to be taught how to use them. If church leaders learn how to use the helps, they can teach their congregations. Anyone who has learned to read can learn to use helps.

For each help listed on the board, discuss how people can be taught to use them. Add anything from the list below that has not been mentioned.

- Introductions: Prepare two or three questions and ask people to find the answers in the introduction. The questions should ask about information that is relevant, that is, information that would help them understand passages in that book better.
  Show them that there are introductions to each book.
- Section titles: Print out a section of Scripture without the section heading. Ask people to read it and tell you what they understand. Then give them the section heading and ask them how this affects their understanding. Then point out other headings in your Bible.
- Notes: Tell them that when they see the symbol for a footnote, to go to the bottom or side of the page and read the information there. It will help them understand the passage better. Then they can return to the text and keep reading it. Give three references that have footnotes in your Bible. The first to find the footnote should stand and read it out loud. Then they can say how it helps them understand the passage better.
- Illustrations: Discuss what people notice in various illustrations in the Bible, and how this helps them understand Bible passages better.
- Glossaries: Give two or three references that have words listed in the glossary. Have people look up these words. The first to find them should stand and read the information out loud. Then they can say how it helps them understand the passage better.
- Maps: As a group, make a map of your location, indicating cities, rivers, national boundaries, and so forth. If possible, have a map of the world and show where Israel is compared with your location. Then look at the maps in your Bible and have people find cities, rivers, countries, and so forth.
- Topical index: Have people find references in the topical index and read them aloud.

Summary

Audiences may know the concepts in Scripture, but lack the specific context associated with those concepts that is needed to understand a passage. They can learn this information if it is presented in a way that is bridged to what they already know. Any information provided needs to be relevant, true, and acceptable to all of the churches represented in the intended audience. At least some of this information can be supplied in-text or out-of-text, depending on the kind of Scripture product being prepared. When information is supplied in extra-textual helps, the materials need to be tested for relevance and approved by the leaders of the churches in the target audience. Audiences need to be taught how to use them.

So what? | Translators need to develop, test, and check extra-textual helps. Then audiences need to be taught how to use them.

Assignment

Choose any three of the Study Bibles below. Use the criteria listed above to say how relevant the information provided on Luke 10:13–14 would be for your audience.

CEV Learning Bible

TEXT: [13] You people of Chorazin are in for trouble! You people of Bethsaida are also in for trouble! If the miracles that took place in your towns had happened in Tyre and Sidon, the people there would have turned to God long ago. They would have dressed in sackcloth and put ashes on their heads. [14] On the day of judgment the people of Tyre and Sidon will get off easier than you will.

> Note #1 on v. 13 Chorazin…Bethsaida…Tyre and Sidon: Chorazin, Bethsaida, and Capernaum were Jewish towns on the northern end of Lake Galilee. Tyre and Sidon were important non-Jewish port cities on the Mediterranean Sea Coast. See the map on p. 2375. While the people in these Jewish towns did not respond to Jesus' message and miracles, Jesus says that the people in cities like Tyre and Sidon would be more willing to turn to God.
>
> Note #2 on v. 13 Sackcloth and… ashes: Sackcloth is dark cloth (see Rev 6:12) made of camel's hair or goat's hair. The Greek word for 'ashes' in this verse refers to a kind of smoky soot. People wore sackcloth or put ashes on their head in times of deep sadness or when they wanted to show that they were sorry for their sins (see Esther 4:1; Job 2:8).
>
> Note #3 on v. 14 day of judgment: This day was expected to be a time when God would judge the people of the world. Those who put their trust in Christ will be saved, but those who did not will experience God's anger and punishment (see Matt 13:47–50; 25:31–46; John 12:44–50). See also the mini-article called "day of the Lord," p. 1622.

African Study Bible

TEXT: [13] "Woe to you, Chorazin! Woe to you, Bethsaida! For if the miracles had been performed in Tyre and Sidon which occurred in you, they would have repented long ago, sitting in sackcloth and ashes. [14] But it will be more tolerable for Tyre and Sidon in the judgment than for you (New American Bible).

> NOTE: The principle applies: to whom much is given , of them much is expected.

The Holy Gospel

TEXT: [13] "How terrible it will be for you, Chorazin! How terrible for you too, Bethsaida! If the miracles which were performed in you had been performed in Tyre and Sidon, the people there would have long ago sat down, put on sackcloth, and sprinkled ashes on themselves, to show that they had turned from their sins! [14] God will show more mercy on the Judgment Day to Tyre and Sidon than to you (TEV).

> Note #1: To reject the good news proclaimed by Jesus is to bring judgment on oneself.
> Note #2: *Miracles* – Literally, powerful acts (Greek *dunameis*), referring to the acts of healing, raising the dead, casting out evil spirits, etc. done by Jesus as signs of God's power.
> Note #3: *Put on sackcloth and sprinkled ashes* – a custom showing sorrow and repentance.

Catholic Study Bible

TEXT: [13] Woe to you, Chorazin! Woe to you, Bethsaida! For if the mighty deeds done in your midst had been done in Tyre and Sidon, they would long ago have repented, sitting in sackcloth and ashes. [14] But it will be more tolerable for Tyre and Sidon at the judgment than for you (New American Bible).

> NOTE: The call to repentance that is a part of the proclamation of the kingdom brings with it a severe judgment for those who hear it and reject it.

HarperCollins Study Bible

TEXT: [13] "Woe to you, Chorazin! Woe to you, Bethsaida! For if the deeds of power done in you had been done in Tyre and Sidon, they would have repented long ago, sitting in sackcloth and ashes. [14] But at the judgment it will be more tolerable for Tyre and Sidon than for you" (NRSV).

> Note #1 on v. 13 The exact location of Chorazin is unknown. *Bethsaida.* See note on 9:10. *Tyre and Sidon,* Phoenician (gentile) seacoast towns which Jesus did not visit. On the need to repent see 3:3, 8; 11:32; 13:3, 5; 15:7, 10; 16:30.

Cross-referenced note on 9:10. Bethsaida had been recently built by Herod Philip on the Sea of Galilee.

NIV Study Bible

TEXT: [13] "Woe to you, Korazin! Woe to you, Bethsaida! For if the miracles that were performed in you had been performed in Tyre and Sidon, they would have repented long ago, sitting in sackcloth and ashes. [14] But it will be more bearable for Tyre and Sidon at the judgment than for you

Note #1 on v 13: *Korazin...Bethsaida*. See note on Mt 11:21. *Sackcloth and ashes*. See Mt 11:21; Rev 11:3 and notes.

Cross-referenced note on Mt 11:21: *Korazin*. Mentioned in the Bible only twice (here and in Luke 10:13), it was near the Sea of Galilee, probably about two miles north of Capernaum. *Bethsaida*. On the northeast shore of the Sea of Galilee. Philip the tetrarch rebuilt Bethsaida and named it 'Julias," after Julia, daughter of Caesar Augustus. *Tyre and Sidon*. Cities on the Phoenician coast north of the Holy Land (see note on Mk 7:31). *Sackcloth*. Here a sign of repentance (see note on Ge 37:34). Cf Rev 6:12. *Ashes*. Also a sign of repentance.

Cross-referenced note on Ge 37:34: *tore his clothes, put on sackcloth*. Tearing one's clothes (see v 29) and wearing coarse and uncomfortable sackcloth instead of ordinary clothes were both signs of mourning (see note on Rev 11:3).

Cross-referenced note on Rev 11:3 *two witnesses*: Modeled after Moses and Elijah (see notes on vv. 5–6). They may symbolize testifying believers in the final period before Christ returns. Or they may be two actual individuals who will be martyred for the proclamation of the truth. 1,260 days. See note on v. 2. These are months of 30 days (42 months x 30 days = 1,260 days). *sackcloth*: A coarse, dark cloth woven from the hair of goats or camels. It was worn as a sign of mourning and penitence (Joel 1:13; Jnh 3:5–6; Mt 11:21).

Note #5 on 10:14 *Tyre and Sidon*. Gentile cities in Phoenicia (see note on 6:17), north of Galilee, which had not had opportunity to witness Jesus' miracles and hear his preaching as the people had in most of Galilee (see note on v. 12).

Note #6 on v. 12 *more bearable...for Sodom*. Although Sodom was so sinful that God destroyed it (see Gen. 18:20 and note: 19:24–28; Jude 7 and note), the people who heard the message of Jesus and his disciples were even more accountable, because they had the gospel of the kingdom preached to them. *That day*: Judgment day.

New Living Application Bible

TEXT: [13] "What horrors await you, Korazin and Bethsaida! For if the miracles I did in you had been done in wicked Tyre and Sidon, their people would have sat in deep repentance long ago, clothed in sackcloth and throwing ashes on their heads to show their remorse. [14] Yes, Tyre and Sidon will be better off on the judgment day than you (NLT).

> Note #1: Korazin was a city near the Sea of Galilee, probably about two miles north of Capernaum. Tyre and Sidon were cities destroyed by God as punishment for their wickedness (Ezekiel 26–28).

Lesson 19

Translating Metaphors and More

Jesus, the Good Shepherd

One Sunday, Peter and John were walking back from church and discussing the sermon. John said, "It helps me to think of Jesus as the Good Shepherd, I know he is looking after me and he knows what I need." Peter smiled a little and said, "That's fine, but I can't help thinking about when I was seven years old, and my father sent me to look after the family goats. We were a small group of young boys, and each day we would go out with the goats to make sure they didn't eat people's crops or stray onto the motor road. We used to throw stones at them if they went the wrong way, and sometimes we beat them. I definitely wouldn't have liked to have been one of our goats! So every time someone says 'Jesus is our Shepherd', I get the wrong picture!"

John replied, "Yes, but I think things were different at the time of Jesus. Remember those Bible background videos we saw of the sheep following the shepherd, and of him protecting them from wild animals?" "Yes," said Peter, "I need to think of that instead. There are other pictures of God, however, that make more sense to me. God is our fortress, for example. You know that high rocky hill where people used to hide when there were wars? I think of God being like that place, a refuge, a secure place, a place that protects us. The nice thing about these pictures is that they help us to think of a lot of things, not just one."

They walked on along the road, and after a few minutes John said, "You know, I've never said this to anyone before, but I have problems with Jesus' words, 'I am the bread of life.' After all, what is bread? For us it is something you buy sometimes as a snack if you have some extra money, or if you are going on a trip. This doesn't seem to be a very good picture of Jesus to me!" Now it was Peter's turn to remind him of the videos they had seen at the seminar. "Remember how the people on the Bible background videos were eating bread with everything," said Peter. "It seems it was a very important food for them." "Yes," said John, "these word pictures of God can help us understand him better, but we need to know what the original audience was imagining. When we get home, maybe this would make a good subject for a series of Bible studies!"

GROUP DISCUSSION

1. Discuss reasons Peter found it hard to think of Jesus as the Good Shepherd.
2. Do you use word pictures in your own language? Give some examples and explain what they mean.
3. There are many word pictures of God in the Bible. Share one of the word pictures that helps you the most.

What are metaphors?

Metaphors are word pictures that talk about one thing in terms of another. For example:

- Your lover as dessert
- Emotions in terms of temperature
- God in terms of a rock

> Metaphors are word pictures that talk about one thing in terms of another.

Metaphors are one way of giving weak guidance to a range of implications. They are not limited to short expressions. Longer texts, like parables, can be extended metaphors. Since metaphors depend heavily on context, they often lead to communication problems in secondary communication.

'Bread' is used in Scripture to refer to actual bread but it is also used as a metaphor to talk about something else. For example, in John 6 Jesus fed 5000 people with five loaves and two fish. After seeing that, the crowd came to him. Jesus tells them that they came because of the bread he gave them but that what they really needed to do was to believe in him. Then they demand that he perform a miracle to prove that he is someone special. They argue that Moses gave the Israelites manna in the desert, implying that Jesus should do something similar. The text continues:

> Jesus said to them, "I tell you the truth, it is not Moses who has given you the bread from heaven, but it is my Father who gives you the true bread from heaven. For the bread of God is he who comes down from heaven and gives life to the world." "Sir," they said, "from now on give us this bread." Then Jesus declared, "I am the bread of life. He who comes to me will never go hungry, and he who believes in me will never be thirsty" (Jn 6:32–35 NIV).

Keeping this context in mind, focus on the expression "*I am the bread of life,*" and discuss these questions:

1. What information did Jesus' audience associate with the concept *bread*?
2. What implications did Jesus intend them to understand from this passage? (Look also at verses 36–51.)
3. Discuss what the expression *life* communicated, especially combined with bread?
4. Discuss why you think Jesus used the expression *bread* here, rather than simply saying, "I am the Messiah."

When Jesus used the metaphor, "I am the bread of life," it helped his audience in the following ways:

1. It linked this part of the text to the earlier part where Jesus had fed bread to the 5000. This gives unity to the passage.
2. It made a wide range of information available:

   - people can't live without bread
   - people get hungry again after eating bread
   - people have to work for bread (v. 27)
   - bread gives us strength
   - God provided bread from heaven for the Israelites in the desert
   - and so forth.

   These led the audience to a wide range of implications. If Jesus just wanted to say one of these things, he could have said it directly. For example, "I give you strength." By using a metaphor, he intended to communicate more meaning.
3. The metaphor of bread tied many different ideas together and made them easier to remember.

Metaphors give weak guidance to a range of implications by joining two ideas in new ways.

Metaphors are a very powerful way of communicating. Like all weakly guided communication, they invite people to think and explore possible implications. Because people exert more effort, they expect and often find more cognitive benefits. Metaphors are widely used, especially in poetry.

Jesus used metaphors a lot, and his listeners often misunderstood them, at least at first. For example, his disciples misunderstood what he meant by the leaven of the Pharisees (Mt 13:13). Nicodemus misunderstood what he meant by being "born again" (Jn 3). The woman at the well misunderstood what "living water" referred to (Jn 4:11). If Jesus was not understood immediately when he used metaphors, secondary audiences of Scripture today should not be expected to understand everything the first time they read or hear them.

Speakers may compare two things by saying one is like another. For example, Jesus said, "Anyone who will not receive the kingdom of God *like a little child* will never enter it" (Mk 10:15). When they use the word *like*, it gives an explicit clue to the audience that this is comparing two things. Audiences still need to use context to understand in which way the two things are similar.

Giving people something to think about and discover is especially important in cultures that value proverbs and symbolic speech. Among the Bafia of Cameroon, for example, important things are always expressed by means of more weakly communicated implications. Things that are expressed directly are not taken as seriously.[1]

GROUP DISCUSSION

Identify the metaphors in these verses. Then think of a range of implications they might communicate:

1. For your arrows have pierced me, and your hand has come down upon me (Ps 38:2 NIV).
2. He lifted me out of the slimy pit, out of the mud and mire (Ps 40:2a NIV).
3. "I tell you the truth, no one can see the kingdom of God unless he is born again" (Jn 3:3 NIV).

Translating metaphors

Where there is no contextual mismatch between the original and secondary audience, metaphors can be translated as in the original without difficulty. Since metaphors rely heavily on context, however, the possibility of contextual mismatches is high.

Certain metaphors are central to the Bible and the church, for example, the Lamb of God, or the cross. Even if there are contextual mismatches between the original and secondary audiences, the secondary audience needs to learn what these metaphors communicated to the original audience.

Other metaphors can be translated in different ways depending on the kind of Scripture product being prepared. Translators can aim to:

Approach #1. Adjust the text to the audience's context so they do not have to learn new contextual information.
Approach #2. Adjust the audience's context where it differs from the original audience's, and keep a higher degree of meaning resemblance to the original.
Approach #3. Something in between.

Audiences need to be able to understand the author's intended meaning, but making one or more of the implications of a metaphor explicit changes the nature of the communication and reduces the meaning resemblance. Here are some solutions translators can consider.

1. Keep the original metaphor

The original metaphors can be kept in the translation. This is a good solution if:

---

[1] Bessong, Dieudonné P. Aroga, 2004, "Translating Samson's enigma (Jg 14:14) into Bafia, a Cameroonian language." Paper presented at Translation and Interculturality: Africa and the West, Translation and Interculturality: Africa and the West, Groningen, the Netherlands, 2004. University of Groningen, Netherlands.

1. The metaphor happens to communicate the same thing in the audience's context.

2. The Scripture product is aiming at a high degree of meaning resemblance and provides ways for their audience to learn the range of meanings the metaphor communicates through extra-textual helps, teaching, videos, and so forth. Section headings can provide clues. For example in Mark 2:21–22, Jesus uses the metaphors of mending an old garment with a new patch and putting new wine into old wineskins. Some translations give this section title, "Jesus spoke to them about his teaching."

Information provided in extra-textual helps should indicate that the implications suggested are some but not all of the possible implications. For example in Isaiah 5:1–5, a note on the metaphor *vineyard* might say:

> In the Bible, the vineyard was often a symbol of the love relationship between a man and a woman and was often used to refer to God's relationship with Israel. He tended her carefully, she produced fruit, he guarded her from his watchtower, he surrounded her with a wall, she gave him great joy, and so forth.

2. Translate the implication directly

Another option for translating metaphors is to express the intended meaning explicitly, without using a metaphor at all. For example, in some languages, "Herod that fox" (Lk 13:32) has been translated as "Herod that sly man," or "Herod the tricky one." This may be a good solution when aiming at a Scripture product that is easy for audiences to understand in their current context. The disadvantage is that the meaning resemblance is reduced. In addition, there is the danger of misunderstanding the metaphor in its original context.

3. Translate the metaphor and one implication

Translators may keep the original metaphor and express one or more of the intended implications in the text. For example, some versions translate "You blind guides" as "You are blind guides because you yourselves are in error and you lead people into error" (Mt 23:24). The range of possible meanings is lost (for example, that they could fall into a hole, they could get lost, they could be a laughing stock to on-lookers, that they had an unrealistic belief in their abilities, and so forth), but the text is easier for audiences who lack the intended context to understand.

4. Substitute a local metaphor

If the original metaphor is unknown, another way to translate it is to use a local metaphor that has similar information linked to it. The range of implications the audience understands may come close to that of the original, but the meaning actually expressed in the text is quite different. For example, "I send you out as sheep in the midst of wolves"

(Mt 10:16), may be translated, "I send you out as sheep in the midst of hyenas" or "I send you out as sheep in the midst of civet cats." The challenge with this solution is to find local concepts that share the same set of meanings as the original. For example, when Jesus refers to Herod as a fox (Lk 13:32), the first audience would have understood that Jesus meant he was sly, cruel, and destructive, and not really important (Translator's Notes).

Translators need to be sure any substitutions would have been possible in the historical period of the original. For example, cars were not known in Israel at the time of Jesus, so to translate James 3:4, "ships are guided by a very small rudder" as "cars are guided by very small steering wheels" would not be correct historically.

Translators can provide the original word in footnotes so readers who compare their translation to translations in other languages will recognize that the translator made the substitution intentionally.

EXERCISE

Assign one of the verses below to each small group.

- I will make you become *fishers of men* (Mk 1:17 RSV).
- You are the *salt of the earth* (Mt 5:13 RSV).
- Unless one is *born anew*, he cannot see the kingdom of God (Jn 3:3 RSV).
- No one sews a patch of unshrunk cloth on an old garment; otherwise the patch pulls away from it, the new from the old, and a worse tear results (Mk 2:21 NASB).

Ask them to:

1. Read the verse in its context. Pay special attention to the metaphor.
2. Discuss the implications that are communicated by the metaphor.
3. Identify the context that is needed to understand them.
4. Decide if your audience lacks any of this information.
5. Translate the verse for your audience in two ways:
   a. Approach #2: If your audience does not share the intended context, write a section title or brief note to provide this information. Be sure that the new information is linked to what they already know.
   b. Approach #1: Translate the verse in a way your audience can understand easily in their current context, using one of the methods suggested above. Decide which of the implications you think are the most important to communicate.
6. Back-translate your translations into English.

7. Share your results with the class. Discuss what is good about each translation and what might be lacking.

Translating other kinds of weakly communicated implications

Speakers can give weak guidance to a range of implications in many ways, not just by using metaphors. What do you understand Jesus intended to communicate in this verse?

Jesus answered, "As long as they [the wedding guests] have the bridegroom with them, they cannot fast" (Mk 2:19 RSV).

Jesus intended a range of implications: that people cannot fast while they are feasting and full of joy, that his disciples could not fast while Jesus was with them on earth, that there is a time for fasting and a time for feasting, this is not a time for fasting, that he was not subject to their religious rules, and so forth. Translators need to use the same principles in translating all forms of weakly communicated implications, depending on the kind of Scripture product they are preparing.

EXERCISE

Read these two passages:

- Matthew 8:19 And a scribe came up and said to him, "Teacher, I will follow you wherever you go." And Jesus said to him, "Foxes have holes, and birds of the air have nests; but the *Son of man has nowhere to lay his head*" (RSV).
- Matthew 3:3 Prepare the way of the Lord, *make his paths straight* (RSV).
1. Discuss the intended meaning of the part of the passages in italics.
2. Identify the context that might lead to these implications.
3. Would your audience understand the intended meaning of this passage?
4. If not, discuss what help you could give them.

Summary

Metaphors are one way of giving weak guidance to a range of implications. Because metaphors rely heavily on context, translators need to be alert for contextual mismatches, both for their own understanding of the range of implications being communicated and their audience's understanding. The way metaphors are translated depends on the approach being used, whether it aims at a high degree of meaning resemblance or a text that is adjusted to the audience's current context so it is easy for them to understand right away. Some metaphors are central to the Bible and the church, and all Christians need to learn them. For many metaphors, however, translators have options: they can keep the metaphor in the text and provide ways for the audience to learn the intended context, translate one of the implications explicitly, translate the metaphor and one implication, or use a local metaphor. Each solution has its advantages and disadvantages. The same options can be used for translating all kinds of weakly communicated implications.

So what?

The way metaphors are translated depends on the communication approach.

Assignment

Take the text on the left as the original and that on the right hand side as its translation. Compare the meaning of the translation with that of the original. Decide how they are the same and how they differ. Discuss the approach in the communication strategy you think the translator is aiming at in each case.

Matthew. 10:16 I send you out as sheep in the midst of wolves (RSV).	When I send you out into the world, it is like sending defenseless sheep out among ravenous wolves.
Acts 16:17 These men…proclaim the way of salvation (RSV).	They tell you how to be saved.
Acts 16:21 They advocate customs which it is not lawful for us Romans to accept or practice (RSV).	They have broken the law by preaching about a god we do not accept.
John 13:14 If I then, your Lord and Teacher, have washed your feet, you also ought to wash one another's feet (RSV).	If I then, your Lord and Teacher, have served you, you also ought to serve one another.

More Clues from the Text

Lesson 20

How We Connect Thoughts

Opening Exercise

Discuss what you think Bob intended to communicate in the following examples.
1. Bob says: I went shopping today. I ran out of milk.
2. Bob says: I went shopping today. It was a beautiful day.
3. Bob says: I went shopping today. A volcano erupted in Mexico.

In the first example, the sentences simply say that Bob went shopping today and that he ran out of milk. We immediately understand more than that, however. We recognize that the second sentence ('I ran out of milk') expresses the reason the speaker went shopping. We understand this because we expect the second sentence to be relevant in the context of the first one. This interpretation gives us a contextual implication (or cognitive benefit), and so we are satisfied that we have understood the speaker's meaning.

In the second example, it is more difficult to see how the second sentence is relevant in the context given by the first. We may understand that Bob went shopping because the weather was so beautiful, and he wanted to get out, or we may understand that Bob went shopping, realized the weather was great, and is now going to talk about what happened next.

In the third example, it is very hard to see how the second sentence can be relevant on the basis of what has been communicated in the first one. We get the impression that the sentences are not related, that it is not really a text.

Leaving the way thoughts are connected implicit

When we process communication, we do not just look for the thoughts sentences communicate. We also look for how those thoughts are connected. We do this because we are looking for a relevant interpretation, that is, cognitive benefits. We take the first interpretation that makes sense as the intended one.

Sometimes speakers leave the way thoughts are connected implicit. They do this because they feel the intended relationship is so obvious that there is no need to draw the hearer's attention to it. For example, if Peter said to John, "I overslept.

My alarm didn't go off," John would understand that Peter's comment about the alarm gives the reason John overslept, because it is very well known that the purpose of alarm clocks is to wake people up on time.

Another reason speakers may leave the way their thoughts are connected implicit is that they may want to only give weak guidance to the relationship between the thoughts. Often, connectors spell out the relationship between thoughts too clearly. For example, the effect of poetry can be destroyed by adding connectors. Compare the effect of the added connectors in Psalm 23:1.

- The Lord is my shepherd, I shall not be in want. He makes me lie down in green pastures.
- The Lord is my shepherd, therefore I shall not be in want, because he makes me lie down in green pastures.

To be able to understand the way thoughts should be connected, we need to know the context the speaker intends. Discuss what you understand from these examples:

1. The river had been dry for a long time. Everybody attended the funeral.
2. Peter was very hungry. He went to McDonalds and ordered a quarter pounder.

The first example is from the Sissala of Burkina Faso. To understand how these thoughts are connected, you need to know that Sissala believe that there are spirits in rivers. If a river has been dry for a long time, they understand that the spirit of that river has died. Whenever there is a death, there is a funeral, and people are expected to attend.

In the second example, hearers need to know that McDonald's is a restaurant, and that a quarter pounder is a kind of food that is sold at McDonald's.

> ## We need context to understand the way speakers intend their thoughts to be connected.

Connecting thoughts explicitly

EXERCISE

1. Pair up with someone. One of you will receive a paper with five words on it. Do not let your partner see these words.
2. Describe the meaning of the words, but do not say the word itself.
3. When the leader tells you to, if you have not already guessed the word, move on to the next one.
4. See how many of the words your partner can guess.

We can define words that represent concepts like cat, dog, rain, and so forth without too much difficulty because they express concepts. Other words like *so, after all, still, too,* and *nevertheless* are more difficult to define. Words like these give hearers clues about how to process the communication rather than express concepts. Languages have many ways of giving these clues.

Connectors are words that give clues about how the speaker's thoughts are to be connected. At times, speakers use connectors to make the way they intended their thoughts to be connected very clear. They may do this if they feel this was not clear or if they want to be sure hearers connect the thoughts in a certain way. For example:

> *Connectors are words that give clues about how the speaker's thoughts are to be connected.*

Mary caught a cold again. She is weak physically.

The speaker could intend the thoughts to be connected in either of these two ways:

Mary caught a cold again because she is weak physically.
Mary caught a cold again and so she is weak physically.

If speakers wanted to be sure the audience understood one or the other of these meanings, they would need to use a connector to make that clear.

Speakers can use connectors to guide hearers to the intended meaning.

EXERCISES

1. Insert different connectors between these two sentences, and imagine a context in which this could be said. Then explain how the meaning that is communicated is changed by adding a connector, and by each different connector.

   The girl was trembling. He gave her a chair.

   She baked bread. Visitors were coming.

2. Read both versions of these lines of poetry. Explain how the connectors in the second version affect the meaning.

Come, let us pick strawberries,
It is not far to the woods.
Let us pick young roses,
They wither so soon.

Come, let us pick strawberries,
After all it is not far to the woods.
Let us pick young roses,
Since they wither so soon.

A variety of connectors

Languages provide speakers with a variety of connectors that they can use to guide their audience to their intended interpretation. Some connectors only give instructions about how to process the communication and have no conceptual content at all. Others have some conceptual content. Some give very strong guidance while others give weaker guidance.

Some connectors guide hearers to look for new implications

In English, speakers can use the connector *so* to indicate that the second part of a text gives a conclusion to what was already communicated. This could be something that was stated explicitly in the first clause, an implication communicated by it, or something brought to mind by the communication situation. Hearers have to supply context to be able to see how the conclusion makes sense. For example:

So says, "Understand the second clause to be a conclusion to what was already communicated."

Peter fell asleep in class

Context: Falling asleep is not allowed in class.
            Falling asleep in class is punished.
            Friends look out for one another.

so John woke him up.

Audiences have to be able to supply the context in order to be able to understand how John waking Peter is a conclusion to the speaker saying that Peter fell asleep in class.

EXERCISES

Supply the context needed to see how the final clause is a conclusion to what has already been communicated.

1. My wife is sick

    -

    -

    -

    so I won't be going to the conference.

2. My wife was sick and we have huge hospital bills,

    -

    -

    -

    so I won't be going to the conference.

3. He decided to clear the land and remove all the tree stumps,

-

-

-

so it would be ready for planting.

Some connectors guide hearers to eliminate thoughts

In English, speakers can use the connector *but* to erase an implication that might have arisen from what was already communicated. For example,

Peter fell asleep in class
Implication: ~~Peter continued sleeping in class.~~
but John woke him up.

The *but* erases the implication that Peter continued sleeping in class. Other connectors that function in a similar way are *however* and *nevertheless.*

But says,
"Be careful! Some of the implications you might have expected are not true."

EXERCISES

What implications does the *but* in each of the following examples eliminate?

1. I want to go to the market *but* I have a lot of work to do in the house.
2. My husband and I were not able to have children *but* we are happy.
3. They want to be teachers of God's law, *but* they do not understand their own words or the matters about which they speak with so much confidence (1 Tim 1:7 GNB).
4. You killed the author of life, *but* God raised him from the dead (Acts 3:15 NIV).

Some connectors guide hearers to strengthen thoughts

In English, speakers can use the connector *indeed* to strengthen thoughts already communicated.

Peter fell asleep in class. *Indeed,* he was even snoring.

In the example, Peter's snoring strengthens the claim that he had fallen asleep.

Indeed says,
"Understand that the text introduced by indeed gives evidence that should convince you to believe what I told you!"

EXERCISES

What instructions does *indeed* give in examples below?

1. He was very ill. *Indeed,* his family was already thinking about his funeral.
2. He will not let your foot slip—he who watches over you will not

slumber; *indeed,* he who watches over Israel will neither slumber nor sleep (Ps 121:3, 4 NIV).

3. Jesus answered, "Everyone who drinks this water will be thirsty again, but whoever drinks the water I give him will never thirst. *Indeed,* the water I give him will become in him a spring of water welling up to eternal life" (Jn 4:13–14 NIV).

In English, the connector *after all* can also guide hearers to strengthen thoughts they already have. Speakers can use it to indicate that the second part of the text serves as a reminder of something the hearer already knows and should use to understand what was already communicated.

> After all says, "This is something you know, and should use to understand what was already communicated.

Peter fell asleep in class. *After all,* it was hot and boring.

EXERCISES

What instructions does *after all* give in the following examples?

1. She is far too young to travel so far alone. *After all,* she is only twelve.

2. Paul to the Corinthians: Now I am ready to visit you for the third time, and I will not be a burden to you, because what I want is not your possessions but you. *After all,* children should not have to save up for their parents, but parents for their children (2 Cor 12:14 NIV).

3. In this same way, husbands ought to love their wives as their own bodies. He who loves his wife loves himself. *After all*, no one ever hated his own body, but he feeds and cares for it, just as Christ does the church (Eph 5:28–29 NIV).

Other kinds of guidance

Connectors can provide other kinds of guidance as well. For example, in English, speakers can use the connector *too* to indicate that the thoughts communicated in the second part of their utterance should be understood in the same way as those communicated in the first. That is, the hearers should expect the same kind of cognitive benefits.

> Too says, "Understand the second part of the text in the same way you did the first."

Peter fell asleep in class, and John did, *too.*

Other expressions that can serve in a similar way are *as well* and *also*. For example, Peter was bored. He was also hot.

EXERCISES

What instructions does *too* give in each of the example?

1. Peter thought he was ready for the test. John did, *too.*

2. (Jesus had healed a blind man, and then addressed the crowd.) Jesus said, "For judgment I have come into this world, so that the blind will see and those who see will become blind." Some Pharisees who were with him heard him say this and asked, "What? Are we blind, *too?*"

Table 3: Kinds of guidance connectors give

Word	Instruction	Type of cognitive benefit
so	Understand the second clause to be a conclusion to what was already communicated	new implications
but	Some of the implications you might have expected are not true	elimination
indeed	understand that the text introduced by Indeed gives evidence that should convince you to believe what I told you	strengthening
after all	This is something you know, but you may not have thought about it just now	
too	understand the second part of the text in the same way you did the first	find similar contexts and similar cognitive benefits

Some connectors give conceptual content

Connectors like *because* and *therefore* are different from the connectors we have seen so far, because they have some conceptual content. *Because* indicates that the clause it introduces gives a cause for what is communicated by the other clause. To understand the intended meaning, audiences have to use context to identify relevant causes.

EXERCISES

Insert *because* between the clauses below. Then give the contextual information you used to infer the intended meaning.

1. Sue took a linguistics course. She wanted to become a Bible translator.
2. This computer doesn't work. The CMOS battery has gone flat.

Some connectors give weaker guidance

Some connectors give very weak guidance to an interpretation. For example, speakers use the connector *and* in English to tell hearers that 1) the two clauses are true, and 2) the thoughts need to be understood together, without specifying exactly how the thoughts should be connected. Hearers are free to discover this, using clues from the context. They may find a variety of ways the ideas are connected: the two events happened one after the other, the two thoughts are joined, or the two thoughts have a logical link. Discuss the guidance *and* gives in each of the sentences below.

She washed the dishes *and* went to bed.

She washed the dishes *and* chatted with her friend.

She likes blue *and* he doesn't.

I ate my dinner *and* got sick.

Translating the way thoughts are connected

People use connectors successfully without ever being able to explain how they function. Translators may encounter several kinds of problems as they work between languages, however. Some reasons connectors are challenging are:

1. Translators may not understand completely how these words function in the source text and so not understand the author's meaning completely or correctly.
2. If translators are not aware of how connectors function in their language, the connectors in the source language can interfere with their abilities to express things naturally in their language.
3. Since connectors are difficult to translate, different translations of the Bible may translate them in different ways or leave them out altogether. Where connectors in different versions communicate different meanings, translators need to research the passage in commentaries and translation helps, or ask a consultant to explain which of the meanings is most likely to be the intended one.

If translators hope to express the biblical author's meaning successfully in their language, they need to become consciously aware of how connectors function, both in the source and receptor languages. They also need to understand the intended meaning of each passage, based on the text and the context, and the exact contribution the connector makes to it. Then they need to express the meaning in their language in the best way possible and be sure their audience has access to the intended context.

EXERCISES

1. Insert *so, and,* and *but* one by one between these two clauses. Imagine a context in which each one could be said. The last one, *but,* will take some creativity. How is the meaning changed by each of these connectors?

   The LORD is my shepherd, I shall not be in want (Ps 23:1 NIV).

2. Look at the relationships between thoughts in one of your texts. Circle all the connectors.
   - Where are they used? Where are they not used?
   - What guidance does each connector give?
3. Make a list of connectors in your language.
   - Can you paraphrase some of them with noun phrases?
   - Do some of connectors seem to give similar clues? If so, can you always substitute the words for each other?

Summary

Speakers not only communicate the content of their thoughts; they also communicate how those thoughts should be connected. They may leave these connections implicit when the context makes the connection clear or when they intentionally want to leave the connection vague. They may connect thoughts explicitly when it is necessary to communicate their thoughts clearly or when they want to make the connection especially clear. There are a variety of connectors, some that only give instructions, some that contain some conceptual content, some that give very lose guidance. In all cases, audiences combine the clues connectors give with the meaning of the text and the context to understand the speaker's meaning. Each language has its own set of connectors. Translators need to understand the clues they give to use them effectively.

> **So what?**
>
> **Translators need to understand the clues connectors give, both in the biblical text and in their own languages.**

Assignment

1. Circle each *but* and *so* in Genesis 4:2b–5 below:

   > Now Abel kept flocks, and Cain worked the soil. [3] In the course of time Cain brought some of the fruits of the soil as an offering to the LORD. [4] But Abel brought fat portions from some of the firstborn of his flock. The LORD looked with favor on Abel and his offering, [5] but on Cain and his offering he did not look with favor. So Cain was very angry, and his face was downcast (NIV).

   Now read through the text without the connectors.

   a. How is your understanding changed?
   b. What context do you supply? What implications are eliminated?

2. Explain the implication the *but* eliminates in the following examples.
   a. Mark 6:47–49 When evening came, the boat was in the middle of the

lake, and he was alone on land. He saw the disciples straining at the oars, because the wind was against them. About the fourth watch of the night he went out to them, walking on the lake. He was about to pass by them, *but* when they saw him walking on the lake, they thought he was a ghost. They cried out, because they all saw him and were terrified (NIV).

b. Romans 7:20 Now if I do what I do not want, it is no longer I that do it, *but* sin which dwells within me (RSV).

c. 1 John 2:19a They went out from us, *but* they did not really belong to us (NIV).

d. 1 John 2:19b For if they had belonged to us, they would have remained with us; *but* their going showed that none of them belonged to us (NIV).

e. Romans 7:14 We know that the law is spiritual; *but* I am unspiritual, sold as a slave to sin (NIV).

Lesson 21

Crafting Bible Stories

Designing products based on Scripture is a good place to begin as a translator, as some of the difficult limitations of Scripture translation are relaxed. The focus is on communicating a message that is relevant to an audience in their current context. Scripture-based products are especially good for introducing people to the Bible. In this lesson we focus on one kind of Scripture-based product—Bible stories.

Selecting passages

Some parts of the Bible are more relevant to an audience than others. Translation projects should begin with the more relevant parts, as audiences will be more motivated to read or listen to them. In time, their interest may grow and they may be motivated to understand other passages. Selecting relevant passages is especially important when crafting Scripture-based products, as only a selection of texts are prepared in this way, not the whole Bible.

Audiences may find some passages more relevant in their current context, such as:

- Passages for which the audience already shares many cultural assumptions with the first audience. The processing costs are lower. For example, cattle-herders may be interested in passages about finding water for cattle in Genesis. Passages that require audiences to learn a lot of new context will seem less relevant. For example, the passage from Hebrews on how Jesus descended from Melchizedek rather than Aaron as a proof that he is a priest of a higher order than Levi would probably not be immediately relevant to most audiences today.
- Passages that address issues the audience finds interesting. They will be more willing to invest effort to understand these. For example, many Australian Aborigines are extremely interested in the origin of the world. One group stayed up all night the first time they got Genesis because they were so fascinated by it. They were not at all interested in Mark, however.
- Passages that help an audience solve a problem they feel they have. Again, they will be motivated to invest more effort to understand these. For example, the Chol of Mexico felt they were at the mercy of spirits and spiritual

powers. They found Jesus' power over these things extremely relevant.[1] People suffering from the trauma of war find passages that address suffering and God's care relevant. The Yanamamo of Venezuela believed that God loved others but not them, and so they find passages about God's love for all people to be especially relevant.

Audiences may find some passages less relevant or even offensive, such as:

- Passages that uphold values they do not share. For example, cattle herders and agriculturalists generally do not get along with each other, so passages about Jesus being the Good Shepherd might not be popular among agriculturalists. Cattle herders may also be scandalized by passages where oxen are used for plowing.
- Passages that contradict their beliefs, such as those that refer to killing the fatted calf among Hindus. Muslims find passages that refer to the Son of God offensive. These may not be the best place to start.

Since the Old Testament provides context for the New Testament, a selection of passages starting with creation can give key points of God's revelation of himself to people. Reading the New Testament without a knowledge of the Old is like starting your education at secondary school without ever going to primary school. Without the Old Testament, people may not realize the need for a sacrifice for sin and so may not understand why Christ was sacrificed for our sins. A set of stories that gives an overview of the Bible is sometimes referred to as a Bible Story Set or a Panoramic Bible. It can be filled in later with more Scripture passages.

After deciding on a series of stories, check to see that it covers the main beliefs of the Christian faith. One way to do this is to compare your story set with the Apostles' Creed (below), since it expresses these beliefs.

> I believe in God, the Father almighty, creator of heaven and earth.
> I believe in Jesus Christ, God's only Son, our Lord, who was conceived by the Holy Spirit, born of the Virgin Mary, suffered under Pontius Pilate, was crucified, died, and was buried; he descended to the dead.
> On the third day he rose again; he ascended into heaven, he is seated at the right hand of the Father, and he will come again to judge the living and the dead.
> I believe in the Holy Spirit, the holy catholic church, the communion of saints, the forgiveness of sins, the resurrection of the body, and the life everlasting.

---

[1] Beekman, John. 1974. A culturally relevant witness. In W.A. Smalley (ed.), *Readings in missionary antropology.* Pasadena, Calif.: William Carey, pp. 132–135.

1. Think of one issue that is particularly relevant to your audience at this time.
2. Discuss how Scripture addresses this issue.
3. Think of several stories in Scripture that address this issue and then pick the best one.

Freedoms and responsibilities when crafting stories

Audience's expectations of meaning resemblance are lower for products based on Scripture than for the genre *Scripture*, so communicators have much more freedom to:

- Add the context the audience needs. For example, this may involve adding that when Jesus wrapped the towel around his waist it was the way slaves dressed (Jn 13:4). Or it might involve filling out the text, for example, that Jerusalem was a city. It may also include contradicting any unintended contexts the audience might use. For example, among groups that believe strongly that witchcraft can be passed on through food, story crafters can say that the bread Jesus gave Judas at the Last Supper did not contain witchcraft.
- Omit details that are not immediately relevant and only increase processing costs. For example, that blind Bartemaeus was the son of Timaeus (Mk 10:46).
- Reorder events so they follow the actual chronological order. Verse numbers are usually omitted.
- Bring several accounts of the same event together in one story, for example, those told in more than one Gospel, or stories in 1 and 2 Kings and 1 and 2 Chronicles. At times, the order or details of the events may be different in different accounts. For example, the order of events of the Last Supper in Matthew and Mark's accounts agree, but Luke has a different order, and John's account is different again. Story crafters have to decide which version to follow.
- Add other things to make it an interesting story: putting narrative text into conversation, adding exclamations, and so forth.

Decisions about what to omit and add when crafting a Bible story are made by considering the audience and the goal of the communication. For example, the story of Simon the Magician in Acts 8 could be told with quite different goals in mind:

1. To communicate that God's power is stronger than magic.
2. To communicate that God's power is stronger than magic but it is a gift, not something that can be bought and owned.
3. To communicate how the early church grew, with the church in Jerusalem taking responsible for its spread.
4. To communicate how the God worked in the early church to help the apostles realize that the Gospel is for everyone, including those they looked down on and avoided.

If you are telling this story with the first goal in mind, there would be no reason to include details about Samaritans, Jerusalem, apostles, and so forth. If you are telling the story with the fourth goal in mind, all these details are necessary as well as some contextual information about Jewish-Samaritan relations, the role of the apostles, the baptism of the Holy Spirit, and so forth.

Each change that is made needs to contribute to the relevance of the story and remain true to the intended meaning of the biblical text. Because communicators preparing this type of product have more freedom to adjust the story to the audience's context, they bear greater responsibility for its truth.

EXERCISE

Read the Bible story version of Acts 16:16–18 in the first column below and answer these questions:

1. For whom might a product like this be appropriate?
2. Compare it with the RSV of this passage in the second column. Identify where the story-teller has:
    *   added contextual information
    *   simplified the text or omitted things
    *   added information that reflects her culture
3. Try to explain how these changes contribute to relevance.

Story Bible	**RSV**
In Philippi there was a young woman who was a fortuneteller. She was not in her right mind, for an evil spirit lived in her and made her say strange things. Many people believed that what she said was sure to happen. They asked her all sorts of questions about the future, and did whatever she told them. Some men of the city had made this poor girl their slave. Every day she had to go out into the streets to tell people's fortunes for money. Her masters became rich through the money she brought back to them.	[16] As we were going to the place of prayer, we were met by a slave girl who had a spirit of divination and brought her owners much gain by soothsaying.
Whenever she saw Paul and Silas and Timothy in the streets, this poor girl followed them, calling out so that everybody could hear, "These men are servants of the Most High God, and they come to tell us how to be saved."	[17] She followed Paul and us, crying, "These men are servants of the Most High God, who proclaim to you the way of salvation."
Of course people stared at the young girl following three strangers and shouting after them. Everybody knew that she was not in her right mind. Those who did not believe in her fortunetelling laughed at the sight.	

Paul did not like this at all. He knew that it was an evil spirit which spoke through the lips of the poor girl. And he did not want people to laugh at his teaching.

For many days the girl followed the missionaries, calling out after them. At last Paul turned and said to the evil spirit that was in her, "I command you in the name of Jesus Christ to come out of her!"

Immediately the evil spirit left her, and the girl was restored to her right mind....[2]

[18] And this she did for many days. But Paul was annoyed, and turned and said to the spirit, "I charge you in the name of Jesus Christ to come out of her." And it came out that very hour.

The process of crafting a story orally

1. Decide who your audience is. And the reason you are telling them this story.
2. Understand the story.
   a. Read the passage, noticing what comes before and after it. Read it in several versions, compare the differences and how they affect what you understand.
   b. Listen to the passage being read, either an audio recording, by someone reading it aloud, or by recording yourself reading it aloud. If you have videos or images of the passage, look at them. Try to see the events in your mind.
   c. Think of the main implications of the story.
   d. Do a verbal sketch of the passage.
   e. Sketch out the story on paper by drawing images that will give you visual clues of the action of the story scene by scean. This is referred to as *story-boarding*.
   f. Identify any contextual mismatches your audience might have.
3. Decide on any adjustments that are needed for your audience.
   a. Should anything be omitted? For example, all the names of people and cities may not be necessary.
   b. Should any context be supplied?
   c. Should anything be re-ordered?
4. Learn the story.
   a. Divide the story into three or four scenes.
   b. Act out the story. Try to imagine how each character felt.
   c. Tell the story in your language to your small group until you feel you are doing it well.
5. Record the story.
6. Check your story against the original. Correct any errors you find. Make sure the main point is clear.

---

[2] Vos, Catrerine F. 1977. *The child's story Bible.* Grand Rapids, Mich.: Eerdmans.

7. Have a consultant check your story. He or she may request a written or oral back-translation.
8. Make a final recording.

Summary

For some audiences, products based on Scripture may be the most relevant. Translators can work with church leaders to select passages that are highly relevant and begin with those. Because they are not claiming to be Scripture, translators have much more freedom to craft a product that is relevant to an audience in their current context, but they also have more responsibility for the many decisions made in the process. They can leave out less relevant details in the texts, as well as add necessary context. These products are well-suited to oral as well as written media.

So what?

Skilled translators know how to prepare a variety of Scripture products.

Work Session K: Crafting the Story of Luke 7:11–17

Use the process described in Lesson 21 to craft a story based on Luke 7:11–17.

Compare these versions of the passage, and observe any differences in meaning.

Text	NIV	TEV	Your Comments/ Observations
[11] And-it-happened soon afterwards he-went into town named Nain and with him came his disciples and a big crowd.	[11] Soon afterward, Jesus went to a town called Nain, and his disciples and a large crowd went along with him.	[11] Soon afterward Jesus went to a town named Nain, accompanied by his disciples and a large crowd.	
[12] As they came near to the gate of the town, and see/ look, there was they carried a dead person, the only son of his mother, and she was a widow, and a lot of people from the town were with her.	[12] As he approached the town gate, a dead person was being carried out—the only son of his mother, and she was a widow. And a large crowd from the town was with her.	[12] Just as he arrived at the gate of the town, a funeral procession was coming out. The dead man was the only son of a woman who was a widow, and a large crowd from the town was with her.	
[13–15] And when the Lord saw her, he had compassion with her and said to her "don't cry." And he drew near and touched the stretcher (stretcher for carrying dead people) and the carriers stopped, and he said: "Young man, I tell you, stand up." And the dead man sat up and started to talk, and he [Jesus] gave him [the deceased] to his mother.	[13] When the Lord saw her, his heart went out to her and he said, "Don't cry." [14] Then he went up and touched the coffin, and those carrying it stood still. He said, "Young man, I say to you, get up!" [15] The dead man sat up and began to talk, and Jesus gave him back to his mother.	[13] When the Lord saw her, his heart was filled with pity for her, and he said to her, "Don't cry." [14] Then he walked over and touched the coffin, and the men carrying it stopped. Jesus said, "Young man! Get up, I tell you!" [15] The dead man sat up and began to talk, and Jesus gave him back to his mother.	

| 16–17 All were filled with fear and praised God saying: "A great prophet has arisen among us" and "God has visited his people." And this word about him went out into all of Judea and in all the surrounding region. | 16 They were all filled with awe and praised God. "A great prophet has appeared among us," they said. "God has come to help his people." 17 This news about Jesus spread throughout Judea and the surrounding country. | 16 They all were filled with fear and praised God. "A great prophet has appeared among us!" they said; "God has come to save his people!" 17 This news about Jesus went out through all the country and the surrounding territory. | |

Develop a communication chart of this passage.

Text	Communicated Ideas	Context
11And-it-happened soon afterwards he-went into a town named Nain and with him came his disciples and a big crowd.		
12As they came near to the gate of the town, and see/look, there was they carried a dead person, the only son of his mother, and she was a widow, and a lot of people from the town were with her.		

^{13–15} And when the Lord saw her, he had compassion with her and said to her "don't cry." And he drew near and touched the stretcher (stretcher for carrying dead people) and the carriers stopped, and he said: "Young man, I tell you, stand up." And the dead man sat up and started to talk, and he [Jesus] gave him [the deceased] to his mother.		
^{16–17} All were filled with fear and praised God saying: "A great prophet has arisen among us" and "God has visited his people." And this word about him went out into all of Judea and in all the surrounding region.		

IVP Bible Background Commentary[3]

Luke 7:11–17 Interrupting a Funeral

Interrupting a funeral was a blatant breach of Jewish law and custom; touching the bier exposed a person to a day's uncleanness (Num 19:21–22); touching the corpse exposed him to a week's uncleanness (cf. Num 5:2–3; 19:11–20). But in Jesus' case, the influence goes in the other direction.

7:11–12 People customarily dropped whatever they were doing and joined in a funeral procession when it passed by. For a widow's only son to die before she did was considered extremely tragic; it also left her dependent on public charity for support unless she had other relatives of means.

7:13 According to custom the bereaved mother would walk in front of the bier, so Jesus would meet her first. Philosophers often tried to console the bereaved

---

[3] Keener, Craig S. 1993. *The IVP Bible background commentary: New Testament.* Downers Grove, Ill.: InterVarsity.

by saying, "Do not grieve, for it will do no good." Jesus' approach is entirely different: he removes the cause of bereavement (1 Kings 17:17–24).

7:14 By touching even the bier, a stretcher on which the body was borne (Jewish custom did not use a closed coffin), Jesus would contract corpse-uncleanness, the severest form of ritual impurity in Judaism. Only those closest to the deceased were expected to expose themselves to this impurity. The young man had not been dead long, because it was necessary to wash, anoint, wrap, mourn over, and then bury the body as quickly as possible to avoid the stench of decomposition.

7:15–17 God had used several earlier prophets (Elijah and Elisha) to resuscitate the dead, but it was a rare miracle. The few pagan stories of resuscitations, especially from the third century A.D. (from Philostratus and Apuleius), are later and not validated by eyewitnesses as the Gospel accounts are; they also often exhibit features missing here, such as reports from the underworld.

Lesson 22

Different Contributions to Relevance in a Text

We'll be famous!

One morning, John and Peter heard that another visitor was coming to speak that afternoon. Peter wondered if this one would be more interesting than the last one who had put John to sleep! Mr. Azi, the guest speaker from a Christian radio station, was introduced and then began by saying, "Today there are many free computer programs available to help you. All you have to do is to download them from the internet." He then went on to explain how freeware works and why people were willing to give away free programs. He continued to explain about freeware at great length. After five minutes or so, John hissed at Peter, "Why in the world is he telling us all this?"

The words were no sooner out of his mouth than Mr. Azi said, "Now I'm going to tell you why I've come to talk to you today! I know you all want to make recordings of your church choirs. There is a free computer program called Audacity, and if you download it, you will be able to record music and then edit it to cut out any unwanted parts. You can record your Bible stories, too, and then put the stories and music together. You can make your own Bible story CDs with music!"

John happened to be a choir director, and he immediately began thinking of the possibilities. He smiled at Peter and said, "We'll be famous!"

GROUP DISCUSSION

What do you think John and Peter thought was the most important part of Mr. Azi's speech?

Not all parts of a text contribute to relevance in the same way

Texts can be as short as a word, like "Stop!" or as long as a whole book. No matter how long or short, we understand longer texts as units that achieve relevance as a whole. Each part contributes to that overall relevance, but in different ways.

Some parts of a text mainly serve to raise expectations of relevance. This kind of information is often given at the beginning of a text, but it can also occur within a text. For example, the story at the beginning of the lesson starts with "One morning, John and Peter heard that there was another visiting speaker coming that afternoon." This provides context for the rest of the text by letting us know what the story is going to be about and when it takes place. We expect the story to continue by telling us something about this speaker. If the story started with "Peter wondered if this one would be more interesting than the last one who had put John to sleep!," we would not be able to understand what was going on. If the story stopped at this point, our expectations of relevance would not have been filled. Both of these sentences raise more expectations of relevance than they fulfill. Until our expectations of relevance are fulfilled, the communication seems incomplete.

Information that mainly raises expectations of relevance does not lead to many cognitive benefits in itself, but it contributes to the overall relevance of the communication by providing context for what comes later. The more information a speaker asks us to process, the more our expectations of relevance increase. If a speaker is asking us to process information, we can expect the benefits to be greater than the processing effort.

Other parts of a text fill those expectations and trigger lots of cognitive benefits immediately. For example, in the story when Mr. Azi says "Today there are many freeware programs available to help you," it fills some of the expectations of relevance created by the earlier information: we now know why he came and what he will be talking about. It leads more directly to some cognitive benefits, but we still wonder what the point of the story will be. If Mr. Azi had stopped there, the participants would have been disappointed. When he says, "There is a freeware program called Audacity and when you download it, you can record music," Peter and John could think of many implications for their own work, so they suddenly were able to derive enough cognitive benefits to justify the effort they used to process the earlier utterances. They felt they understood why Mr. Azi has come. The communication seemed complete.

Information in a text falls on a scale between raising expectations and filling them. In addition, the same information can fill some expectations and raise others at the same time.

EXERCISES

Go through the texts below and explain how expectations of relevance are raised and filled. You may benefit from looking up the passages in their larger context. Remember, some information leads to more cognitive benefits than other information, and any part of a text that has already been processed provides context for the next part of the text.

1. Jesus sat down opposite the place where the offerings were put and watched the crowd putting their money into the temple treasury. Many rich people threw in large amounts. But a poor widow came and put in two very small copper coins, worth only a fraction of a penny. Calling his disciples to him, Jesus said, "I tell you the truth, this poor widow has put more into the treasury than all the others. They all gave out of their wealth; but she, out of her poverty, put in everything—all she had to live on." (Mk 12:41–44 NIV).

2. If I must boast, I will boast of the things that show my weakness. The God and Father of the Lord Jesus, who is to be praised forever, knows that I am not lying. In Damascus, the governor under King Aretas guarded the city of Damascus in order to seize me, but I was let down in a basket through a window in the wall, and escaped from his hands (2 Cor 11:30–33 RSV).

Sometimes speakers give special guidance

There are many ways speakers can indicate the way they intend the parts of a text to contribute to relevance. They can tell hearers explicitly what is most relevant, as in the story at the beginning of this lesson when Mr. Azi said, "Now I'm going to tell you why I've come to talk to you." In oral communication, intonation and stress can communicate what is most important. For example, pastors often speak louder at the most directly relevant part of their sermon. In a classroom, a teacher might indicate the most directly relevant part of a lecture by writing it on a blackboard. Languages also have structures that speakers can use to guide hearers to the way different parts of their text are meant to be relevant. Audiences take in these language clues along with the other clues from the context to understand the speaker's meaning.

One way speakers can indicate the way information contributes to relevance is by verb forms. They can use certain verb forms to signal information that directly fills expectations of relevance, and other verb forms to signal information that mainly raises expectations. For example in English, verbs like *had eaten* raise expectations that the speaker is going to say something about what happened next. These expectations can be filled with other verb forms, such as the past tense:

I had eaten my dinner and suddenly I felt very sleepy.

Sometimes speakers give clues about contributions to relevance by the way they use clauses. *Clauses* are the smallest grammatical unit that can be used to describe an event, process, or state. There are two types of clauses: main clauses and dependent clauses. Main clauses express thoughts that are complete enough to occur on their own. This is not the case for dependent clauses. For example, "if you're going to town" is a dependent clause and hearers expect a main clause to be able to understand what the speaker wants to communicate.

In sentences with several clauses, often speakers express the most directly relevant information in the main clause. Often they use dependent clauses to express information that gives the context for the information in the main clause, such as when or where or why the action of the main clause occurred. For example, in the sentence, "After five minutes or so had passed, John hissed at Peter," the first clause is dependent. It gives the context for the second clause, which is the main clause.

Clauses are the smallest grammatical unit that can be used to describe an event, process, or state.
Main clauses can occur alone.
Dependent clauses cannot.

EXERCISE

Underline the dependent clauses:

1. When you download Audacity, you will be able to record music or speech.
2. I think I will leave early, unless you give me a good reason why I should not.
3. I will go to the market if I can find a taxi.
4. Since it is Saturday, I am not working on translation.

Although speakers often use dependent clauses to indicate information that raises expectations of relevance, this is not always the case. Sometimes they express the most directly relevant part of a sentence in a dependent clause. For example, in a story of a woman who was so angry at her husband she left him, the author writes, "The door slammed while she dashed out of the room in anger." In the context of the story, the most directly relevant part of the sentence is that the woman dashed out of the room in anger, not that the door slammed. That is what fulfills the readers' expectations of cognitive effects. They may think, "Oh! So she left him in the end!" The fact that the door slammed does not fulfill those expectations.

In some languages, speakers can indicate the relevance of information by using a short word or suffix whose meaning is difficult to define on its own. We refer to these as *particles*. Their role is to communicate how to process what follows. Some particles alert the audience to the way that part of the text contributes to relevance. For example, in the Adioukrou language of Côte d'Ivoire, if a clause or phrase ends with the particle *a*, in most cases the audience will expect the clause to communicate information that mainly raises expectations of relevance. That is, they will expect the speaker to say something more before they feel satisfied that they have understood. This clue reduces the processing effort for the audience.

A particle is a short word or suffix whose meaning is difficult to define on its own.

Speakers may give extra clues about the most relevant information of a sentence by placing it in a construction like "It was…that…". For example, if the audience knows that someone built a house, but does not know who did it, a speaker might say:

It was John who built the house.

This construction gives a clue that the most relevant information is "John" and not another part of the sentence. On the other hand, if the audience knew that John had been building something, but wasn't sure what it was he was building, a speaker might say:

It was a house that John built.

In this case, it is clear that "a house" is the most directly relevant part of the sentence.

In some languages, speakers move a word or words out of their normal place in a sentence to the front. Often in English, the speaker puts a pronoun in its normal place. For example, instead of saying "She ate all of the apple," a speaker could say, *"The apple*, she ate the whole thing."* This is referred to as *front-shifting*. The front-shifted word or words raise expectations of relevance, which the rest of the sentence fulfills.

> Front-shifting is shifting a word or words from their normal place in the sentence to the beginning.

Speakers have many ways of indicating the way information contributes to relevance, and hearers understand it by a number of clues coming together. Often, this is clear without using any special features of the language to do so.

EXERCISES

In one of your texts in your language:

1. Identify three dependent clauses.
2. Identify any particles that occur.
3. Identify any front-shifted parts of sentences.
4. Explain how these structures contribute to relevance: do they signal that expectations should be raised or fulfilled?

Raising and filling expectations of relevance in translation

Translators need to be sure that their translations lead their audiences to the main point of the text without confusion. The language they are translating into may indicate degrees of relevance in different ways than the language they are translating from. For example, in many Bantu languages in Africa, the part of a sentence that contributes most to relevance is placed at the end. In English, it is placed at the beginning. In English, Matthew 3:9d reads, "Out of these stones God can raise up children to Abraham" (NIV). If translators followed this word order in many Bantu languages, readers would not realize that the main relevance is contributed by the phrase "out of these stones." They would understand the main relevance to be "children to Abraham". To communicate the intended meaning in Bantu languages, translators would have to reverse the order and say, "God can raise up children to Abraham out of these stones."[3]

Summary

Not all parts of a text are intended to be equally relevant. Some parts serve to provide the context for other parts and so are only indirectly relevant. They raise expectations of relevance. Other parts of a text lead directly to cognitive benefits, fulfilling those expectations of relevance. Sometimes speakers give special guidance to their audience in how different parts of a text contribute to relevance. They have many means at their disposal to do so: intonation, the words they use, structures of the language, and so forth. They use a combination of these clues to get their message across in a relevant way.

> **So what?**
>
> Translators need to translate in such a way that audiences are led to the main point of the text without confusion.

Assignment

1. What part of the following sentences raises expectations of cognitive benefits? What part fulfills those expectations, that is, leads directly to cognitive benefits?
   a. In the cupboard under the sink is where I put the frying pan.
   b. When I was sixteen, I got my first job.

2. Read Mark 6:45–52. Underline the parts that fulfill expectations of relevance and give the most direct cognitive benefits.

> [45] Immediately Jesus made his disciples get into the boat and go on ahead of him to Bethsaida, while he dismissed the crowd. [46] After leaving them, he went up on a mountainside to pray. [47] When evening came, the boat was in the middle of the lake, and he was alone on land. [48] He saw the disciples straining at the oars, because the wind was against them. About the fourth watch of the night he went out to them, walking on the lake. He was about to pass by them, [49] but when they saw him walking on the lake, they thought he was a ghost. They cried out, [50] because they all saw him and were terrified. Immediately he spoke to them and said, "Take courage! It is I. Don't be afraid." [51] Then he climbed into the boat with them, and the wind died down. They were completely amazed, [52] for they had not understood about the loaves; their hearts were hardened (NIV).

[2] Levinsohn, Stephen. 2008. Bible translation and the audience's language type. Paper presented at BT08, European Training Program, Horsleys Green, UK, Feb 4–6, 2008.

Work Session L: Expectations of Relevance in your Texts

1. Look at your text(s) and explain how expectations of relevance are raised and filled.
2. Can you identify clues from the text that guide the audience's expectations?

Work Session M: Retelling Order

Communicators may tell things out of the order in which they happened to guide hearers to the intended interpretation. Translators need to be sure they understand the order in which events happened because they cannot translate what they do not understand. In some languages, it may not be possible to tell events out of the order in which they happened. In these cases, translators may need to make adjustments.

1. Read this story:
    > At that time Herod the tetrarch heard the reports about Jesus, and he said to his attendants, "This is John the Baptist; he has risen from the dead! That is why miraculous powers are at work in him."
    >
    > Now Herod had arrested John and bound him and put him in prison because of Herodias, his brother Philip's wife· for John had been saying to him: "It is not lawful for you to have her." Herod wanted to kill John, but he was afraid of the people, because they considered him a prophet.
    >
    > On Herod's birthday the daughter of Herodias danced for them and pleased Herod so much that he promised with an oath to give her whatever she asked. Prompted by her mother, she said, "Give me here on a platter the head of John the Baptist." The king was distressed, but because of his oaths and his dinner guests, he ordered that her request be granted and had John beheaded in the prison. His head was brought in on a platter and given to the girl, who carried it to her mother. John's disciples came and took his body and buried it. Then they went and told Jesus (Mt 14:3–12 NIV).

    This is the order in which the events are retold:
    a. Herod governs in Galilee.
    b. Herod hears Jesus.
    c. Herod tells his servants "John has risen from the dead."
    d. Herod arrests and imprisons John.
    e. John tells Herod, "You should not have that woman as your wife."
    f. Herod has his birthday.
    g. Herod's daughter dances.
    h. Herod makes a promise.
    i. The mother tells her daughter to ask for John's head.
    j. The daughter asks for John's head.
    k. Herod gets sad.
    l. Herod gives the order to behead John.
    m. They take John's head to the daughter on a plate.
    n. The daughter gives the head on a plate to the mother.

    o. John's followers arrive.

    p. John's followers take his body and bury it.

    q. John's followers tell Jesus about John's death.

Reorder them in the order in which they occurred.

Discuss what the author achieves by telling the events out of the order in which they happened.

2.   Identify the parts of this story that are retold out of order. Discuss what the author achieves by telling the events out of the order in which they happened.

²⁶ They sailed to the region of the Gerasenes, which is across the lake from Galilee. ²⁷ When Jesus stepped ashore, he was met by a demon-possessed man from the town. For a long time this man had not worn clothes or lived in a house, but had lived in the tombs. ²⁸ When he saw Jesus, he cried out and fell at his feet, shouting at the top of his voice, "What do you want with me, Jesus, Son of the Most High God? I beg you, don't torture me!" ²⁹ For Jesus had commanded the evil spirit to come out of the man. Many times it had seized him, and though he was chained hand and foot and kept under guard, he had broken his chains and had been driven by the demon into solitary places. ³⁰ Jesus asked him, "What is your name?" "Legion," he replied, because many demons had gone into him. ³¹ And they begged him repeatedly not to order them to go into the Abyss. ³² A large herd of pigs was feeding there on the hillside. The demons begged Jesus to let them go into them, and he gave them permission. ³³ When the demons came out of the man, they went into the pigs, and the herd rushed down the steep bank into the lake and was drowned.

³⁴ When those tending the pigs saw what had happened, they ran off and reported this in the town and countryside, ³⁵ and the people went out to see what had happened. When they came to Jesus, they found the man from whom the demons had gone out, sitting at Jesus' feet, dressed and in his right mind; and they were afraid. ³⁶ Those who had seen it told the people how the demon-possessed man had been cured. ³⁷ Then all the people of the region of the Gerasenes asked Jesus to leave them, because they were overcome with fear. So he got into the boat and left.

³⁸ The man from whom the demons had gone out begged to go with him, but Jesus sent him away, saying, ³⁹ "Return home and tell how much God has done for you." So the man went away and told all over town how much Jesus had done for him (Lk 8:26–39 NIV).

Lesson 23

Communicating Additional Layers of Meaning

The King James Bible

There was a lively discussion going on down the hall that evening after the session. The participants were getting to know each other well after living together for so many days. The program was very intense with sessions from morning until evening, and many of them were missing their families. People became irritated easily.

During the day, one of the leaders had said that the King James Bible was the most widely sold book in the world. Peter and John went on to discuss which version of the Bible was the best for their churches today.

John: My father always used the King James. He was a wise man. And besides, isn't it the most widely sold book in the world?

Peter: But we do not speak English like that anymore. Hast thou not noticed? Only people who have been in church all their lives understand the King James, and even they do not always.

John: Excuse me! Would you be so kind as to stop insulting the true Bible? Blasphemy is unforgivable, you know.

Peter: Do you know what you are talking about?

John: What was good enough for St. Paul is good enough for me!

GROUP DISCUSSION

1. What did John mean when he said, "Isn't it the most widely sold book in the world?"
2. What did Peter mean when he said, "Hast thou not noticed?" Was he really wanting to know whether John had noticed, or was he meaning something else?
3. What did John mean when he said, "Excuse me!" Was he commanding Peter to excuse him? Requesting him to do so? Or did he mean something else entirely?
4. What did John mean when he said, "Would you be so kind as to stop insulting the true Bible?" Did he expect a yes or no answer? What did he mean?

5. What did Peter mean when he said, "Do you know what you're talking about?"
6. When John said "What was good enough for St. Paul is good enough for me!" he was retelling what someone had said earlier. Did he agree with it or disagree with this statement?

Communicating attitudes towards what we say

In addition to the content of what we say, we can also communicate an attitude towards that content and this can affect the intended meaning significantly.

Sometimes we express an attitude explicitly. For example, imagine I just bought a used car and the salesperson said, "What a great deal!" After driving it one day, the car breaks down and I say, "What a great deal! Ridiculous!" I have made it very clear by the second part of what I said that I do not agree with the first part at all. Although I am retelling what the salesperson said, I am distancing myself from it.

We can also communicate an attitude implicitly. For example, in the same situation, I might say, "What a great deal!" Even without saying it explicitly, hearers would understand that I am distancing myself from what the salesman said, since no one would consider a car that breaks down the first day a great deal. We refer to this as *irony*. I am communicating, "(It's ridiculous to say that) it's a great deal." This is the only interpretation that makes sense in the context, so I can count on my audience to understand what I mean.

> Irony is when speakers retell what was said or thought earlier and distance themselves from it, without doing so explicitly.

On the other hand, we may communicate a positive attitude toward what we say. Suppose that I buy a used car for a low price, again on the salesperson's recommendation that it is a great deal. I take a long trip in it, and the car shows no signs of problems. I say, "What a great deal!" In this context, hearers would understand that I am echoing the thoughts of the dealer with an approving attitude.

Another way we can communicate an attitude when we communicate orally is by our intonation. For example, if we say "Really," it could be with a questioning attitude, an exasperated attitude, or an attitude of agreement. We also use facial features and gestures. In written communication, sometimes punctuation can communicate these things, but not always.

EXERCISES

1. Say this sentence with as many different intonations as you can. Give a context in which each one would make sense and say what would be understood: "He left yesterday."

2. I am intent on buying a used car that is clearly not a good one. My friend says, "Go ahead and waste your money!" What is my friend communicating? How do you know?

3. In Matthew 27:28–30, explain what the soldiers were communicating when they said "Long live the King of the Jews!" Tell which clues guided you to understand them in this way.

> ^{28} They stripped off his clothes and put a scarlet robe on him. ^{29} Then they made a crown out of thorny branches and placed it on his head, and put a stick in his right hand; then they knelt before him and made fun of him. "Long live the King of the Jews!" they said. ^{30} They spat on him, and took the stick and hit him over the head (TEV).

4. In 1 Kings 22, Jehoshaphat and the king of Israel called on their prophets to advise them whether or not to attack Ramoth Gilead. All four hundred of them said that they should attack and God would make them victorious. Jehoshaphat was still not convinced and asked if there was any other prophet they could ask. The king of Israel replied, "There is still one other by whom we may inquire of the LORD, Micaiah son of Imlah; but I hate him, for he never prophesies anything favorable about me, but only disaster" (22:8). They sent a messenger to get Micaiah. Read what happened:

> ^{13} The messenger who had gone to summon Micaiah said to him, "Look, the words of the prophets with one accord are favorable to the king; let your word be like the word of one of them, and speak favorably." ^{14} But Micaiah said, "As the LORD lives, whatever the LORD says to me, that I will speak."
>
> ^{15} When he had come to the king, the king said to him, "Micaiah, shall we go to Remoth Gilead to battle, or shall we refrain?" He answered him, "Go up and triumph; the LORD will give it into the hand of the king." ^{16} But the king said to him, "How many times must I make you swear to tell me nothing but the truth in the name of the LORD?"
>
> ^{17} Then Micaiah said, "I saw all Israel scattered on the mountains, like sheep that have no shepherd; and the LORD said, 'These have no master; let each one go home in peace.' " ^{18} The king of Israel said to Jehoshaphat, "Did I not tell you that he would not prophesy anything favorable about me, but only disaster?"

a. Why did the king reply as he did in verse 16? How did he understand what Micaiah said in verse 15?
b. What tone of voice do you think Micaiah used?
c. How could you help your audience understand what Micaiah meant in verse 15?

Questions and additional layers of meaning

Questions are typically requests for information. They are thoughts that need to be completed to be relevant. For example, if I ask "Where are you going?" I expect to have a location provided, as in "I'm going to the store." The answer to this question is relevant to me. My thought about where you're going is incomplete, and your answer completes it.

Sometimes the answer to a question is relevant to the hearer rather than the speaker. For example, teachers ask students questions they already know the answers to. Why? Because by answering, the student shows the teacher they understand the material. The answer is relevant to the student—to get a good grade!

Whenever speakers ask questions they already know the answer to, they may be communicating additional layers of meaning. In the story at the beginning of the lesson when John said, "Isn't it the most widely sold book in the world?" Peter knew that John was not asking whether or not this statement was true, because they had already agreed on that point. John was saying this to support his belief that the KJV was the best translation available. At the same time, he was reminding Peter of this fact and communicating that he should have known this, that everyone knows this, and so forth. If all John wanted to do was to state that this was true, he could have done that with the simple statement, "This is the most widely sold book in the world." This would have been easier for Peter to process.

Hearers use contextual information as they process the meaning of questions. Some of this contextual information is cultural. Questions themselves are used in different ways by different cultures. In some cultures, if someone says "Would you like something to eat?" people would not understand it as a genuine question. They would understand the speaker to mean that he did not want to offer him any food at all. If he wanted to offer food, he would use a command, "Come eat!" Sometimes questions that are intended to ask for information may be understood as accusations. For example, in many places in Africa if a wallet goes missing and someone asks the house cleaner, "Have you seen my wallet?" the house cleaner would consider it an accusation rather than as a request for information.

> To understand questions, ask:
> Who is the answer relevant to?
> Is anything else being communicated?

Exercises

1. Imagine a young girl comes into the kitchen in her house. Her mother could ask any of these questions. What does each one communicate? Who is the answer of the question relevant to? Are any additional layers of meaning being communicated? If so, what are they?
   a. Did you buy milk?
   b. Who bought the milk?
   c. Who told you that you could take money from my wallet?

2. Think of situations in which someone might ask the following questions. What is the speaker trying to communicate by the question? Who is the answer relevant to? Is any extra meaning being communicated by using a question form? Is so, what is it?
   a. Mother to son: Why did you bring all this mud into the house?
   b. How many languages already have the Bible in Asia?
   c. Why don't you open the window?
   d. Would you like some salt?

3. What is the biblical author communicating by the following questions? (Notice that some versions of the Bible do not translate these as questions.) Who are they relevant to? If not the speaker, is any extra meaning being communicated? If so, what is it?
   a. For what does it profit a man, to gain the whole world and forfeit his life? For what can a man give in return for his life? (Mk 8:36–37 RSV).
   b. 'Lord, Lord, did we not prophesy in your name, and cast out demons in your name, and do many mighty works in your name?' (Mt 7:22 RSV).
   c. Then what becomes of our boasting? It is excluded. On what principle? On the principle of works? No, but on the principle of faith (Rom 3:27 RSV).
   d. Who shall separate us from the love of Christ? Shall tribulation, or distress, or persecution, or famine, or nakedness, or peril, or sword? (Rom 8:35–36 RSV).

Different meanings communicated by command forms

The typical function of command forms is to get someone to do something. The thing that is expressed is thought to be both desired and possible. But desirable to whom? They may be desirable to the speaker. For example, when a person says "Bring me a chair," he or she communicates, "I would like you to bring me a chair." In other cases speakers use command forms to indicate something that is desirable for the hearer. For example, "Take an umbrella with you when you go." The speaker is telling the hearer, "It would be desirable for you and you are able to take an umbrella with you when you go." Often we call these kinds of command forms advice.

Not all command forms communicate commands. Imagine this conversation at the train station:

> Woman to the man at the information booth: Which train goes to London?
> Man at the information booth: Take the train on Platform 4.

Speakers may use command forms to make simple statements.
The man is not commanding the woman to take this train. He
probably does not care what she does. He is simply providing information using a command form. He is really saying, "It is desirable for you and within your ability to board the train on Platform 4."

In all cases, the search for relevance and contextual information leads us to the intended meaning. After we have understood what a speaker is communicating by a command form, we can label it as a plea, a command, advice, or a prayer. Before we have understood the meaning, all we know is that it is a command form. For example, "Give him the money," could mean different things in different situations:

- A child might be asking his parents for money, and the mother may say this to her husband to plead on her child's behalf. In this case it is a plea or request.
- An employer may say this to the cashier when an employee is asking for money. In this case, it is a command.
- Peter might be discussing with John whether it would be good for him to give money to some friend of theirs. In this case it is advice.

Our knowledge of the relationship of the speaker to the hearer is one part of the contextual information we use to assess the strength of the command. A suggestion by a high-ranking person might well be understood as a command. In prayers, we often use commands to request help from God. When neither party has the ability to perform the action, a command is simply a wish, as in "Get well soon".

Often information from the culture affects how command forms are interpreted. For example, in many language communities in Côte d'Ivoire, commands are the polite way to make a request.

EXERCISE

To whom are the commands in the examples below relevant? How strong is the command? Is it an order, a request, a wish, or what? Explain your response.

- Husband to wife: Please shut the window. I am getting cold.
- Pedestrian to someone asking for directions: If you want to get to John's garage, take the first left at the lights.
- Pastor to congregation: Be seated.

> To understand commands, ask:
> * Who is the action desirable for?
> * Who is able to bring about the action?
> * Is anything else being communicated?

Translating additional layers of meaning

Translators need to understand any additional layers of meaning the biblical authors are communicating. To do this, they need to know the context. For example, in The Parable of the Talents in Matthew 25:26–27, recognizing the speaker's attitude affects the meaning we understand.

> The lazy servant: "Master," he said, "I knew that you are a hard man, harvesting where you have not sown and gathering where you have not scattered seed…"

> The master: "You wicked, lazy servant! So you knew that I harvest where I have not sown and gather where I have not scattered seed? Well then, you should have…" (NIV).

It is unlikely that the master is confessing to having behaved in this way. It is much more likely that he is retelling what the servant accused him of and distancing himself from it. He is saying something like, "You believe that I reap where I have not sowed and gather where I have not winnowed. Even if this is what you believe about me, you should have…."

Once translators understand the meaning of the original, they need to think about how to communicate that meaning to their audience. How can their text give their audience the best clues to the intended meaning? Questions may not be best translated as questions, and commands may not be best translated as commands. Translators also need to be alert to contextual mismatches and adjust them so that their audience is able to understand the additional layers of meaning the biblical authors intend.

Summary

We can communicate layers of meaning when we speak in addition to the content of what we say in several ways. We can communicate an attitude towards what we say, either agreeing with it strongly or disagreeing with it. We can use sentences in ways that communicate additional layers of meaning. Whenever speakers use questions but are not requesting information, we should look for additional layers of meaning. We do this because it requires more effort to process than a simple statement would require. Speakers may use sentences in command form to communicate things that are desirable and possible for either the speaker or hearer. Context guides hearers to recognize and uncover any additional layers of meaning.

> **So what?**
>
> ## Translators need to be aware of additional layers of meaning in order to communicate them to their audiences.

Assignment

1. What does the speaker mean by the following questions? If he could have said it in a statement, is any extra meaning communicated by the question form? Look up the verses and read them in context, if necessary.
   a. Job 38:4 Where were you when I laid the foundation of the earth? (RSV).
   b. John 18:35 "Am I a Jew?" Pilate replied (NIV).
   c. John 18:38 "What is truth?" Pilate asked (RSV).
2. What do you think the speakers' attitude is in these utterances? Do they agree or disagree with what they are saying? What do they mean?
   a. Mother to child who has just broken a plate: "Well, that's great!"
   b. John, speaking of a member of his translation team: "He knows everything about computers, even how to turn them on!"
3. When Jesus was crucified, Pilate put a sign on his cross which said, "Jesus of Nazareth, The King of the Jews." The Jewish leaders were unhappy. They wanted him to change the sign to say that he claimed to be the king of the Jews (Jn 19:17, 21). Was Pilate describing or retelling? What are the implications? Why did the Jewish leaders want him to add "He claimed to be the King of the Jews?" How did this affect what people might understand?
4. Find two places in Matthew 15:21–28 where Jesus may be echoing the beliefs of others rather than expressing his own beliefs.

Work Session N: Communicating Jonah 1:1–7

Translate Jonah 1:1–7 using Approach #3—a translation that is somewhat adjusted to the audience's context. Use the translation process summarized in Appendix 3. You may skip the oral recording of your translation if you wish. Some helps are provided in this chapter.

Comparing Versions	Jonah 1:1–7			
ESV	**NIV**	**TEV (GNB)**	**NLT**	**Your comments**
¹ Now the word of the LORD came to Jonah the son of Amittai, saying,	¹ The word of the LORD came to Jonah son of Amittai:	¹ One day the LORD spoke to Jonah son of Amittai.	¹ The LORD gave this message to Jonah son of Amittai:	
² "Arise, go to Nineveh, that great city, and call out against it, for their evil has come up before me."	² "Go to the great city of Nineveh and preach against it, because its wickedness has come up before me."	² He said, "Go to Nineveh, that great city, and speak out against it; I am aware of how wicked its people are."	² "Get up and go to the great city of Nineveh! Announce my judgment against it because I have seen how wicked its people are."	
³ But Jonah rose to flee to Tarshish from the presence of the LORD. He went down to Joppa and found a ship going to Tarshish. So he paid the fare and went on board, to go with them to Tarshish, away from the presence of the LORD.	³ But Jonah ran away from the LORD and headed for Tarshish. He went down to Joppa, where he found a ship bound for that port. After paying the fare, he went aboard and sailed for Tarshish to flee from the LORD.	³ Jonah, however, set out in the opposite direction in order to get away from the LORD. He went to Joppa, where he found a ship about to go to Spain. He paid his fare and went aboard with the crew to sail to Spain, where he would be away from the LORD.	³ But Jonah got up and went in the opposite direction in order to get away from the LORD. He went down to the sea-coast, to the port of Joppa, where he found a ship leaving for Tarshish. He bought a ticket and went on board, hoping that by going away to the west he could escape from the LORD.	

⁴ But the LORD hurled a great wind upon the sea, and there was a mighty tempest on the sea, so that the ship threatened to break up.	⁴ Then the LORD sent a great wind on the sea, and such a violent storm arose that the ship threatened to break up.	⁴ But the LORD sent a strong wind on the sea, and the storm was so violent that the ship was in danger of breaking up.	⁴ But as the ship was sailing along, suddenly the LORD flung a powerful wind over the sea, causing a violent storm that threatened to send them to the bottom.	
⁵ Then the mariners [=sailors] were afraid, and each cried out to his god. And they hurled the cargo that was in the ship into the sea to lighten it for them. But Jonah had gone down into the inner part of the ship and had lain down and was fast asleep.	⁵ All the sailors were afraid and each cried out to his own god. And they threw the cargo into the sea to lighten the ship. But Jonah had gone below deck, where he lay down and fell into a deep sleep.	⁵ The sailors were terrified and cried out for help, each one to his own god. Then, in order to lessen the danger, they threw the cargo overboard. Meanwhile, Jonah had gone below and was lying in the ship's hold, sound asleep.	⁵ Fearing for their lives, the desperate sailors shouted to their gods for help and threw the cargo overboard to lighten the ship. And all this time Jonah was sound asleep down in the hold.	
⁶ So the captain came and said to him, "What do you mean, you sleeper? Arise, call out to your god! Perhaps the god will give a thought to us, that we may not perish."	⁶ The captain went to him and said, "How can you sleep? Get up and call on your god! Maybe he will take notice of us, and we will not perish."	⁶ The captain found him there and said to him, "What are you doing asleep? Get up and pray to your god for help. Maybe he will feel sorry for us and spare our lives."	⁶ So the captain went down after him. "How can you sleep at a time like this?" he shouted. "Get up and pray to your god! Maybe he will have mercy on us and spare our lives."	

[7] And they said to one another, Come, let us cast lots, that we may know on whose account this evil has come upon us. So they cast lots, and the lot fell on Jonah.	[7] Then the sailors said to each other, "Come, let us cast lots to find out who is responsible for this calamity." They cast lots and the lot fell on Jonah.	[7] The sailors said to each other, "Let's draw lots and find out who is to blame for getting us into this danger." They did so, and Jonah's name was drawn.	[7] Then the crew cast lots to see which of them had offended the gods and caused the terrible storm. When they did this, Jonah lost the toss.	

Communication Chart of Jonah 1:1–7

Text: Jonah 1:1–7	Communicated ideas	Context
[1,2] And-it-was the word of YHWH to Jonah, son of Amittai saying: Get-up go to Nineveh the great city and cry against her _ki_ ('that') her evil deeds have gone up to my face.	God commanded Jonah, the son of Amittai the following: Travel to Nineveh and warn the people of Nineveh that the evil deeds of the people of Nineveh has come to God's special attention. God is about to inflict judgment on the people of Nineveh. God is about to destroy the people of Nineveh. God calls Jonah to be a prophet.	'The word of God' in the prophets was the authoritative speech of God, usually a command or verdict, addressed to someone. God speaks to prophets rather than to normal persons. God tells prophets what to do. A prophet is a devout person who gladly does what God tells him to do. Prophets obey God, otherwise God would not call that person to be a prophet. When God says that the sins of people have come to his special attention, then he is about to inflict judgment on them. Judgment for sin consists of destruction.

³ And-got-up Jonah to-flee to Tarshish away from the face of YHWH And-went-down to Joppa And-found a ship that was going to Tarshish And-gave the coins And-went down into-it to go with them to Tarshish away from the face of YHWH.		
⁴ And-YHWH stirred up a strong wind on the sea And-it-was a great storm on the sea And-the-ship was-about to break up.		
⁵ And-they-feared the seamen and-they-called everyone to his god and-they-threw the containers [jars] that were in the ship into the sea in order to lighten it from them.		
And-Jonah went-down into the farthest-away-place of the vessel [different word from 'ship'] and-laid-down and-slept.		
⁶ And-came-near head of the seamen [other word] and-said to him: What to you sleeping? Get-up cry to your god. Maybe the god will remember us and we will not perish.		
⁷ And-said man to one's friend: 'Come and let us throw lots and we know because of whom this evil is to-us' And-they threw lots and-fell the lot on Jonah.		

Translator's Notes-adapted

Introduction

Jonah was a prophet from the town of Gath Hepher in northern Israel. He was the son of Amittai of the tribe of Zebulon (2 Kings 14:25). He lived while Jeroboam II was the king of Israel. At that time the Assyrians were enemies of the Israelites. Nineveh was the capital city of Assyria. The book of Jonah is the account of how the LORD commanded Jonah to go to Nineveh and tell the people there that their city would soon be destroyed because of their wickedness. However, because the people of Assyria were enemies of Israel, Jonah refused to obey the LORD's command. He did not want to give the people of Nineveh an opportunity to hear this message and to repent. If they did, Jonah knew that the LORD would have mercy on them and spare them.

Book Summary

The book of Jonah shows the LORD's compassion and concern for all people. This is seen in the way he acted toward his servant, Jonah, who was a prophet from Israel. First, the LORD commanded Jonah to go and tell the people of Nineveh that he was going to judge them for their wicked behavior. Since the people of Nineveh were the enemies of Israel, at first Jonah refused to do this and tried to escape by going in the opposite direction, to the city of Tarshish. Jonah was concerned that if he did as the LORD commanded, the people of Nineveh would repent from their sins and then the LORD would have mercy on them and forgive them. This, of course, is what the LORD wanted to happen. And this is what did happen after Jonah finally obeyed the LORD and went to Nineveh. So this book helps us understand the LORD's character and compassion.

Notes

1:1 **The word of the LORD came to Jonah son of Amittai:** The expression the word of the LORD came to Jonah refers to the message which the LORD communicated to Jonah. We do not know how Jonah received this message. It could have been in a vision or a dream, or perhaps the LORD spoke directly to him. **LORD:** LORD represents the Hebrew YHWH, the personal name of God. **Jonah son of Amittai:** Jonah was the son of a man called Amittai. Nothing more is recorded about Jonah's background in this book. The important thing to keep in mind is that he was an Israelite and the LORD told him to deliver a message to the people of Nineveh, who were enemies of the Israelites.

1:2 **Go to the great city of Nineveh:** Nineveh is called a great city because it was very large and many people lived in it. It was so large that it took a person three days to walk through it (3:3). More than 120,000 people lived there (4:11). **Go to...Nineveh:** In Hebrew this verse begins with two verbs *qum* and *lek* which literally mean "arise, go." When the verb *qum* is followed by another motion verb, many scholars believe that it has lost its Word-for-word meaning and that instead

it signals the beginning of an action. In this case it may also signal the urgency of the action, as reflected in "Leave at once for Nineveh" (GW) or "Go at once to Nineveh" (NJPS, NRSV).
Other translations do not include the idea of "rise" at all: Go to…Nineveh (NIV, TEV, CEV).

and preach against it: The rest of the story shows that what Jonah was told to preach was a message which condemned the people of Nineveh. Therefore, expressions such as "cry out against it" (NRSV), or "speak against it" (TEV) show that this was a message of judgment.

it: This refers to the city of Nineveh. Although the text says that Jonah was to preach against "the city of Nineveh," it meant that he was to preach against the people of the city because of the wicked way they were behaving.

its wickedness: Here the wickedness and sinful behavior of the people of Nineveh is referred to as if the city were a person.

has come up before me: Or "has come to my attention." TEV has: "I am aware of how wicked its people are."

1:3 **But:** TEV has: "however". This verse clearly contrasts with verse 2.
Jonah ran away from the LORD: This is literally "to flee from before the face of the LORD," that is, "to flee from the presence of the LORD". As an Israelite, Jonah knew that the LORD was everywhere—yet he tried to flee from his presence.
and headed for Tarshish: Jonah had no intention of obeying the LORD or of going to Nineveh. Instead, he went in the opposite direction, towards the city of Tarshish. This was probably in the country now known as Spain. In Jonah's time, it was considered to be at the western end of the world. Nineveh, however, was northeast of Israel.
He went down to Joppa: Joppa was a city on the coast of the Mediterranean Sea. Ships would stop there to pick up passengers and cargo.
went down: Jonah went from higher land down to the coast.
where he found a ship bound for that port: There in Joppa, Jonah found a ship which was ready to sail to Tarshish. The sailors (the men who worked on the ship) were not Israelites but were probably from the country of Phoenicia.
After paying the fare: The text does not tell us to whom Jonah paid the money. If it is necessary in your language to supply this information, you could say, "to the owner of the ship".
he went aboard and sailed for Tarshish: RSV has: "to go with them to Tarshish". Most commentators agree that "with them" (omitted by the NIV) refers to the sailors. TEV makes this explicit: "went aboard with the crew to sail to Spain".
to flee from the LORD: This is the second time this expression has occurred in this verse. The phrase is probably repeated to emphasize it.

1:4 **Then the LORD sent a great wind on the sea:** The word-for-word expression is that the LORD "hurled" or "threw" the wind on the sea. This image may not be clear or natural in your language. Because it is not a natural image in English, the NIV has: "the LORD sent a great wind". If possible, use a term which expresses how violent and sudden the action was.

and such a violent storm arose that the ship threatened to break up: As a result of the strong wind, the waves started to hit against the ship with great force and the ship was about to break into pieces.

a violent storm: Choose the most natural word in your language to describe a severe storm.

1:5 each cried out to his own god: In Jonah, there is a distinction made between "God"—that is, the LORD—and "god/gods". It is possible that these sailors were from different nations and each nationality had its own gods. However, it is more likely that these sailors were all Phoenicians, who believed in many different gods.

And they threw the cargo into the sea to lighten the ship: As well as praying to their gods to rescue them, they did their best to help the ship remain floating. A heavy ship floats lower in the water than a light ship and therefore has a greater chance of water splashing into it and causing the ship to sink. Therefore, the sailors threw the cargo overboard to make it lighter.

the cargo: If you do not have a term for cargo in your language, you could say "the things the ship was carrying".

But Jonah had gone below deck, where he lay down and fell into a deep sleep: It is not clear whether Jonah went down into the hold of the ship and went to sleep before the storm started or during it. Many English versions retain this ambiguity. Other versions make it clear that it was before the storm. For example, the CEV has "All this time, Jonah was down below deck, sound asleep." Most other versions use the connecting word "Meanwhile", which also makes it clear that Jonah had gone to sleep before the storm. It is recommended that you follow this interpretation.

1:6 The captain went to him: The captain of the ship, that is, the man who was in charge of the ship, found Jonah asleep and was surprised.

How can you sleep? His question to Jonah was not a real question, but a rhetorical one. He was scolding Jonah for being asleep when he should have been praying to his god for help. If rhetorical questions cannot be used in your language for scolding, you may need to use a statement here instead of a question.

Get up and call on your god! The captain ordered Jonah to pray fervently to his god for help. Notice NIV uses "god" without a capital "g". The captain, at this point, did not yet know that Jonah's god was the true God, so he talked about him as if he were just one of many gods.

Maybe he will take notice of us, and we will not perish: The people from the nations near Israel believed that storms were caused and controlled by various gods and that they had the power to stop or even start storms. Therefore, the captain felt that it was very important that everyone on the ship ought to be praying to their gods so the people on board the ship would be spared and not die.

1:7 Then the sailors said to each other: There is a jump in the story at this point. Between 1:6 and 1:7, the sailors had noticed that their prayers did not seem to be working. Also, the captain and Jonah had had time to get back to the deck of the ship. **Come, let us cast lots to find out who is responsible for this calamity:** As the situation became more dangerous and their prayers did not work, the sailors decided that the storm had happened because someone on the ship had done something to offend one of the gods. So they decided to cast lots to find out who the guilty person was.

Come: You should probably not translate this literally. The Hebrew word here has the sense in English of "come on, let us do something".

cast lots: People often cast lots to determine the cause of events which puzzle them. The way the lots were actually cast on this occasion is not known. Perhaps the sailors threw dice or drew straws. Another possibility is that each person's name was written on small tablets or pieces of wood. One of these tablets was then picked at random. The person whose name was on the chosen tablet would be the person who was at fault. You should try, if possible, to use an expression which does not identify a particular method of casting lots.

the lot fell on Jonah: Jonah was picked out by lot. This proved to the others on the ship that he was the one responsible for the storm, or at least that he knew something about why it had happened.

Other Issues

Lesson 24

Special Issues: Names, Weights, Measures, and Money

Have you heard people talking in any of these ways about a translation?

"I don't want to read that new translation of the Bible because they have spelled the name of Jesus like the Catholics spell it."

"I find the translation of the Bible in my language difficult because of all those strange names of people and places. I simply can't pronounce them and so I'm embarrassed to read it aloud in public."

"Why have they taken all the proper names from the Lingala Bible? That is not our language!"

"In the Bible in our language, it says the worker earned a day's wages. In the King James Bible, it says he earned a denarius. I don't trust our translation. It's changed things."

Weights, measures, and money may all be unknown concepts for an audience. Translators need to find ways to express them in the language and help their audience build the concepts. Names are numerous and need to be addressed in a logical and consistent way.

Writing names in the mother tongue

There are over one thousand names in the New Testament, and more than six thousand in the Old Testament. Many names in the Bible have meaning, even the names of Bible books. For example, *Genesis* means *Beginnings*. Translators have several options when translating names, and they may use different solutions for different names. They can translate the meaning of the name in the text, and put the original name in a footnote, or they can put the original name in the text, and the meaning in a footnote. Another alternative is to put both the name and its meaning in the text. For example, "When she gave birth to a son she said, 'This time I will praise the LORD.' So she named him Judah, which means *Praise*" (Gen 29:35). In cultures where names have meanings, providing the meaning of names is particularly important.

Since there are so many names in the Bible, it is important to establish rules for writing them in the receptor language that can be applied consistently throughout the Bible. If you do not have a system for this early in your translation process, an enormous amount time can be wasted trying to correct them all. To develop rules for spelling names, work with church leaders and any review committees. Put a sample of names on the board. As they make choices about the spelling, try to work out general rules that can apply to all proper names.

Some of the possible choices are:

1. Use all the names as they stand from an existing Bible in a more prestigious language that people use.
2. Take the names from a translation people use and apply spelling rules to make them conform to the sound system of the mother tongue, for example:
    a. Two consonants may not occur without a vowel between them. The vowel is taken from the preceding syllable.
    b. The letters *ph* will always be written *f.*
    c. All double letters will be written as a single letter, for example *Zillah* would be written *Zilah.*
3. Names known by people in the area follow Rule 1 above. Unknown names follow Rule 2. Some names that are very similar may need some adjustment, such as Jehoaddah or Jehoaddan.

People can have surprisingly strong emotional reactions to the way things are written in their language, so decisions about how names will be written need to be made with church leaders, reviewers, and other leaders. Start discussing the names of the Bible books and of the Old and New Testament first. Important names, like those for God and Jesus, may need serious discussion, especially in Islamic areas.

Once agreed on, check to make sure that a name is written the same every time it occurs in the text. There are two main ways to do this:

1. In the early stages of the translation project, one way is to post a list of commonly used names on the wall in front of each translator. If they find names that they are not sure they know how to spell, they can write them down in a notebook reserved for this, and discuss it with the translation team at some point in the week. Develop a way of keeping a running record of the names as they are decided. This may be done in a computer file or on index cards in a file box.

2. Computer checks are the only way of being sure that the names are spelled consistently. Checks should be run on each book or product as it is finished. A general check should be done on the whole Bible or New Testament before it is published. Your translation advisor or consultant can help you learn how to do this.

EXERCISES

Use Bible helps to find out the meaning of the italicized names below. All the references are from the RSV.
1. Genesis 38:29 And ever after he was called *Perez.*
2. Ruth 1:20 "Don't call me *Naomi,*" she told them, "Instead call me *Mara.*"
3. Matthew 4:25 And great crowds followed him from Galilee and the *Decapolis* and from Jerusalem and Judea and from beyond the Jordan.
4. 1 Samuel 1:20 She named him *Samuel.*

Money

In most cases, we have a reasonably clear idea of what the Hebrew and Greek words represented in terms of distance, weight, and monetary value. You can find this information in a study Bible, Bible dictionary, or encyclopedia. The Greek and Jewish systems are different, however. For example, one shekel is worth four denari. Some translations give these amounts in terms of the original systems, and others translate them into a system their audience understands more easily. For example, in The Parable of the Talents (Mt 25:14–28), the RSV says the first servant was given five talents. The Good News Bible expresses this as five thousand golden coins.

Figure 26. Jewish coin

GROUP DISCUSSION

1. Compare the way three different versions translate the salary of the workers in the vineyard in Matthew 20:1–18.
2. Imagine you are translating for a language group using Approach #2—a high meaning resemblance translation. Discuss how you would translate the following verses. What extra-textual helps would you provide?
   - Mark 14:5 For this perfume could have been sold for over three hundred denari,… (NASB).
   - Mark 12:42 A poor widow came and put in two small copper coins, which amount to a cent (NASB).
   - Matthew 18:24 …one who owed him ten thousand talents was brought to him (NASB).

Weights and measures

Measurements of length in the Bible were based on the human (male) body. For example, a span is the distance on an outstretched hand from the thumb to the little finger. A cubit is the distance from the elbow to the tip of the index finger. This is approximately 21½ inches or 550 mm. The New Testament uses furlongs, which are 202 yards (185 meters), and miles which were one thousand paces.

EXERCISES

1. Think of your audience and the kind of translation product they prefer. Decide how you are going to translate the following:
   a. Genesis 6:15 This is how you are to make it: The length of the ark three hundred cubits, its breadth fifty cubits, and its height thirty cubits (RSV).
   b. John 11:18 Bethany was nigh unto Jerusalem, about fifteen furlongs off (KJV).
2. Decide how you would translate the following weights or measures into your language, first for church leaders who want to know as much as possible what the original says, and then secondly for an audience of new Christians who are just beginning to understand the Bible.
   a. Matthew 20:9 When those hired about the eleventh hour came, each one received a denarius (NASB).
   b. John 19:39 Nicodemus, who had first come to him by night, also came, bringing a mixture of myrrh and aloes, about a hundred pounds weight (NASB). (See also NIV.)

General principles

1. Know your intended audience.
2. Know whether to use the metric or non-metric system. If your audience needs both, you could put one system in the text and the other in notes.
3. Numbers should normally be rounded off to the nearest round number. The authors did not usually intend to give every minute detail. Processing this detail would lead your audience to expect more benefits than the author intended.
4. Look at a variety of translations and see which is the most appropriate for your audience.
5. Giving modern equivalents of weights and measures works well, but giving the modern equivalent of the value of money does not, because the value of money changes with inflation and devaluations, and this would change the meaning of the text.
6. Translations that use biblical measures and money, and weights and measures should give the receptor culture equivalents at the end of the Bible.

Summary

A system to write names needs to be agreed on by all the groups that make up the intended audience. This will take time and may even cause conflict between groups, especially for important names like Jesus and the names of the books of the Bible. A system needs to be agreed on as early as possible in the translation process so that it can be used. Correcting seven thousand names is a long task! To translate weights, measures, and amounts of money, translators need to understand the amount referred to, and then help the church or community leaders decide the best way to communicate this to their intended audience.

So what?

Translators need to have a system for translating names, weights, measures, and money in Scripture.

Assignment

In Bingola the translation team and the church leaders set up the following rules for writing proper names in Bingolan:

- No two consonants can come together except for *l* or *r* plus another consonant.
- If a vowel needs inserting between or after consonants, then the vowel used is the same as the nearest previous vowel. If there is no previous vowel, then the following vowel is taken.
- *F* or *ph* are always written p (there is no *f* in the language).
- *Sh* is written s, *ch* is written *tch*, *j* is written as *y*, *th* as *t*, *y* as *i*.
- All double letters are written as a single letter.
- No word may end in a consonant. Add a final vowel according to Rule 2.

Now work out how you would write the following proper names in Bingolan:

Artemis	Egypt	Paul
Abednego	Jerusalem	Eliphaz
Ptolemais	Timothy	Cnidus
Nebuchadnezzar		

Lesson 25

From Draft to Publication

Disaster!

David Akosa was a newly appointed translation consultant in Bingola. He had visited a couple of translation projects with a senior consultant, and now for the first time he was off to check translation alone. After a long and tiring journey, he arrived at Sebi, the town where the Katiri translation project had its offices. He was warmly welcomed by the team, and after a good night's sleep, he was ready to start checking the Gospel of Luke.

By 8 a.m., he was sitting around a table with the three translators and a secretary. He started by asking them general questions about the project. He found out that there were about half a million people who spoke Katiri, and that the major churches in the area were the Presbyterians and the Catholics. Having been told that, he was rather surprised to hear that all three translators were from the Baptist church.

When the time came to start checking the translation, the team asked the secretary to make some print-outs of Luke 1. After prayer, the checking started, and they had only got as far as the second verse when one of the translators realized that they were working from an old version that had many mistakes that had already been corrected. After this was sorted out, David noticed three different spellings of Zechariah in the first few verses. The translators admitted that they had not checked for consistency. The checking proceeded slowly until they stopped for a much needed cup of coffee.

During the break, the translators told David that the churches were simply not interested in using the translation. As David listened to the reasons for this, he realized that the church leaders had had no input whatsoever in the choice of the translators, the choice of biblical key terms, the type of translation being produced, or the media in which the translation was being distributed. As David asked about checking the translation with people outside the team, he found that there were no review committees, and that the only people who had seen the translation so far were a handful of members of the local Baptist church.

After the break as they returned to work, an argument broke out between two of the translators about whose fault it was that half of Luke 4 was missing. "Even if it isn't in the computer, I'm sure it is on one of these papers," said the secretary, as he hunted through papers piled in a cupboard. By the end of the morning the whole team was shouting at each other and no one seemed to be in charge. David was more than ready to pack his bags and go home.

GROUP DISCUSSION

Many things had gone wrong in this project. List some of their problems.

The translation process

Making a first draft

Throughout this course, you have learned the process of making a first draft of a Scripture product. Although this takes a lot of time and effort, it is only the first step in the process.

Testing the draft

Translators can usually understand what their translation means, but can anyone else? Early in the process, translators need to find out how their audience understands their translation. Getting this audience perspective is vital to successful work.

One way to get this feedback is by asking someone to do a back-translation of the translation, following the procedure in Appendix 2. A native speaker of the language who did not work on the translation needs to do this, without looking at any Bibles.

Another way to get this kind of feedback is by asking people to read the text aloud, if they are able. Note where they hesitate or stumble, as this may indicate a problem in the translation.

Yet another way to get feedback is to ask questions about what people understand from the translation. In some cultures, people are afraid to answer these comprehension questions because they feel the answers are so obvious, the tester must have another reason for asking, for example, to shame them. It is very important to find a culturally appropriate way to ask about comprehension. Be sure people understand why you are asking them these questions.

To do comprehension checking, use your communication chart of the passage. Read a section of the text and go over the following topics with people from your target audience.

1. Are they *filling out the text* in the intended way? This means identifying the participants correctly, filling in parts of sentences that are left out, understanding the intended senses of words, and so forth. Ask them to tell the text again in their own words. Listen for anything that is missing or incorrect. Listen also for better ways to express things!

2. Are they able to supply the *intended context*? If you have prepared helps to accompany the passage, test these at the same time as you test the translation. Between the text and the helps, are people able to supply the intended context?

    • For the notes, is the new information understandable?
    • Is the new information adequately connected to what the audience already knows?
    • Do the notes help people understand the text?
    • What do people understand by the titles, illustrations, and so forth?

3. Are they able to tell you the *intended implications* the first readers understood from the text? Ask them to tell you the main point(s) of the section.

4. Are they able to tell you the thoughts that were *strengthened* or *eliminated* for the first audience?

Study the feedback from these sessions. Problems in comprehension may be due to the individual, the translation, or contextual mismatches. Some of the feedback will be helpful but not all, so evaluate it carefully and revise your work as necessary.

Initially translators should do testing themselves, but once they have a good feel for their audience, they can train others to do it. They need to train the testers to write down problem areas and explain them to the translators.

GROUP DISCUSSION

1. Have you ever tested a translation? If so, share your experiences. If not, pair up with someone who has.
2. Write three questions you would ask when testing the story of Jesus visiting Simon's house (Lk 7:36–50).

The consultant check

GROUP DISCUSSION

If you are part of an existing translation project, explain how your translation has been checked. Can you see ways of improving this?

All translations must be checked by a translation consultant before they can be published. This is both to assure that the translation is faithful to the original, and also as a way to train the translation team so they improve their translation skills. Translation consultants may also be able to give advice about other aspects of the program, such as linguistic and orthography questions, literacy publications, Scripture Engagement, computer use, funding, and so forth. Ideally, a beginning translation team

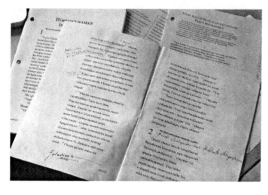

should have their work checked after they have completed one hundred verses. In the early stages, the translation should be checked before it is sent to review committees. At a later stage, it is good if the consultant check is done just before publication.

Most translation consultants ask teams to send a written back-translation to him/her before the checking session. (See Appendix 2 on how to make a back-translation.) The consultant may also ask the team to have someone present during the checking sessions who has not been involved in the work, and who can give an oral back-translation and answer the consultant's questions.

Preparing the translation for publication

When you feel that your translation of a book or section of Scripture is as good as you can make it, you can print or record a small number of copies as a trial edition to test the translation with a wider audience. Label them as trial editions, and ask readers and listeners for comments. Be sure church and community leaders receive a copy. Listen as people read the text aloud, use it in Bible studies, or discuss it.

When you have incorporated the feedback from the people who used the trial edition, then you can publish or record the Scripture portion for wider distribution. Do this with some shorter Scripture portions as they are completed rather than waiting until the whole New Testament or Bible is completed.

How to work together as a team

Over time, translation teams develop ways of working together that help them make good progress. This will vary from project to project. The following list shows a typical order in a project with three translators, a typist, and five review committee members. The order may well change due to factors like the availability of electricity or consultants.

Stage 1: Generating the first draft of books of the Bible

1. Translator A studies Chapter 1, either with the translation advisor or independently, noting any questions to ask the translation advisor later.

2. Translator A makes the first draft, using the process summarized in Appendix 3. This includes drafting any extra-textual helps.
3. The typist types up the draft.
4. Translator A proofreads the printout, makes any corrections, and passes it on to translator B.
5. Translator B reads the translation without referring to Bibles in other languages. He pencils in suggestions for changes where the draft is not clear.
6. Translator A looks at the suggestions and inks in the ones that he or she accepts.
7. Periodically Translators A and B meet to discuss those points which Translator A has not accepted so far.
8. The exegete or team leader checks the chapter exegetically using Bibles in other languages and Hebrew/Greek.
9. All the changes up to this point are entered into the computer, a fresh printout is made and Translator A proofreads the chapter again.
10. Basic computer checks are run to check that all the verses are there.
11. Illustrations are selected and captions written.
12. This continues until all of the book or the section is complete.

Stage 2: Checking and testing

1. The translation is sent to one or more of the review committee members.
2. Local testing is done with a sample of the intended audience.
3. The back-translator makes a back-translation of the translation.
4. Translator A checks the back-translation and the comments from the review committee members or local testing, and makes any needed changes to the translation. If needed, a new printout is made.
5. A translation consultant checks the work. The typist enters all the changes and, if needed, another printout is made.

This book is then put to one side unless it is going to be printed as a separate book or recorded for audio use.

Stage 3: Publication

1. Computer checks are run on the whole book to correct spelling, checking that the key terms and the formatting are consistent.
2. The whole translation team takes turns reading the book aloud, and changes are made so that it flows well.

Begin with a book or set of passages and take it through all of these steps. What you learn from the review committee members and consultant checks will feed into the drafting of the next book or set of passages.

Keeping things organized

Translation teams need good systems in place to keep track of all of their documents as well as key decisions they have made.

Keeping track of documents

1. Agree together about the steps your team will use as they translate. Make a chart for each book or set of stories. Across the top, list the chapters of the book or the titles of the stories you are translating. Down the side list the steps of your process. Post it on the wall of the translation office. As each step is finished, the person who finished it marks it off on the chart. The secretary should play a part in keeping things organized.

2. For each book of the Bible, one translator should be responsible for seeing that it goes through all the steps in the process. He or she is also responsible to see that the typist puts in corrections properly and prints out the most up-to-date version.

Table 4. Translation progress chart

Philippians	1	2	3	4
Generating the Draft				
Draft by Translator A	√	√	√	
Typed, proof read/changes entered	√	√	√	
Read and revised by Translator B	√	√		
Comments read by Translator A	√	√		
A and B discuss	√			
Exegetical check	√			
. . . .				

3. Each book of the Bible should have its own folder where the latest printout is kept. Earlier printouts should be kept in an archive file. Each translator also needs his own folder in which he keeps the translation that he or she is working on.

4. Designate one copy of the translation as the master copy, both on the computer and in the print-outs. Make all corrections on the master copy. It is helpful if the printouts all have the date printed as a default footer.

5. Back up your computer files at least every week! Keep copies of all your translation on CDs or other storage devices somewhere away from your office in case of fire or theft. If the country is politically unstable, copies should be kept in another country. Sending files by email to someone who keeps them in a safe place can be one way of doing this.

GROUP DISCUSSION

1. Think of an existing translation project you know. Discuss how the procedures of that project different from the description in this chapter. Do you see ways of improving that project?
2. Add some other ideas to the section on practical ways of keeping things organized.

Keep track of terms used for concepts

Keep a record of the decisions about terms used for important or difficult concepts and write a definition for them in your language. Here is an example of such a record:

> Priest – *ngangga 'da Gale*
> Used to describe priests in the Bible. This was a group of people that first came into being at the time of Moses. The first priest was Aaron. One of their main tasks was to sacrifice animals to God. Do not confuse this word with *sango* – used for modern day Catholic priests.
>
> righteous – *wi bolo zu*
> This word describes a person who is upright before God and obeys his commandments – literally a straight head.
>
> Temple – *gab toe da Gale*
> Literally this means the big house of God. This is the phrase used for the big building in Jerusalem where the priests offered sacrifices to God.

A record like this can allow translators to compare the way a word is translated in different passages. It can also help them be consistent and use the same word widely for a biblical concept. Computer programs can identify all the places a word occurs in Scripture, and make a list of all the ways it has been translated. The record of key terms with their explanations can be published to help people learn how to express these things in their language. This is especially important for those who preach or do spontaneous interpretation in church services.

Summary

Translators must first internalize the text and understand the author's intended meaning before they are ready to begin drafting. This involves reading the text in different versions and using the helps available. Drafting of narrative is best done orally by translators working together, because it lessens the direct influence of the source language on the translation and allows the natural structures and expressions in the language to surface. After the translators become more experienced, they may decide to work on drafting separate books, and they may do so in writing rather than orally. After there is a first draft, the translation is ready to be tested in the community, through back-translation and/or with reviewers. Good organization of the work is vital for the smooth, efficient running of the work. A team needs to work well together, each one knowing his/her particular role. Records of the terms used for difficult concepts in the translation can help translators use terms consistently, and can be of interest to others who are learning how to refer to biblical concepts in their language.

<table>
<tr><td>So what?</td><td>Translators need to be able to organize their program, people, papers, and files!</td></tr>
</table>

Assignment

Imagine you are working on a translation team. Make a chart for 2 Timothy for your project. List the major steps in the process you think your team is likely to use.

Lesson 26

Translation Programs

GROUP DISCUSSION

Discuss who is responsible for a community understanding the Bible.

Church growth, Scripture engagement, and language

Church leaders are concerned about the growth of their churches, both the number of Christians and their spiritual maturity. One of their main tasks is to help their people understand Scripture and apply what they have understood to their lives. In some communities, people cannot understand Scripture because it is not available in a language they understand well and like to use in religious activities. Where this is the case, a translation program may be necessary. Translation programs take a long-term commitment of prayer, personnel, and funding. Before beginning work, church leaders must be sure that a translation of Scripture in a local language is what they need and that they are willing to commit to it. This takes time and thought. Beginning a translation program before a community has decided that it is something they need and are willing to work for is premature and leads to problems that can plague a translation program for a long time.

Some communities have no churches. In these cases, community leaders can be involved in making decisions. Often there are churches or organizations outside the community that want to bring the Gospel to them. The leaders of these churches can also be involved in decision-making and can function on behalf of the community until a church is established.

GROUP DISCUSSION

Discuss who should be involved in making decisions about what your community needs.

Translation Committee

If church leaders decide that a translation of the Bible is what is needed, they need to work out exactly what they hope to achieve through it. Leaders from all of the main churches need to work together to develop products and programs that can serve the entire language community. Some communities may already have organizations that bring all of the churches together and these can be used to discuss the translation program, at least initially. Other communities may need to form a new committee. As interest in the translation grows into action, a more formal translation committee may be necessary. This group needs to decide things like:

- Who is the audience?
- What is the major goal?
- Who should do the work?
- Where will they work?
- What kind of translation product would be most effective?
- What media would be most effective?
- How will the audience learn the intended context?
- What terms should be used for key concepts in our Scripture?
- How will names, measures, and so forth be translated?
- How will the translation be distributed?
- How will the work be funded?

Translation advisors can help church leaders understand the role of translation in church growth, the way communication functions, the different kinds of Scripture products and kinds of translations, and so forth. It may be necessary to bring in respected outsiders with expertise in Bible translation to do this, as church leaders may be more open to them than to their own people. Bringing church leaders together in seminars allows them to discuss and come up with ideas together as well as develop relationships with each other. National church leaders that affect decisions on the local level need to be included in such seminars. By thinking through their situation carefully and creatively, they may decide to begin translation with a product they had not thought about before. For example, they may realize that their real concern is that children hear Scriptures in their mother tongue. Consequently, they may decide to begin with Bible stories that can be used in Sunday school and family devotions rather than starting with the full books of the Bible.

Translators may have their personal preferences about the type of product, media, and selections, but in the end, it is the church that needs to decide. If the churches are not involved in the decision, they will make their preferences clear later by not using the translated Scriptures.

Decisions made by the translation team or even the translation committee need to be tested in the wider community, and they may not be accepted. For example, decisions about the Guarani New Testament in Brazil were accepted by the translation team and translation committee, but the intended audience wanted a different style of translation, and the whole thing had to be revised, a process which took another five years' work. Among the Anyi of Côte d'Ivoire, translators agreed that a hymnbook for the Protestant church should be formatted on horizontal half-sheets but at the dedication ceremony the people were angry. "This is a Catholic book!" they said. "We're Protestants! Protestant books don't look like this!"

Translation committees can represent the translation project to the community. They are often responsible for publicity and vision-sharing. They may raise funds to support the translation project and may pay salaries. They make decisions about staff, goals, and organize celebrations of progress. Even after completing the translation of the entire Bible, there are revisions and other Scripture products churches need, so the work of a translation committee is on-going.

> Church leaders need to decide on
> their main communication goal,
> where they should start,
> and where that should lead.

GROUP DISCUSSION

1. Discuss why it is important that church leaders take responsibility for Bible translation in their language. Think about negative effects if outsiders make key decisions.
2. Discuss if there is an existing structure in your community that brings all or most of the churches together, where decisions about Scripture needs can be discussed, at least initially.
3. Discuss the kind of structure that would work best in your community long term.
4. Consider the kinds of training which church leaders in your community need to be able to make good decisions about communicating Scripture to their audience.

Bible Translation Organizations

Local communities need the help of an organization with expertise in Bible translation. Many such organizations exist: SIL, Wycliffe, United Bible Societies, Lutheran Bible Translators, Pioneer Bible Translators, and so forth. They offer consulting services, both in designing translation programs and checking translations so that they can be approved for publication. Each publisher has its own rules for what it will accept in terms of footnotes and extra-textual helps. A relationship with a translation organization needs to be established from the beginning of a project so that no time or effort is wasted preparing a translation in a way they will not publish. The relationship between the Bible agency, the translation committee and the full-time translation team varies from project to project, but must be clear and acceptable to everyone from an early stage.

The translation team: full-time roles

> On the board, list some full-time roles you know of on a translation team. Mark those which are essential with a +.

Translation work is not a part time job! A project will be seriously handicapped if translators are trying to do another job at the same time. Projects differ greatly, but normally a translation team should have between two and four translators. One person working alone is likely to become discouraged. He or she will not have the encouragement and feedback that comes from working and discussing with at least one other person. More than four translators make a project much more complicated to organize. The team also needs a place where they can work without too many interruptions. Depending on local factors, one person may fill more than one of the roles listed below, or one role can be filled by several people.

Translators

How are translators selected? One solution is for churches to select candidates they feel would represent them well in the work. A translation consultant can run an assessment course for these candidates to determine who has the best natural ability for the work. The church can then take other factors such as their character and reputation in the community into consideration and make their selection. If possible, one translator should come from each of the major church traditions. A translation team benefits from having members with higher education as well as those who are gifted speakers of the language, especially when translating poetry.

An exegete

An exegete must have received training in biblical studies, biblical languages, exegesis, and translation checking. He or she may be one of the translators. It is best if the exegete is a mother-tongue speaker of the language, but this is not obligatory. The exegete also needs to be well respected and accepted by the local churches.

A team leader

One person needs to be responsible for the day-to-day administration of a translation project. This can involve reporting to funding agencies and translation organizations, planning the work, ordering supplies, arranging the distribution of draft translations to review committees, meeting with church leaders to report on the progress of the project, trouble-shooting problems between translators, and so forth. The team leader may be one of the translators, the exegete, or another member of the team. The main qualifications for the position of team leader are that he or she has good administrative and leadership skills. He or she needs to be someone the team members respect and are willing to follow. The person with the highest education may not always be the best choice for this position.

Secretary

Although translators can do their own typing and printing, the project will go much more quickly if there is a full-time secretary who can enter drafts into the computer, make needed corrections, print out copies, proofread to be sure corrections are entered correctly, and keep files in order. Good secretaries can also correct punctuation errors as they type the manuscript.

Scripture engagement and literacy workers

The goal of translating the Bible is that people will use it. One or more people need to organize the promotion of the oral and/or printed Scripture products and help churches use them in their services and programs in appropriate ways. They may be involved in preparing recordings for radio stations or for listening groups. They may organize and supervise literacy programs for adult learners. Translators can take responsibility for these parts of the program, but this will mean that the translation will progress more slowly.

Reviewers, testers, back-translators: part-time roles

All translations need to be checked and reviewed by people outside the translation team before they are published. This allows the translators to see how their audience understands the translation and whether or not they accept the many decisions the team has made in the course of their work.

Reviewers

Reviewers receive printed copies of the translation as it becomes available. When translators cannot decide on different ways of translating a word or expression, they may give alternatives marked by brackets and ask the reviewers to cross out the one they do not like. For example:

The man was carrying a [jar] [pitcher] on his head.

They study it on their own before meeting together as a group. Face-to-face discussions are necessary to get good feedback.

Reviewers usually serve as volunteers. Recruiting influential leaders such as senior church leaders, teachers, doctors and other medical personnel, and government officials can be good for a project. They need to be trained for their work so they understand communication and translation principles. This can be done in a short course of a few days. Each church tradition should be represented in the group of reviewers, especially those that are not represented on the translation team.

Reviewers should be organized in a way that works well in the culture. Some will form a committee and elect a president, vice president, and so forth. Other communities may prefer a less formal structure.

When working together, a review committee can check about six pages typed, double-spaced A4 in a half day.

Testers

Another way to find out what people understand from a translation is to test it with the audience by reading it to them and asking them questions. In some translation programs, the translators do this testing, but in other programs, they train people to do it.

Back-translators

Translations are translated back into a language of wider communication at various points in the translation process, depending on the team's process. These back-translations help consultants to see if the translation is communicating clearly. It is extremely important that people who have not worked on the translation do the back-translation. They need training and mentoring in how to do this special kind of translation.

Funding translation programs

Translation programs cost money. It can come from several sources. One important source is from the community itself. Contributing something is important for a sense of ownership and self respect. Some contributions can be in kind, such as food for the translators or for seminars, office space, working in a development project to raise money for the translation project. No community is so poor it cannot contribute something, and many communities can contribute substantial amounts if they really want the Bible in their language.

Funds from outside the community can be requested to supplement local funding. Applying for funding requires understanding the donor organization's interests and procedures. Donor organizations sometimes change their priorities, so funding from the outside may not be a reliable long-term solution.

GROUP DISCUSSION

> Discuss which of all the issues mentioned in this chapter needs more attention in your language community.

Summary

Bible translation programs involve an enormous amount of effort and resources. Church leaders need to evaluate carefully if local language Scriptures are needed, and if so, they need to decide exactly what their goals are, where to begin, and how to proceed. Bible translation programs involve full-time and part-time roles. Relationships with Bible Translation organizations are necessary from the beginning to avoid wasted effort. Developing materials in a language for use in the church is an on-going task.

So what? Translators need to help church leaders understand the many issues involved in translation programs so that they can make decisions that serve their goals.

Work Session O: A Second Look

Look at the translation of the creation story you did at the beginning of the course.
Compare it with the original. On the basis of what you've learned in this course,
what would you change? Why?

Appendixes

Appendix 1

Glossary

Active sentences are sentences in which the subject does the action.

Approach #1 aims at communicating Scripture in a relevant way to an audience in their current context, without requiring them to learn any extra information outside the text about the original context. Where contextual differences between the original and secondary audience are large, this strategy often leads to preparing Scripture-based products that do not claim to be a translation and so do not raise expectations of high meaning resemblance.

Approach #2 aims to allow audiences to understand the meaning of their translation in a way that resembles the author's meaning as much as possible. Where the audience does not know the intended context, there needs to be some way for them to be able to learn it outside the Scripture text.

Approach #3 is somewhere between strategy #1 and #2. It aims to increase ease of understanding somewhat by making some adjustments in the text to the audience's current context, and provides other contextual information outside the text to adjust their context.

Back-translations are word-for-word translations back into a trade or national language. They allow someone who does not know the local language understand what is expressed by the text.

Clauses are the smallest grammatical unit that can be used to describe an event, process, or state. Main clauses can occur alone. Dependent clauses cannot.

Cognitive benefits are changes in our thoughts that result from incoming information. They can strengthen thoughts, eliminate thoughts, or combine with thoughts we already have to form new implications.

Concepts are ideas about things, processes, qualities, or relationships. They are entry points to networks of information in our minds.

Connectors are words that give clues about how thoughts expressed in a text are related.

Context is all of the contextual information we use to understand what the speaker means. We already know it before hearing (that part of) a text. It must fill all three of these conditions: it must come to mind quickly, it must be information we think we share with our communication partner, and it must lead to adequate cognitive benefits.

Contextual information is the bits of information that come to mind from everything we know as we try to understand a communication. Together it forms the context for processing a communication.

Contextual mismatches are when the context intended by the speaker does not match the context the audience supplies. They can be of three kinds: unrecognized context, unintended context, and unknown context.

Contextual knowledge is everything a person knows or could know.

Culture is ideas, beliefs, and practices that are long-lasting and widely shared by a group of people.

Dependent clauses are clauses that cannot stand alone.

Describing is telling about something. It is judged by the criteria of truth.

Eliminating is a kind of cognitive benefit in which an existing thought is eliminated.

Explicit information is information that is expressed in words.

Filling out what was said means processing exactly what speakers are referring to, using the text and context. This involves determining who pronouns refer to, the intended meaning of words and expressions if more than one is possible, filling in ellipses, providing actors for passive verbs, and so forth.

Front-shifting is shifting a word(s) from its usual place to the beginning of the sentence.

Genre are culturally defined kinds of communication that raise audience's expectations for a specific kind of relevance.

Idioms are expressions in which several words together have a special meaning.

Implications are one kind of cognitive effect. They are the new things we know after we hear that part of the text.

Implicit information is information that is meant but is not expressed in words.

Irony is when speakers retell what was said or thought earlier and distance themselves from it, without doing so explicitly.

Key biblical concepts are concepts that occur frequently in Scripture and are very important for the message of the Gospel.

Main clauses are clauses that can stand alone. Dependent clauses cannot.

Meaning resemblance is the degree to which a retelling communicates the same ideas as the original communication.

Metaphors are word pictures that talk about one thing in terms of another.

New implications are thoughts that result from new information combining with things we already know.

Path of least effort means taking the contextual information that come to mind most easily (and requires the lowest processing effort) as we search to understand what a communicator means. If that information does not lead to an interpretation that satisfies our expectations of relevance, we search more widely and stop as soon as we find an interpretation that satisfies our expectations.

Particles are short words or suffixes whose meaning are difficult to define on their own.

Passive sentences are sentences in which the subject has the action done to them.

Primary communication is communication that is addressed to an audience directly.

Processing effort is the effort it takes us to understand something.

Relevance is determined by the difference between effort and cognitive benefits.

Retelling is telling again what someone said or thought earlier. It is judged by whether it is faithful to the original in relevant respects.

Scripture products are any product that is related to Scripture, both those that claim to be Scripture and those that claim to be based on Scripture.

Scripture-based products do not claim to be Scripture and so are free to adapt the text enough to the audience's current context that they experience enough cognitive effects to consider the communication relevant. This may involve omitting some of the original, adding in contextual information, or other kinds of adjustments.

Secondary communication is when a second audience is trying to understand a communication designed for another audience.

Shared knowledge is information that we share with our communication partner. If we realize we share this information, we will access it as we process communication. If we do not realize that we share it, we will not access it. Or we may assume information is shared when in fact it is not.

Strengthening is a kind of cognitive benefit which causes us to believe an existing thought even more.

Strong guidance to implications is when hearers receive strong guidance to a specific implication. Also referred to as *strong communication.*

Unintended context is a kind of contextual mismatch in which hearers think they share the intended context with the speaker when, in fact, they do not.

Unknown context is a kind of contextual mismatch in which hearers do not know the intended context and are quite aware of the fact they do not know it.

Unnatural translations are translations that require audiences to increase processing effort with no increase in cognitive benefits. They are often the result of translating word-for-word from the original language.

Unrecognized context is a kind of contextual mismatch in which hearers may share the intended context with the speaker, but do not realize they share it.

Weak guidance to implications is when hearers receive weak guidance to a range of possible implications.

Appendix 2

How to Make a Back-Translation

What is a back-translation?

Back-translations are word-for-word translations back into a trade or national language. For example, a local language Bible translation can be translated back into English. The back-translation reflects the content and grammatical structure of the local language as much as possible. It allows someone who does not speak that language to understand how the text is expressed in it. A back-translation is not a proper translation. It will not sound natural because it shows the grammatical patterns that are used in the original language, not those of English.

> Back-translations are word-for-word translations back into a trade or national language. They allow someone who does not know the local language to understand what is expressed by the text.

What is the purpose of a back-translation?

One purpose of making a back-translation is to help a translation consultants, or someone else who does not know the language, be able to discuss the translation with the translator. Although it will not give consultants as full an understanding as they would have if they knew the language, it will at least give them some insight and serve as a starting point for further discussion and explanation. It is important that the back-translation be well made. If not, it will mislead the consultant. Back-translations are also a way of testing the translation. Places where the translation is inaccurate or unclear are often discovered through back-translations.

A translator can check the back-translation and add notes to help the consultant, but they should never change what was written by the person doing the back-translation.

Different kinds of back-translations

One kind of back-translation is *word-for-word*. Although slight adjustments of word order may be made, it follows the original text almost entirely word by word. Here is an example:

Ne	NWA	toa	hã	Abrama	na:	"Mo	kúlú	ngo, …"
Then	Lord	said	to	Abram	that	you	get	up,

Another kind of back-translation is a *free back-translation*. In this type of back-translation, although the content of the original version is still followed very closely, more grammatical adjustments are made in the back-translation so that it is easier to read and follow.

Often the best type of back-translation to help a consultant is a word-for-word translation, which may well be generated by a computer program, with a free translation of the sentences and phrases underneath. Here is an example:

Ne	NWA	toa	hã	Abrama	na:	"Mo	kúlú	ngo, …"
Then	Lord	said	to	Abram	that	you	get	up,

Then the Lord said to Abram, "Leave!"

How to make a back-translation

The back-translator should not look at any text except the translation while making the back-translation. All other Bibles should be closed. Do not under any circumstance look to see what other versions say. The back-translation should reflect only what this translation says.

If at any point the back-translator is not sure what the translation means, it shows that at that point the translation is not clear. The back-translator should leave a space, or mark what he supposes it means with a question mark.

The back-translation should be made by someone other than the translators. This is because translators have previous knowledge of the passage and know what the translation is meant to say. They no doubt feel the translation communicates the correct meaning or they would not have translated that way. This does not guarantee that the correct meaning would be understood by someone else.

The person doing the back-translation should be someone who has the same knowledge as the target audience. For example, if the translation is being prepared primarily for church members, a person from that background should do the back-translation. If the translation is targeting non-Christians, a person from that background should do the back-translation.

Training back-translators

Making a good back-translation is not easy. It takes teaching and practice. It is best if the back-translator starts by translating a non-biblical text, such as a short folk story. Feedback needs to be given and two or three other short texts back-translated with feedback before he/she begins doing this for biblical passages.

Format of the back-translation

If the translation is entered into a computer, format it so that there are large spaces under each line. The back-translator gives the free translation under each line, either on the computer or on a printout.

If the translation is written by hand, a space should be left underneath the translation so that the back-translation can be written in underneath the text. It is helpful if the back-translation is written in a different color ink or pencil from the translation itself.

Appendix 3

Generating a First Draft: A Summary

Understanding the biblical author's intended meaning

1. **Get the bigger picture:** Read an introduction to the book or other material that will give you a general overview of the book. Try to understand who wrote to whom in what situation and for what purpose.
   Read the larger section of Scripture around the passage you intend to translate. This may mean reading the whole chapter, several chapters, or the whole book.

2. **Compare versions:** Read the text carefully and try to understand what the author was trying to communicate to his first audience. Read the passage to be translated in several versions, and in more than one language, if possible. Notice how the translations have expressed the meaning differently.

3. **Verbal sketch:** Make a verbal sketch of the passage. Imagine you are telling it to someone in one minute, 45 seconds, 30 seconds, and 15 seconds.

4. **Act it out:** Act out the story, if possible. Try to imagine how each character felt.

5. **Study the passage using biblical helps:** Read materials on the book and passage, using study Bibles, translator's helps, Bible dictionaries, and/or commentaries. Study any problem areas in detail.

6. **Make a communication chart:**
   a. Determine how the author intended the text to be filled out: pronoun reference, filling out of words, supplying parts of sentences that are not stated, and so forth. Notice anything in the grammar that gives clues to the intended meaning.
   b. Identify the context the author expected his audience to supply.
   c. Identify the ideas that the author intended to communicate.

7. **Note down questions:** Write any questions you cannot answer in a notebook reserved for questions to ask your consultant or exegete.

Communicating the author's intended meaning

1. **Picture your audience:** Think of a specific group of people in your home church you want to tell this passage to, for example, youth, lay preachers, children, older women.

2. **Make the first draft**: Three options for drafting:
    a. *Oral drafting:*
        - Close all of your books and Bibles, and have each person in the group tell the story in the receptor language in turn while the others listen. Comment on expressions or sentences that sound really good.
        - When you feel you are telling the text well, choose one person to record it. Listen to the recording. If you are not satisfied, try to discover why and then tell the story again.
        - Have everyone in the group transcribe this recording. Leave three blank lines between every line of text.
    b. *Written drafting:* Discuss how to express the author's meaning in the receptor language together and when you agree, have one person write it down. Leave three blank lines between each line of text.
    c. *Group drafting or individual drafting:* When a translation team first begins its work, it is best to work together on a passage. After they have gained experience, each team member can draft a separate book of the Bible, and then they can read each other's drafts and give feedback.
3. **Contextual adjustment strategy:** Think about the context that your audience is lacking and how it can be supplied. If any of it should appear in extra-textual helps as part of the printed Bible, write these footnotes or glossary items. Indicate any illustrations you think should be inserted. Do not forget section titles and introductions.
4. **Checking your draft:**
    a. *Check for accuracy:* Compare your translation with the original to check for accuracy. Is anything missing? Anything added? Anything incorrect? Make any revisions that are needed.
    b. *Check for naturalness:* Read the text aloud. Is it natural? Make any revisions that are needed.

The translation is now ready to be tested with native speakers, reviewed by church leaders, and checked by a consultant (see Lesson 25).

Appendix 4

Topical Indexes

Topical Index

Adultery (and fornication)
Matthew 5:27–30; John 8:2–11; Romans 13:8–10; 1 Corinthians 5:9–11, 6:9–20; Galatians 5:19; Ephesians 5:3; Colossians 3:5–6; 1 Thessalonians 4:1–8; Hebrews 13:4; Jude 7.

Baptism
Matthew 28:18–20; John 3:22, 4:1–2; Acts 2:37–42, 8:12, 8:36–38, 10:44–48, 16:14–15, 16:31–33, 19:1–7, 22:12–16; Romans 6:1–4; Galatians 3:26–27; Colossians 2:12; 1 Peter 3:20–22.

Cleansing from sin by Christ's death
Matthew 26:26–29; Romans 3:25, 5:9–10; Ephesians 1:7; Hebrews 9:11–14; 1 John 1:6–7; Revelation 7:14–17.

Church of Jesus Christ
Matthew 16:13–20; Acts 2:41–42; Romans 12:4–8; 1 Corinthians 12:12–30; Ephesians 1:22–23, 2:19–22, 4:1–16; Colossians 1:18; Hebrews 10:24–25; 1 Peter 2:4–10; Revelation 19:5–10.

Church leaders qualifications and appointment of church leaders (pastors, elders and deacons)
Acts 6:1–6; Acts 14:23; 1 Timothy 3:1–13; Titus 1:5–9.
- Instructions to church leaders: Matthew 28:18–20; Luke 22:24–27; Acts 20:17–35; 1 Thessalonians 2:1–12; 1 Timothy 4:1–16; 2 Timothy 2:1–26, 3:10–17, 4:1–5; Titus 2:7–8; 1 Peter 5:1–4.
- Respect due church leaders: 1 Corinthians 9:14; Galatians 6:6; 1 Thessalonians 5:12–13; 1 Timothy 5:17–22; Hebrews 13:7, 13:17.

Creation
Matthew 19:4; John 1:3; Acts 14:15; 17:24–26; 1 Corinthians 8:6; Colossians 1:15–16; Hebrews 1:2; 11:3; Revelation 4:11.

Death
John 6:39–40, 11:17–27, 14:1–4; Romans 8:10–11, 8:38–39, 14:7–9;
1 Corinthians 15:12–58; 2 Corinthians 5:1–10; Philippians 1:20–24;
1 Thessalonians 4:13–18; Hebrews 2:14–15; Revelation 14:13, 21:1–4, 22:1–5.

Divorce
Matthew 5:31–32, 19:3–9; Luke 16:18; Romans 7:2–3; 1 Corinthians 7:10–16.

Drunkenness
Romans 13:13; 1 Corinthians 5:11, 6:9–11; Galatians 5:19–21; Ephesians 5:18;
1 Timothy 3:1–3; Titus 1:7; 1 Peter 4:3–5.

Eternal life
Eternal life is that new life which Jesus Christ gives to those who believe in him.
Matthew 19:16–30; Luke 10:25–28; John 3:1–16, 5:19–29, 10:10, 11:25–26, 14:6,
17:2–3, 20:31; Romans 5:21, 6:5–14, 8:10–17; 2 Corinthians 5:17; Galatians
2:20; Ephesians 2:1–6; Colossians 2:13; 3:1–4; 2 Timothy 1:10; Titus 3:4–7;
1 Peter 1:23; 1 John 5:11–13.

Faith
Believing faith for salvation: John 1:12, 3:15–18, 3:36, 6:47, 14:6, 20:31; Acts
4:12, 16:30–31; Romans 3:20–22, 10:9–10; Galatians 2:16; Ephesians 2:8–9.
Faith for the Christian life: Mark 11:22–25; Luke 17:5–6; John 14:1; Romans 5:1–
2, 14:22–23; 1 Corinthians 13:13; 2 Corinthians 5:6–7; Galatians 5:6; Hebrews
11; James 1:2–8, 2:14–26; 1 Peter 1:3–9.

Family life
- Husbands and wives: Matthew 19:4–6; 1 Corinthians 7:1–16; Ephesians
  5:21–33; Colossians 3:18–19; Titus 2:3–5; Hebrews 13:4; 1 Peter 3:1–7.
- Children: Matthew 15:3–6; Luke 2:51; Ephesians 6:1–3; Colossians 3:20;
  1 Timothy 5:4, 5:8; Hebrews 12:7–11.
- Parents: Ephesians 6:4; Colossians 3:21; 1 Timothy 3:4–5.
- Widows: Acts 6:1; Romans 7:2–3; 1 Corinthians 7:39–40; 1 Timothy
  5:3–16; James 1:27.

Fasting
Matthew 6:16–18; Mark 2:18–20; Acts 13:1–3, 14:23.

Fellowship with believers
Matthew 18:19–20; Acts 2:41–47; Romans 12:4–8; Ephesians 1:22–23, 4:11–16;
Colossians 3:15–17; 1 Timothy 4:13; Hebrews 10:24–25.

Forgiveness
God forgives our sins: Matthew 26:28; Mark 11:25–26; Acts 5:31, 10:43, 26:18; Ephesians 1:7; Colossians 1:13–14, 2:13–14; Hebrews 10:17–18; 1 John 1:8–2:2.
We should forgive the sins of others: Matthew 6:12–15, 18:21–35; Mark 11:25; Luke 6:37, 17:3–4; 2 Corinthians 2:5–11; Ephesians 4:31–32; Colossians 3:13.

God
Mark 10:27, 12:29–30; Luke 1:37, 6:35–36; John 4:24; Acts 14:14–17, 17:22–31; Romans 1:18–23, 11:33–36; 1 Corinthians 8:4–6; 2 Corinthians 1:3; 1 Timothy 1:17, 6:15–16; Hebrews 4:13, 10:30–31; James 1:17; 1 Peter 1:14–17; 1 John 1:5, 4:7–12, 4:16; Jude 24–25; Revelation 4:8–11, 15:3–4.

Government
Matthew 22:15–22; Acts 5:27–29; Romans 13:1–7; 1 Timothy 2:1–4; Titus 3:1; 1 Peter 2:13–17.

Heaven
Luke 12:32–34; John 14:1–3; 2 Corinthians 5:1–8; Philippians 1:23; Colossians 3:1; 1 Peter 1:4–5; Revelation 4.1–11, 21:1–4, 21:22–22:5, 22:14–15.

Healing
Matthew 4:23–25, 9:35, 11:2–5; Acts 3:1–6, 8:4–8, 19:11–16, 28:8–9; 1 Corinthians 12:9, 12:29–30; 2 Corinthians 12:7–10; 1 Timothy 5:23; 2 Timothy 4:20; James 5:14–15.

Hell
Matthew 10:28, 13:41–42, 47–50, 25:41; Luke 16:23–26; 2 Thessalonians 1:9; Revelation 20:10–15, 21:8.

Helping others
Matthew 6:1–4, 7:12, 25:31–46; Luke 3:10–11, 6:38; Acts 11:27–30; 1 Corinthians 10:24; 2 Corinthians 8:1–15, 9:1–15; Galatians 6:9–10; Philippians 4:14–19; Hebrews 10:24, 13:1–3, 13:16; James 1:27, 2:15–16; 1 John 3:16–18.

Holy Spirit
Matthew 28:19; Mark 1:9–11, 3:28–30; Luke 1:35, 3:16, 4:1, 11:13, 12:12; John 1:32–34, 3:5–8, 7:37–39, 14:15–17, 14:26, 15:26, 16:7–15, 20:19–23; Acts 1:4–5, 1:8, 2:1–18, 2:38–39, 4:31, 5:3–5, 8:14–17, 10:44–48, 13:2–4, 15:28, 16:7–10, 19:1–7; Romans 5:5, 7:6, 8:9–16, 8:26–27; 2 Peter 1:20–21; 1 John 2:20, 3:24, 4:13, 5:6–8.

Humility
Matthew 5:3–12, 18:1–5; Luke 14:7–11, 18:9–14; Ephesians 4:2; Philippians 2:3–11; Colossians 3:12–13; James 4:5–10; 1 Peter 5:5–7.

Idol worship and sorcery
Matthew 4:10, Acts 13:4–12, 17:22–31, 19:11–20; 1 Corinthians 5:1, 6:9–11, 8:1–13, 10:1–22; 2 Corinthians 6:14–18; Galatians 5:19–21; 1 Thessalonians 1:9–10; 1 John 5:21; Revelation 21:8, 22:15.

Jesus Christ
Jesus Christ is the Son of God: Matthew 11:27–30, 16:13–17; Luke 1:35; John 1:1–18, 5:19–29, 6:35–40, 8:58, 11:25–27, 14:5–11, 17:1–5, 20:26–31; Acts 3:13–16, 4:10–12; Romans 1:3–4; 1 Corinthians 3:11; 2 Corinthians 4:4–6, 5:21; Galatians 4:4–5; Philippians 2:5–11; Colossians 1:15–20, 2:9–10; Hebrews 1:1–14, 7:26–28; 1 John 2:1–2, 5:20; Revelation 1:12–18, 19:11–16.

- The Son of God was born as a human being: John 1:14; Luke 1:26–38; Matthew 1:18–25; Luke 2:1–20; Matthew 2:1–23; Galatians 4:4–5; Philippians 2:6–7; Hebrews 2:14–18.
- Jesus taught the people and healed those who were sick: Matthew 4:23–25, 7:28–29, 9:35–36, 11:1–6; Luke 4:14–44; Acts 10:36–38, John 20:30–31.
- Jesus did many miracles: Matthew 8:1–4, 8:5–13, 8:14–15, 8:23–27, 8:28–33, 9:1–7, 9:18–26, 9:27–31, 9:32–33, 12:9–14, 12:22, 14:15–21, 14:22–32, 15:22–28, 15:32–38, 17:14–18, 20:29–34, 21:18–22; Mark 1:21–28, 7:32–37, 8:22–25, Luke 5:4–8, 7:11–15, 13:10–13, 14:1–4, 17:12–14, 22:50–51; John 2:1–11, 4:46–54, 5:5–9, 9:1–7, 11:11–44, 21:4–6; Acts 2:22.
- The leaders arrested Jesus and sentenced him to death: Matthew 26:47–68, 27:1–2, 27:11–31; Mark 14:43–65, 15:1–20, Luke 22:47–53, 22:63–71, 23:1–25; John 18:1–14, 18:19–24, 18:28–19:16.
- Jesus was crucified: Matthew 27:32–56; Mark 15:21–41; Luke 23:26–49; John 19:17–37.
- Jesus was buried: Matthew 27:57–66; Mark 15:42–47; Luke 23:50–56; John 19:38–42.
- Jesus arose from death and was seen by others: Matthew 28:1–20; Mark 16:1–8; Luke 24:1–49; John 20:1–21:14; Acts 1:3–8, 2:24–32, 3:15, 4:10, 4:33, 10:39–43, 13:29–39, 17:2–3, 17:30–31; Romans 1:4, 4:24–25; 1 Corinthians 15:3–8, 15:12–21; Revelation 1:18.
- Jesus went up to heaven: Luke 24:50–51; Acts 1:9–11, 2:32–36, 5:30–31; Romans 8:34; Ephesians 1:20–23; Philippians 2:9–11; Hebrews 1:3–11, 2:9, 4:14–16, 7:25–26, 10:12–14; 1 Peter 3:22.
- Jesus will come back to earth: Matthew 24:29–44; John 14:1–3; Acts 1:10–11, 3:19–21; Philippians 3:20–21; Colossians 3:4; 1 Thessalonians 1:9–10, 3:13, 4:13–5:11; 2 Thessalonians 1:6–10, 2:1–4; 1 Timothy

6:13–15; 2 Timothy 4:8; Hebrews 9:28; 2 Peter 3:1–18; 1 John 3:1–3; Revelation 1:7, 22:12–13.

Judgment of God through Jesus Christ
Matthew 7:21–23, 16:24–27, 25:31–46; John 3:18–21, 5:24–29; Acts 17:30–31; Romans 2:1–11, 14:10–12; 1 Corinthians 3:10–15, 4:5; 2 Corinthians 5:9–10; 2 Thessalonians 1:5–10; Hebrews 9:27–28, 10:26–31; 1 Peter 1:17, 4:3–5; Revelation 20:11–15.

Justification
Acts 13:38–39; Romans 1:16–17, 3:21–26, 5:1, 5:9–10, 5:18–19; Galatians 2:16, 3:6–9; Titus 3:7.

Lawsuits, court cases
Matthew 5:25–26, 5:38–42, 18:15–17; Romans 12:14–21; 1 Corinthians 6:1–8.

The Lord's Supper /Holy Communion/Mass
Matthew 26:26–30; Mark 14:22–26; Luke 22:14–20; 1 Corinthians 10:14–22, 11:17–34.

Love   God loves us
John 3:16; Romans 5:8; Ephesians 2:4–5; 1 John 4:9–10.
- We should love God: Matthew 22:37–38; Mark 12:28–30; John 14:21; 1 Peter 1:8; 1 John 5:3
- We should love one another: Matthew 5:43–48, 22:39; John 13:34–35, 15:12–17; Romans 12:9–10, 13:8–10; 1 Corinthians 13:1–13, 16:14; Galatians 5:13–14; 1 Thessalonians 4:9–10; 1 Peter 4:8; 1 John 2:9–11, 3:11–18, 4:7–21.

Money, possessions
Matthew 6:19–21, 6:24–34; Luke 12:13–21, 12:32–34; Acts 20:35; 1 Timothy 6:6–10, 6:17–19; Hebrews 13:5–6; James 2:1–9, 5:1–6.

Obedience to God
John 14:15, 14:21, 14:23–24, 15:10–17; Romans 13:8–10; 1 Peter 1:14–16; 1 John 2:3–8, 3:22–24; 2 John 5–6.

Overcoming Satan and troubles
Matthew 4:1–11, 6:13; Luke 22:31–32; John 17:14–19; Romans 8:31–39, 12:12, 16:19–20; 1 Corinthians 10:12–13, 16:13; 2 Corinthians 12:7–10; Ephesians 3:20–21, 6:10–18; Philippians 4:13; 1 Thessalonians 3:5–8; 2 Thessalonians 3:3; 2 Timothy 1:7–8; Hebrews 2:18, 4:14–16, 12:1–2; James 4:7; 1 Peter 1:5, 5:8–11; 1 John 4:4, 5:3–5; Revelation 12:7–12.

Persecution
Matthew 5:10–12; Mark 13:9–13; Luke 12:4–9; John 15:18–21, 16:1–4; Acts
5:41; Romans 8:35–37, 12:12–14, 12:17–21; 1 Corinthians 4:11–13;
2 Corinthians 4:8–11, 12:10; Philippians 1:28–29; 2 Thessalonians 1:4–8, 3:2–4;
2 Timothy 3:10–13; Hebrews 10:32–39, 12:3–4; 1 Peter 3:13–17, 4:12–19;
Revelation 2:10.

Prayer
Instructions about prayer: Matthew 6:5–13, 7:7–11, 18:19–20; Mark 11:24–25;
Luke 11:1–13, 18:1–8, 21:36; John 14:13–14, 15:7, 16:23–26; Romans 8:26–27,
12:12; Ephesians 2:18, 6:18; Philippians 4:6–7; Colossians 4:2; 1 Thessalonians
5:17; 1 Timothy 2:1–4, 2:8, 4:4–5; Hebrews 4:16, 10:19–22; James 1:5–8, 4:2–3,
5:13–18; 1 Peter 4:7; 1 John 3:21–22, 5:14–15.
Examples of praying: Matthew 11:25–26, 14:23, 19:13–15; Mark 1:35; Luke
5:16, 6:12, 22:32, 22:39–46; John 11:41–42, 17:1–26; Acts 4:24–31, 16:25, 20:36,
21:5; Romans 1:9–10, 10:1–2.

Providence
Matthew 6:25–34, 10:29–31; Acts 14:15–17; Romans 8:28, 11:36; Colossians
1:17; Hebrews 1:3; James 4:13–16.

Repentance
Matthew 4:17; Mark 6:12; Luke 13:1–5, 15:1–31, 24:45–47; Acts 2:37–40,
3:19–20, 17:29–31, 20:21, 26:19–20; 2 Corinthians 7:8–11; 2 Peter 3:9;
Revelation 9:20–21.

Sacrifices of animals
Matthew 9:13; Mark 12:33; Romans 12:1; Hebrews 9:6–10:18.

Salvation
John 3:16–17; Acts 2:37–39, 4:11–12; Romans 5:1–11, 10:9–13; Ephesians
2:1–10; 1 Timothy 1:15–16, 2:3–7; 1 Peter 1:3–5.

Satan
Matthew 13:19, 25:41; Luke 4:1–13, 22:3–4; John 8:42–44; 2 Corinthians
2:10–11, 4:4, 11:13–15; Ephesians 2:2; 1 Thessalonians 2:18; 2 Thessalonians
2:9–12; 1 Peter 5:8–9; 1 John 3:8–10; Revelation 12:7–12, 20:1–3, 20:10.

Scriptures
Matthew 4:1–4, 5:17–20, 22:29; John 8:31–32, 20:31; Acts 20:32; Romans 15:4,
16:26; Colossians 3:16; 1 Thessalonians 2:13; 1 Timothy 4:13; 2 Timothy
3:14–17; Hebrews 4:12; 1 Peter 1:22–25; 2 Peter 1:19–21; 2 John 9–10;
Revelation 1:3.

Sin

- What sin is: Romans 1:18–32, 8:5–8; Galatians 5:19–21; Ephesians 2:1–3, 5:3–5; Colossians 3:5–10; James 4:17; 1 Peter 4:3; 1 John 3:4–5.
- All people have sinned: John 8:7–9; Romans 3:9–20, 3:23, 5:12; Galatians 3:22; 1 John 1:8–10.
- People need to be saved from punishment for their sins: Matthew 10:28, 13:41–42; John 3:18–20, 3:36; Acts 17:30–31; Romans 1:18–19, 6:23; Galatians 6:7–8; Colossians 3:5–6; 2 Thessalonians 1:7–9; Hebrews 9:27, 10:26–31; 1 Peter 1:17, 4:3–5; Jude 7; Revelation 20:11–15.

Suffering

Romans 8:18–25, 8:28; 2 Corinthians 1:4, 4:16–18; James 1:2–4; 1 Peter 1:6–9, 2:19–21, 5:8–10.

Thankfulness

Luke 17:11–19; John 6:11; Romans 1:21; Ephesians 5:20; Philippians 4:4–7; Colossians 2:7, 3:17, 4:2; 1 Thessalonians 5:18; 1 Timothy 2:1, 4:4–5.

CPSIA information can be obtained at www.ICGtesting.com
Printed in the USA
BVOW020817080513

320192BV00004B/64/P